T0382871

Industrialisation for Employment and Growth in India

India initiated liberal economic reforms in 1991 to transform a slow-growing, large, inward-oriented, state-led economy into an open, market-led, export-oriented industrialising economy, seeking to emulate the East Asian success story. After nearly three decades, however, the outcomes are different. Though economic growth has accelerated, industrialisation has suffered from the manufacturing sector's share in GDP stagnating, and labour-intensive sectors failing to improve their share in India's exports. With rising industrial imports, there is growing apprehension of India becoming prematurely de-industrialised. In response, the government launched the Make in India initiative in 2015, aimed at raising the manufacturing sector's share in GDP to 25 per cent, and to create an additional 100 million jobs by 2022.

Though official estimates show an optimistic image of small scale industries' contribution to industrial output and employment, they do not explain why India failed to boost labour-intensive industrial production as expected of the reforms. Why did they fail to keep the domestic market, let alone expand exports? Given the employment potential of small industry, what would it take to meet the ambitious policy goals of the Make in India initiative?

This book attempts to address these questions. It looks at a series of case studies of the small industry to obtain an in-depth understanding of specific industries, locations and clusters in order to draw meaningful conclusions. It brings together scholars with intimate knowledge and experience of the industries and locations who explore the modern labour-intensive industries, ranging from the sports goods industry and knitwear clusters to foundries and ceramic tile clusters. It seeks to offer rich insights into the current state of the small industry in India that is often overlooked in official statistics and nation-wide surveys. The book also explores the impact of growing automation on manufacturing employment.

R. Nagaraj is currently affiliated with the Centre for Development Studies, Trivandrum. He was formerly Professor of Economics at the Indira Gandhi Institute of Development Research, Mumbai. He has worked extensively on India's economic growth and industrialisation, public sector performance and industrial labour market. He coedited *Political Economy of Contemporary India* with S. Motiram, which was published by Cambridge University Press in 2017.

Industrialisation for Employment and Growth in India

Lessons from Small Firm Clusters and Beyond

Edited by

R. Nagaraj

CAMBRIDGE
UNIVERSITY PRESS

CAMBRIDGE
UNIVERSITY PRESS

University Printing House, Cambridge CB2 8BS, United Kingdom

One Liberty Plaza, 20th Floor, New York, NY 10006, USA

477 Williamstown Road, Port Melbourne, VIC 3207, Australia

314–321, 3rd Floor, Plot 3, Splendor Forum, Jasola District Centre, New Delhi–110025, India

103 Penang Road, #05–06/07, Visioncrest Commercial, Singapore 238467

Cambridge University Press is part of the University of Cambridge.

It furthers the University's mission by disseminating knowledge in the pursuit of education, learning and research at the highest international levels of excellence.

www.cambridge.org
Information on this title: www.cambridge.org/9781108832335

© Cambridge University Press 2021

First published 2021

Printed in India by Thomson Press India Ltd.

A catalogue record for this publication is available from the British Library

Library of Congress Cataloging-in-Publication Data

Names: Nagaraj, R., editor.
Title: Industrialisation for employment and growth in India / edited by R. Nagaraj.
Description: Cambridge, United Kingdom ; New York, NY : Cambridge University Press, 2021. | Includes bibliographical references and index.
Identifiers: LCCN 2021015100 (print) | LCCN 2021015101 (ebook) | ISBN 9781108832335 (hardback) | ISBN 9781108935920 (ebook)
Subjects: LCSH: Industrialization–India. | Industrial policy–India. | Labor market–India. | Employment (Economic theory)–India. | Economic development–India. | BISAC: BUSINESS & ECONOMICS / Development / Economic Development | BUSINESS & ECONOMICS / Development / Economic Development
Classification: LCC HC435 .I83275 2021 (print) | LCC HC435 (ebook) | DDC 338.0954–dc23
LC record available at https://lccn.loc.gov/2021015100
LC ebook record available at https://lccn.loc.gov/2021015101

ISBN 978-1-108-83233-5 Hardback

Contents

List of Tables   vii
List of Figures and Maps   xi
Preface and Acknowledgements   xiii

1. Introduction   1
   R. Nagaraj

2. Garment Cluster in Kolkata: The Untold Story of Expansion
   Relying on Low-end Domestic Demand   24
   Satyaki Roy

3. Constraints to Upgrading and Employment Expansion in
   the Tiruppur Knitwear Cluster   49
   M. Vijayabaskar

4. Determinants of Employment in the Indian Automobile Industry   72
   Madhuri Saripalle

5. Upgrading Technology and Space as Collective Strategy:
   Creation of Jobs and Market Potential in Gujarat's
   Ceramic Clusters   100
   Keshab Das

6. Sports Equipment Manufacturing in India: A Firm-level Inquiry
   into Growth and Employment Dynamism   129
   Varinder Jain

7. Aligarh Lock Cluster: Unravelling the Major Impediments   153
   Tareef Husain

8. Continued Misery or a Change in Fortune? The Case of the
   Howrah Foundry Industry   173
   Judhajit Chakraborty

9. Redevelop and Perish, or Survive and Grow? The Case for
   Supporting Informal Leather Enterprises in Dharavi, Mumbai   196
   Kshiti Gala

10. Growth Performance, Competitiveness and Employment in
    MSMEs: A Case Study of the Rajkot Engineering Cluster   223
    Dinesh Awasthi and *Amita Shah*

11. Manufacturing and Automation   250
    Sunil Mani

About the Contributors   277
Index   280

Tables

1.1	Definition of MSME	5
2.1	Accounts of a simple pair of jeans trousers produced in home-based units	36
2.2	Average monthly occupational wages	39
3.1	Share of fabrics in ready-made garment (RMG) exports of India (in %)	52
4.1	Employment by 3-digit NIC categories in the automobile industry	75
4.2	Export and import shares of vehicles and component manufacturers in 2018–19	76
4.3	Research and development intensity	80
4.4	Descriptive statistics	87
4.5	Estimation results	90
4A.1	Employment, trade and R&D in sample tier 1 auto component firms	93
4A.2	Profile of firms interviewed in the Tamil Nadu small-scale auto cluster	95
5.1	Aspects of ceramic industry in Gujarat, 1999–2015	102
5.2	Main products manufactured by sample units	109
5.3	Number of workers in sample units	110
5.4	Monthly average income by skilled and unskilled workers in sample units	111
5.5	Technology used until the mid-1990s in sample units	114
5.6	In-house changes/innovations undertaken in sample units	115
5.7	Expectations from the state	123
6.1	Selected indicators of the organised sports equipment industry in India	131
6.2	Size of sports goods clusters in Jalandhar and Meerut	133
6.3	Sample size of the study	133
6.4	Selected characteristics of sample enterprises	134
6.5	Various constituents defining the resilience scale	138
6.6	Various constituents defining functional literacy scale	138
6.7	Prevalent piece-based wages (in ₹) for home-based workers	145

6.8   Average monthly wages paid in major exporting units in
      sample clusters   146
6.9   Average incidence of work-related insecurity among wageworkers 147
6.10 Specific interventions aimed at promotion of India's sports
      equipment industry   150
7.1   Average import and export of locks from 2004–08 to 2014–18   156
7.2   Number of enterprises, employment and capital investment in
      the Aligarh lock industry   159
7.3   Trends in employment and sale during the last five years by
      firm size   160
7.4   Education of firm owners by their size   161
8A.1 Manufacturing employment and gross domestic product
      (GDP) in India   191
8A.2 State-wise share of manufacturing in total employment,
      1991–2011   191
8A.3 State-wise distribution of manufacturing workers (main),
      1981–2011   192
8A.4 State-wise ranking, by the share of manufacturing workers,
      1981–2011   192
8A.5 Shares of the top three and bottom three states in net state
      domestic product in total manufacturing at constant prices
      among seventeen major states   193
8A.6 Share of the top and bottom 50 districts in total
      manufacturing employment, 1991–11   193
9.1   Awareness and membership of industry organisations   213
9.2   Entrepreneurs' view on the impact of international
      competition and national policy changes on their businesses 215
10.1 Characteristics of enterprises   227
10.2 Sectoral annual compound rates of growth 2012–13 and 2017–18 231
10.3 Number of firms engaged in outsourcing and/or subcontracting 232
10.4 The proportion of outsourcing as a share of sales turnover   234
10.5 Strategies to face competition   236
10.6 Sources of social capital   239
10.7 Advantages of operating in Rajkot engineering cluster   240
10.8 The direction of changes in business environment in Rajkot   243
10.9 Perceived impact of recent policies and government campaigns 244
10.10 Policy wish list of firms in the Rajkot engineering cluster 245
11.1 Industry-wide distribution of the operational stock of
      industrial robots worldwide (percentage shares)   261

11.2 Task-wise distribution of industrial robots in world
 manufacturing 2011–16 (percentage shares)   262
11.3 Trends in operational stock of industrial robots in India (number) 264
11.4 Trends in the number of delivered robots   265
11.5 Task-based operational stock of industrial robots in India,
 2011–16   267
11.6 Extent of the diffusion of automation technologies in India
 compared with other countries, 2015 (density of industrial
 robots per 10,000 manufacturing employment)   270
11.7 Industrial robot usage in MNC affiliates in India's automotive
 industry   270

Figures and Maps

Figures

1.1 Share of manufacturing and industry in GDP   1

2.1 An *ustagar* with his son in a home-based unit in Chota, South
24 Parganas   38

2.2 Metiabruz: inside ABM *haat* in a weekly market, Kolkata   41

2.3 Regent Garment Park at Barasat, North 24 Paraganas   43

4.1 Growth in total vehicle production   75

4.2 Exports and imports from 2000–18   77

4.3 Ambattur automotive cluster   82

4.4 Real wage rate: 2000–16   88

4A.1 Gross turnover in ₹ millions (deflated by WPI)   94

5.1 Export and import of ceramic products: India, 1988–2017   103

5.2 China's share (%) in India's exports and imports of ceramic
products, 1988–2017   104

5.3 Trade balance in ceramic products: China, 1992–2016   105

5.4 Trade balance in ceramic products: India, 1988–2017   105

5.5 Share of exports of ceramic products by type: India, 1988–2017   106

5.6 Share of imports of ceramic products by type: India, 1988–2017   107

6.1 (a) Small firms' average growth (%) in sales by plant size,
2013–18 periods (b) Exporting firms' sales (in ₹ crore) over the
2013–18 period   136

6.2 Firm-level variation in resilience scale   139

6.3 Region-wise trend of India's export of sports equipment,
US$ million   141

7.1 Average net export (export–import) for 2004–08, 2009–13
and 2014–18 by types of locks in US$ million   155

9.1 Daily wage rate skilled workers doing product pacakaging and
quality control   202

9.2 Workers polishing and smoothening tanned leather procured
from Kolkata that would previously be tanned in Dharavi   205

9.3 Spatial constraints are evident as three-fourths of the
enterprises are crunched up in less than 500 square feet   207

9.4 The Indian Leather Art Co. is a space-constrained enterprise, like many others in Dharavi, with narrow steps and a rope for climbing to the manufacturing enterprise   208

9.5 A 15-year-old Juki machine, bought second hand, exemplifying the need to upgrade machinery   210

9.6 Lack of training and vocational skills constrain Dharavi's leather entrepreneurs   210

9.7 Conventional marketing methods prevail   211

9.8 The Leather Goods Manufacturers' Association head office in Dharavi   213

9.9 A buyer negotiates and bargains; as a result, the entrepreneur cuts prices, because every retail sale matters for his business to stay afloat   215

11.1 Trends in operational stock of industrial robots in the world and in India (in thousands)   259

11.2 Estimated worldwide operational stock of industrial robots in the 15 largest markets, 2016   259

11.3 Density of industrial robots across both developed and developing countries, 2016   260

11.4 Industry-wise operational stock of industrial robots in India, 2006–16   266

11.5 Trends in density of industrial robots in India, manufacturing versus automotive industry   269

11.6a Trends in employment in India's automotive manufacturing industry   272

11.6b Share of automotive sector employment in total organised manufacturing sector employment   273

Maps

1.1 Location of the case studies   7
2.1 Kolkata garment cluster: location of places   31
5.1 The Morbi ceramic clusters trapezoid   124
5.2 The Kandla Port link roadway to Morbi ceramic clusters trapezoid   125
8.1 Howrah cluster map   175
9.1 Map of Dharavi area   198

Preface and Acknowledgements

By the middle of the 2010s, India's economic boom had tapered off after the global financial crisis. India did not suffer as much as the advanced economies did because of its large domestic market and relatively modest exposure to international capital flows. However, India's growing import dependence and rising share of short-term capital inflows in managing the balance of payment deficit became increasingly evident.

The widely accepted view of industrial stagnation gave rise to the clarion call for 'Make in India' – as coined by the then newly elected government. Such a policy goal resonated well with the public in response to growing import dependence on China for even simple consumer goods, such as kites or Ganesha idols. Modest output performance also meant a lack of manufacturing employment growth.

Around the time, I reviewed academic research status on India's industrialisation trends and patterns for the Indian Council of Social Science Research (ICSSR), analysing the reasons for India's modest industrial performance. During a discussion with Srinivasan Iyer of the Ford Foundation and P. S. Vijayshankar of Samaj Pragati Sahayog, Bagli, Dewas, an idea emerged for a research programme on the theme of manufacturing growth, employment and livelihood issues. There are many accounts of industrial performance at the aggregate level. However, our understanding of what has happened at the ground level in recent times seems acutely lacking. Likewise, though there is considerable scholarship on labour and employment, the current academic focus on manufacturing production and its implication for jobs and skills appears sparse.

The above idea, it appeared to me, offered an opportunity to bring together scholars to undertake detailed studies into how the labour-intensive industries, locations and clusters were performing. And what would it take to realising the national goal of 'Make in India'?

Our effort was, in other words, an attempt to do in India's development discourse what the late Alice Amsden graphically described, 'Bring Production Back In'. Why has India not performed well even in simple consumer goods? After deliberations with many concerned scholars over a year, the programme took root in 2016 at the Indira Gandhi Institute of Development Research (IGIDR), Mumbai.

I mentioned the idea to S. Mahendra Dev, Director, Indira Gandhi Institute of Development Research (IGIDR). He enthusiastically welcomed it, agreeing to host the research initiative at the institute. I am grateful to the director for the project's smooth functioning and successful accomplishment of its goals. I thank the registrar and the institute's administrative staff for their valuable support; I am particularly grateful to Sayli Charatkar and Pratiksha Worlikar, who gladly shouldered the project administration responsibility.

Kshiti Gala, who initially joined the project to assist me with the academic spadework, did a fine job undertaking the literature review, identifying potential issues for research and scholars with credible research record. I thank her for her help in launching the initiative. During her work, Kshiti became interested in the problems we were investigating. She expressed her desire to conduct an independent inquiry by herself into the Dharavi leather goods cluster, located close to her residence, about which she had personal acquaintance. I encouraged her academic curiosity.

Before formally initiating the project, we had an informal advisory group consisting of Sudip Chaudhuri, Sunil Mani, K. V. Ramaswamy, P. S. Vijay Shankar and C. Veeramani, whose advice was valuable. I am indebted to them all for all their enthusiastic support and their keen interest in our inquiries.

We held a series of workshops to initiate, review and disseminate the research findings in Mumbai and Delhi. We thank Suresh Babu, Mukesh Gulati, Radhicka Kapoor, K. Narayanan, Vikas Rawal, Tamal Sarkar and Padmini Swaminathan for their contributions during these events and for offering their valuable comments and suggestions to the contributors. I thank them all for their sincere and constructive comments.

To disseminate the research finding among academics, civil society organisations and policymakers, we held a workshop in Delhi 2019. I thank K. P. Krishnan, former Secretary, Ministry of Skill Development and Entrepreneurship, for enthusiastically supporting our effort and participating in the workshop. I also thank Guruprasad Mohapatra, Secretary, Department for Promotion of Industry and Internal Trade; Anand Bhal, former Principal Economic advisor, Government of India; and many other officials for their enthusiastic response to our initiative.

Anwesha Rana, commissioning editor, Cambridge University Press, was very enthusiastic about our research effort right from the beginning. We have worked closely for over two years to bring this book project to fruition. I most sincerely thank her for showing interest in our initiative and being patient with me and the contributors to get our work to completion. I also thank the publisher's anonymous referees, whose comments and suggestions were valuable. They helped us bring out the finding more clearly and improve the quality of reporting of the results. I also thank the publisher's production team, led by Aniruddha De, to efficiently bring out the volume and for their professionally competent job.

More than anyone else, Srinivasan has been a constant source of strength and support throughout the endeavour, without ever interfering in the conduct of research or drawing conclusions and disseminating the results to a broader audience. He was always available to us with constructive suggestions and wise counsel. I am deeply indebted to him. I also thank Seema Sharma and Sundari Kumari of the Ford Foundation, Delhi office, for their consistent and unassuming support for our effort.

Trivandrum   R. Nagaraj
18 March 2021

CHAPTER 1

Introduction

R. NAGARAJ

The Context

In 2017–18, the manufacturing sector (industry) accounted for 18 per cent (31.2 per cent) of India's gross domestic output (GDP) at constant prices. The corresponding ratio for employment is 12.1 per cent (27 per cent), as per the periodic labour force survey (PLFS) data. As the ratios have barely inched up for over 25 years (Figure 1.1), it is a sign of industrial stagnation (Nagaraj 2017). Moreover, after initiating the liberal (free-market) economic reforms in 1991, import and technological dependence have risen (Chaudhuri 2013; Mani 2018).

However, a boom in information technology (IT) services and their exports has more than compensated for industrial stagnation, as India's output growth accelerated. After joining the World Trade Organisation (WTO) in 2001, if China came to be known as the world's factory, many believed that India was

Figure 1.1 Share of manufacturing and industry in GDP

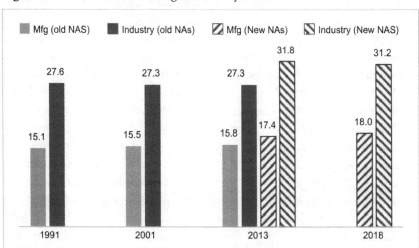

Source: National Accounts Statistics, various issues.

on its way to becoming the world's back office. For a while, India seemed to be on course, catching up with China, but it faltered suddenly.

The global financial crisis in 2008, the great recession after that and the rising threats of a trade war have taken the sheen out of India's performance and put paid to its global ambition. Meanwhile, China has graduated from assembling low-quality consumer goods to a technologically dominant nation – for example, Huawei's pole position in the telecom technology market – with world-beating firms and brands, both in high-tech manufacturing and IT services.

Realising the limits to the growth of the new services without the backing of a sound manufacturing base, the National Manufacturing Policy, 2011, sought to raise the sector's share in GDP to 25 per cent and to create 100 million additional manufacturing sector jobs by 2025. Though the policy failed to take off, the document helped articulate the need for industrialisation – or re-industrialisation – as an imperative for long-term national development.

In 2015, the policy was recast as the 'Make in India' initiative, with the following objectives:

1. The target of an increase in manufacturing sector growth rate to 12–14 per cent per annum over the medium term.
2. An increase in the share of manufacturing in the country's GDP from 16 per cent to 25 per cent by 2022.
3. To create 100 million additional jobs by 2022 in the manufacturing sector.

What has Make in India managed to accomplish? For output growth, there are two competing estimates. Between 2012–13 and 2017–18, National Accounts recorded an annual industrial growth rate of 7.5 per cent. The index of industrial production (IIP) shows an annual growth rate of less than half of that figure, that is, 3.8 per cent. As the GDP growth rate is probably overestimated due to methodological issues in the current series of National Accounts with 2011–12 as the base year (Nagaraj and Srinivasan 2016), industrial growth rate is probably around 5–6 per cent per year, as per the Annual Survey of Industries (ASI). To gain a perspective, during the boom years of 2003–08, industry grew at close to 10 per cent per year. The modest output growth during the last decade was accompanied by massive job losses: the manufacturing sector lost 3.4 million jobs between 2011–12 and 2017–18 (Mehrotra and Parida 2019).[1]

Widespread unease with poor industrial performance goes beyond the aggregate numbers. Imports of even simple consumer goods seem to have displaced domestic production; for example, from Ganesha idols and kites to electric toasters and fans are imported from China.[2] Rising imports have reduced many domestic manufacturers to distributors and retailers of Chinese goods, selling imported goods under their labels. Though credible and granular data on production and imports of such items are hard to come by, there seems to be merit in the public perception that industrial performance has taken a serious beating.

In this context, we initiated a research programme on how to reimagine industrialisation for jobs and growth. The promotion of labour-intensive goods and their exports – to recall the theoretical arguments – was the primary reason for initiating liberal economic reforms, to encourage industrialisation in line with India's comparative advantage.

The outcomes turned out to be different, however. Skill- and capital-intensive IT outsourcing services boomed, while manufacturing languished. Undoubtedly, the ability to move into (higher value-added) IT services – building on domestic industrial capabilities, including electronics hardware and technical education – was a creditable achievement. However, doing so by undermining domestic manufacturing was probably costly. Here is a telling evidence: in 1985, capital goods' share in industrial production in China and India was about 20 per cent. By close to the year 2000, China's share had risen to 30 per cent, while India's share had shrunk to 15 per cent (Nagaraj 2007). The decline in capital goods' share meant missing out on the positive externalities of productivity gains of manufacturing technologies (including information and communication technology [ICT] hardware) for the rest of the economy – following Verdoorn's law (Dasgupta and Singh 2015; Felipe 2018). No large economy has moved up the development path without traversing the stage of industrialisation, history shows (Perkins and Syrquin 1989).

With industrial wages now rising in China, many labour-intensive industries are moving out to other labour-abundant countries such as Vietnam, Cambodia and Bangladesh. Can India attract such footloose global capital to reindustrialise to realise the Make in India goals? As a first step, can India retake the light manufactures that seem to have slipped out?

In light of the foregoing discussion, the research question posed is the following: How to promote employment and output growth in labour-intensive industries or labour-intensive segments of capital-intensive industries? Historically, state support for such industries has been vital (Wade 1990; Amsden 2001). So, what kind, variety and scale of state assistance could potentially help achieve the policy goals? Parenthetically, we were also interested in finding out how Chinese imports may have affected these industries and the possible policy response to it. The research findings reported in this volume seek to answers some of these questions at the level of industrial districts, clusters and locations.

The introduction has three sections. Section I explains the research strategy and the modes of inquiry, section II offers a bird's-eye view of findings, and section III concludes the chapter by drawing a few policy lessons.

I

Research Strategy

Research Design: Ideally, answering the foregoing questions requires detailed firm and factory (or establishment) level production and sales information. The ASI is a credible data source for factories employing 10 or more workers using power (that is, the organised sector), accounting for nearly two-thirds of the manufacturing output and about one-fifth of the employment. For the remaining, the economic census and its follow-up enterprise surveys of non-agricultural enterprises, conducted by National Sample Survey Organisation (NSSO) since 1977, are the sources. The latest one was conducted in 2015–16.[3] However, the economic census is known to understate employment, and its output and investment data are weak (Manna 2010). Thus, using secondary data for studying labour-intensive industries that span the organised and unorganised sectors seems a difficult task.

The official data on registered micro, small and medium enterprises (MSMEs) – small industry, for short – is the other major source. Investment in plant and machinery is the defining criteria for registration under the MSME Development Act. The investment limits are periodically revised upwards; the current limits are as in Table 1.1.[4] Since 1973–74, official agencies have conducted four censuses of registered MSMEs; the fifth census was scheduled for 2016 but was not conducted. Though a valuable source, the census results are not comparable as investment limits (cut-offs) to qualify as an MSME have been revised.

In 2016–17, MSMEs' gross value added (GVA) was ₹44,05,753 crore, accounting for 29 per cent of GDP at current prices. In 2015–16, there were 196.65 lakh MSMEs in the manufacturing sector, employing 360.41 lakh workers (accounting for 31 per cent of value added and 32 per cent of all MSMEs respectively) (*Annual Report, 2018–19*, Ministry of MSMEs).[5] These

Table 1.1   Definition of MSME

Classification	Manufacturing Enterprise (Investment in Plant and Machinery)	Service Enterprise (Investment in Equipment)
Micro	Up to ₹25 lakh	Up to ₹10 lakh
Small	Above ₹25 lakh and up to ₹5 crore	Above ₹10 lakh and up to ₹2 crore
Medium	Above ₹5 crore and up to ₹10 crore	Above ₹2 crore and up to ₹5 crore

Source: RBI (2019)

Note: 1 lakh = 100,000; 1 crore = 10 million.

estimates are based on the NSSO survey of unincorporated non-agricultural enterprises (excluding construction), 2015–16.[6] Evidently, these estimates do not refer to the contribution of registered MSMEs.

The requirement for registration of enterprises under the MSME Development Act, 2006, is ambiguous. As the filing of information after the commencement of production is not mandatory, there is no record of working MSMEs, as evident from the following official statement:

> As per the provisions of the Act, MSMEs file Entrepreneurs Memorandum (Part-I) at District Industries Centres (DICs). After commencement of the project, the entrepreneur concerned files Entrepreneurs Memorandum (Part-II)/[EM-II]. Prior to enactment of the Micro, Small & Medium Enterprises Development Act, 2006 (MSMED Act, 2006) there was a system of registration by small scale industrial units to the DICs. *Now, filing of EM-II is discretionary for micro, small and medium enterprise engaged in both manufacturing and services.* However, it is mandatory for medium scale enterprise engaged in manufacture or production of goods pertaining to any industry specified in the First Schedule of the ID&R Act, 1951.[7]

The official MSME data are not compatible with the ASI or the economic census estimates, as their defining characteristics are different. Moreover, a large segment of small enterprises lies outside the registered MSME sector.

Considering the foregoing problems with the official data, we chose to initiate detailed case studies of labour-intensive/industries/products/locations/clusters. We have not identified industries strictly by labour intensity criterion – as ideally required – but on shared knowledge about such industries and their activities. For instance, the automotive industry is known to be capital intensive, but many auto component industries and processes are known to be relatively labour intensive.

Admittedly, the case-study approach has its limitations, as it does not provide aggregate or a macro picture of the MSME sector. However, hopefully, these case studies will offer rich insights with realistic accounts to compensate for the lack of quantitative information, which will be helpful in drawing meaningful policy lessons. To ensure that our studies help secure an aggregate picture, we sought to spread case studies geographically as widely as possible.

For identifying locations for field surveys, ideally, one should be able to get quantitative information on labour-intensive industries. Such data are not available. Moreover, to undertake the fieldwork of factories and firms is a difficult task, requiring considerable local knowledge, language proficiency and prior experience. Social and personal connections to get access to entrepreneurs/government officials/trade representatives is a valuable resource for surveys.

Therefore, we sought to identify scholars (mostly) with prior fieldwork-based industrial research expertise (Table 1.1). In 2018, we initiated nine such case studies – from the sports goods industry in Jalandhar (Punjab) and Meerut (Uttar Pradesh) to the knitwear industry in Tirupur (Tamil Nadu), and the foundry cluster in Howrah (Kolkata urban region) to the ceramic tile industry in Morbi (Gujarat) (Map 1.1). The researchers addressed the question mentioned earlier from their preferred analytical perspectives – avoiding a cookie-cutter approach – which explains why we have used more general terms such as industrial location, cluster and district interchangeably.

Most economists believe in labour-intensive industrialisation as a proven route to development. However, scholars studying the (on-going) fourth industrial revolution – that is, artificial intelligence, virtual reality, internet of things, and robotics – have raised apprehensions over the prospects of large-scale job losses. Frey and Osborne (2013), for example, have suggested that up to 47 per cent of the total employment in the United States (US) is in the high-risk category of being automated quickly, in a decade or so.

Such dire prediction could have devastating implications for India, in an open globalised economy. In response, we considered it prudent to invite an economist specialising in technology to inform us of the potential threat of automation. The findings reported in the volume have used a unique database that tracks the application of industrial robots in India at the level of 'tasks' (against commonly used occupational classification). The findings suggest a sober view. Contrary to apocalyptic predictions, robots are not likely to steal manufacturing jobs, at least not yet (Chapter 11). These results, reassuringly, seem consistent with Frey's (2019) revised, realistic, re-assessment.

Map 1.1   Location of the case studies

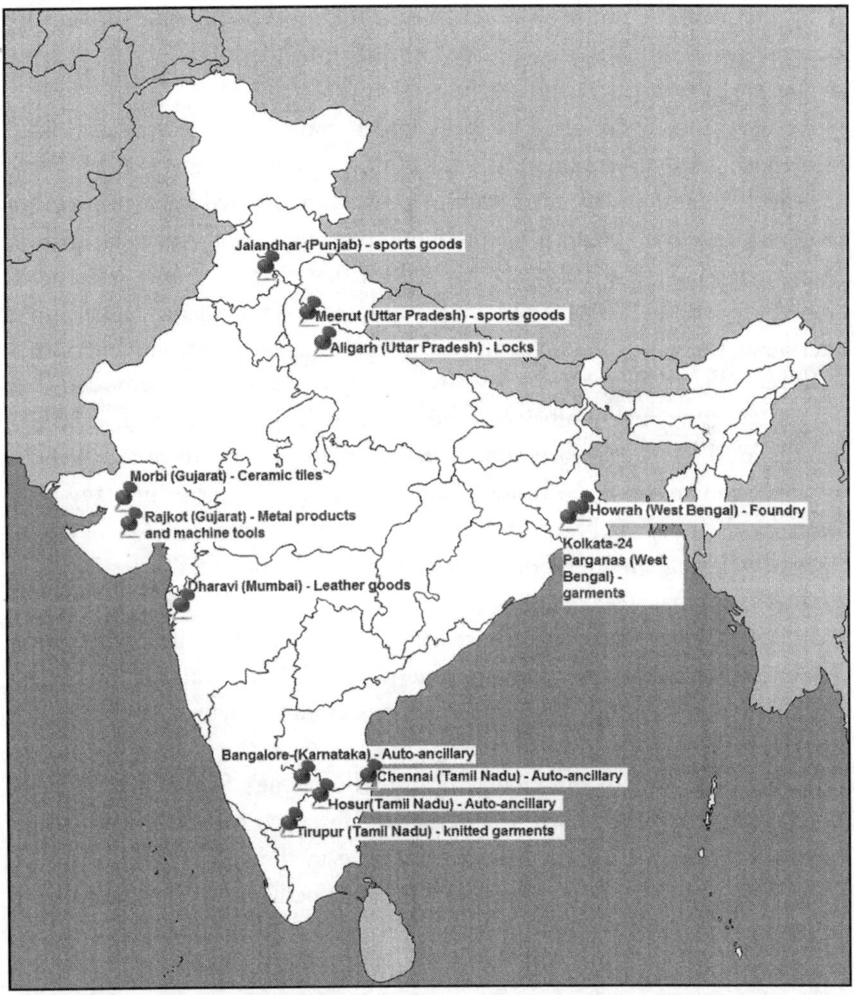

Jalandhar (Punjab) - sports goods

Meerut (Uttar Pradesh) - sports goods

Aligarh (Uttar Pradesh) - Locks

Morbi (Gujarat) - Ceramic tiles

Rajkot (Gujarat) - Metal products and machine tools

Howrah (West Bengal) - Foundry

Kolkata-24 Parganas (West Bengal) - garments

Dharavi (Mumbai) - Leather goods

Bangalore (Karnataka) - Auto-ancillary

Chennai (Tamil Nadu) - Auto-ancillary

Hosur (Tamil Nadu) - Auto-ancillary

Tirupur (Tamil Nadu) - knitted garments

Source: Prepared by author based on map downloaded from d-maps.com.
Note: Map not to scale and does not represent authentic international boundaries.

Fieldwork Methodology

Ideally, fieldwork-based research should follow a well-defined statistical sampling procedure to obtain a representative account. However, often, it is not possible to get a reasonably complete list of factories and firms working in a location or an industry. District Industries Centres (DICs), the official nodal agency at the micro level, often lacks credible and up-to-date information. The list of registered factories available with the inspectorate of factories – a factory being the primary unit of industrial production – is often quite at variance with the ground reality, as a large proportion of factories do not get (or avoid getting) registered under the Factories Act, 1948.[8]

As industrial firms often operate under commercial secrecy and with ambiguous legal or commercial status, entrepreneurs many a time refuse to provide quantitative information or even spare audited balance sheet for academic research. Hence, we preferred personal, anonymous interviews. Thus, doing industrial fieldwork could be a daunting (at times, hazardous) task.[9] However, rich details obtained by close observation and open-ended interviews, we believe, would compensate for the lack of quantitative accounts.

Given the challenges, the researchers followed mixed methods. They interviewed government officials at the state and district levels (such as DICs), and the local industry association(s), and sought their help in conducting the surveys. Scholars' prior professional and social acquaintances – in many cases based on their past field research in the location – often came in handy to get entry through many doors. However, to avoid potential selection bias, scholars consciously sought to survey and interview as diverse a set of firms and entrepreneurs as possible. Moreover, the information is invariably cross-checked or verified with knowledgeable people. We are thus confident that the survey material and their interpretations are a fair representation of the industry or location.

To get a glimpse of the ground reality, to wet one's feet in the fieldwork (and perhaps to whet one's curiosity), the volume editor spent 2–3 days at each location (barring one) when the scholars were in the field. As most surveys were conducted around the same time, the editor perhaps had the advantage of drawing lessons from a comparative experience of the clusters. Thus, what follows is a glimpse of the research findings – avoiding summarising each chapter – reported in the case studies as well from the editor's observations and field notes.

II

A Glimpse of Finding and Policy Lessons

Wide Variations in Output and Employment Performance

Ceramic tiles (in Morbi) and engineering goods (in Rajkot) were booming. The auto-ancillary cluster (in Hosur and Chennai) and the Kolkata and Tirupur garment clusters were performing well with stable demand conditions. The iron foundries in Howrah, leather goods in Dharavi, sports goods in Jalandhar and lock manufacturing in Aligarh appeared stagnant or declining. These are bold generalisations based on extensive interviews and anecdotal evidence; no comparable hard data are available.

Employment generation appeared similar. If Rajkot reported a shortage of skilled workers, Jalandhar faced widespread underemployment, as many manufacturers turned traders and retailers, selling Chinese sports goods. Tirupur seemed to face labour shortages, and employers offered free bus service to ferry workers from nearby villages. Foundries in Howrah faced labour shortages, as the work was strenuous and hazardous, and the local workers (especially younger ones) found easier and better-paying jobs in the services in urban areas (such as running a battery-operated 3-wheeled *to-to*, ubiquitous in the town).

Demonetisation of high-valued currency notes in November 2016 and the introduction of the (ill-designed) goods and services tax (GST) in early 2017 seem to have hit hard the smaller among the enterprises surveyed in most locations. The bigger firms were able to get through with GST filing, as the entrepreneurs were better educated and had the ability to hire accountants for filing the returns frequently.

The inability of smaller and self-employed enterprises to cope with GST is not merely on account of their propensity to evade taxes (as alleged popularly and by many GST proponents). They are also mostly poor and illiterate, and cannot afford to engage a chartered accountant to file the GST returns. Such enterprises usually survive on the strength of skilled work and ability to use the owners and their families' (unpaid) labour intensely with thin profit margins (with zero opportunity cost in a labour-surplus economy). As the high GST rates and the compliance costs seem to undercut the labour cost advantage of such enterprises, they are getting edged out of the market. The GST exemption limit seems too meagre to compensate for the compliance cost.

Effect of Chinese Imports

Jalandhar (sports goods) and Aligarh (locks) are adversely affected by Chinese imports. Lately, in Dharavi, Chinese imports have made inroads into the higher-end corporate market, leaving the cluster with lower-end, low margin mass market.

Jalandhar seems stuck in a 'low-level equilibrium' producing mainly traditional wood- and leather-based sports goods for football and cricket, albeit with a stable demand. Chinese firms have captured the cream of the market, that is, exports. Newer sports items (such as badminton and tennis goods) are met by Chinese and Japanese imports (more about it later).

Aligarh has faced intense competition in the low-end domestic market from China. Demand for newer products such as automobile locks was met by imports from East Asia, as global auto firms prefer to source components from their ancillary partners in their home countries. This is a clear indication of the lack of India's domestic capability.

Morbi's ceramic tile industry offers a counterexample where the Chinese imports are pushed back as domestic capabilities have expanded (more about it later).

Export Performance

Most clusters primarily cater to the domestic market, though a small fraction of firms in these locations specialise in exports (though hard to get their estimates, either as quantities or output shares). Such firms mostly tend to be secretive and refuse to grant interviews or share information (we had some bitter experiences in Howarh and Aligarh). Hence, our information on export-oriented enterprises is sparse. Tirupur is mainly an export-oriented cluster, and Morbi has reportedly seen a rising share of exports lately.

Tirupur and Morbi are both relatively dynamic industrial centres. Firms in these locations perceive exports as the way to grow, with scope for learning by producing, and through better value addition to the raw materials – though, at the moment, they mostly produce relatively low-end (low value-added) items.[10] These clusters, expectedly, face fierce competition in external markets, where large monopsonistic buyers squeeze profit margins (by comparing costs and delivery schedules on a real-time basis across clusters and countries). Nevertheless, entrepreneurs in Tirupur and Morbi firmly believe in the gains from exports lying in large production volumes, in the prospects of moving up the value chain and of the potential for 'learning by doing'.

In Jalandhar, hand-stitched footballs/rugby balls are an essential export item, produced by a few relatively larger firms, supplying to wholesale traders in London (apparently, not to leading brands directly). Similarly, in Howrah, reportedly, a few large foundries export manhole (or utility hole) covers – a sanitary item – to Europe and the Middle East, historically a vital market that got eroded. The business press often suggests substantial exports from Howrah, but we did not find definitive estimates. Considering that advanced economies have prohibited the manufacturing of such environmentally polluting products as manhole covers, the reported rediscovery of these markets lately did not appear surprising.

Dharavi is a compelling case of growth in leather goods exports during the economic boom of the 2000s (2003–08) when it reportedly emerged as a sourcing point for leading international brands.[11] After the global financial crisis of 2008, Dharavi's global presence seems to have disappeared.[12]

Domestic-market-oriented Clusters

The Kolkata garment cluster that produces almost entirely for the lower-end domestic market that is reportedly expanding steadily. These goods have a 'commodity' character (unlike higher-end garments sold via long-term supply contracts under specific brands with well-defined quality specifications). The cluster's output is mostly sold in Metiabruz, a locality on the outskirts of Kolkata, and in Howrah – reportedly, one of India's largest weekly markets for garments drawing retail traders from all over the country.

Apparently, the Kolkata cluster has also given rise to (or mostly supports) the luxury Indian ethnic clothing brand Manyavar. The cluster produces intricate embroidery work (requiring considerable traditional skills) via a tight-knit subcontracting or outsourcing network. Kolkata's outskirts are also home to leading domestic innerwear brands such as Rupa or Dollar. The Bata Shoe Company and the adjacent areas of the 24-Parganas districts in the Kolkata metropolitan region are now reportedly home to low-end knitwear goods and jeans production for the domestic market.

In machinery manufacturing (including the automotive industry), assembly is a skill-intensive activity. Many auto-ancillary firms in Bangalore and Hosur producing relatively capital-intensive products and sub-assemblies are part of global value chains and production networks of their parent firms. Indian firms are primarily exporting through their affiliates, or to tier 1 multinational suppliers, who are members of free trade zones. These firms supply the domestic market, but also feed the global chains depending on relative profitability and subject to export-restriction clauses imposed in the technology-import agreements. Being part of the networks, such firms have an opportunity to upgrade their technologies. Reportedly, some skilled workers get a few opportunities for working in other countries, though it is difficult to quantify their effect.

Skill Requirements/Development

Barring the auto-ancillary industry and the Rajkot engineering industry (requiring skilled workers with formal training in Industrial Training Institutes [ITI] and engineering diplomas), in most other locations labour is recruited in the traditional ways, that is, by on-job training. Illiterate (often migrant) workers enter the cluster as unskilled labour, become 'helpers' in due course and (many) eventually become skilled workers. In the Kolkata garment cluster, reportedly, middle-school children start working as helpers in family- and community-run enterprises, as they find little prospects of employment outside (after completing schooling). A polar opposite case is in Rajkot's precision engineering firms, such as machine tools, where ITI trained workers, or even engineering graduates, are put through in-house training programmes before joining the production line.

However, many entrepreneurs in Rajkot also contended that, in the long run, it should be the government's responsibility to create training facilities to bridge the skill gap. They also expressed the need for several 'finishing schools', at least one tool room, a design school and testing facilities, as investment in such facilities are beyond the technical capability and wherewithal of the Rajkot industry.

In most case studies, acquiring skills seems to offer a tiny window of opportunity for upward mobility. The progression seems quicker and steeper for educated and technically qualified workers. Further, workers with social capital – of caste and regional affinity – seem to move up as self-employed workers, or by setting up their own enterprises. Such microenterprises usually start as 'job-workers', that is, undertaking standardised (machining or foundry) jobs for a fixed piece rate. Such work may improve their earnings marginally, but it allows the entrepreneurs to work intensely with limited machines to learn by doing (and acquire a few elementary organisational skills needed to become an entrepreneur).[13]

In most of our studies, formal skill imparting institutions have played only a marginal role. Often, such institutions appeared dysfunctional or unrelated to the industrial needs. For example, a government polytechnic for leather technology in Bandra East, set up in the 1930s, a stone's throw from the Dharavi cluster, is a case in point. Yet it has no technical and commercial linkages with the Dharavi cluster, which, as mentioned earlier, exported leather products worth up to $500 million for leading global brands (*Economist* 2005). The polytechnic, with its technical facilities frozen in time, mainly offers a diploma in leather tanning for students in small batches, but has little to offer to Dharavi's finished leather goods production.

The poor state of public skill development institutions seems to be true of the other locations as well. In Aligarh, the National Small Industries Corporation's (NSIC) – a public sector promotional agency – training centre located in the industrial estate does offer a few short-term skill development courses in using modern machines in the lock industry. In Jalandhar, state-sponsored skill development and sport-goods promotional facilities created in the 1970s are reportedly lying idle now (we did not get an opportunity to visit the facility).

In contrast, in Hosur (on Bangalore's outskirts, along the border with Tamil Nadu), private engineering colleges seem to have a close technical association with the auto-ancillary industry in offering job-oriented training to skilled workers to become supervisors. Many auto-ancillary firms have internalised the training cost and developed in-house tool rooms and personalised on-the-job courses to train workers.

Technical Progress and Development of New Products in the Clusters

Did we observe any perceptible technical progress among the clusters? Some noteworthy cases are discernible. In Rajkot, a manufacturer for small diesel engines for agriculture purposes, set up some three decades ago, has moved up the technology ladder to now produce an entire 25 horsepower tractor for India's largest tractor producer (as an original equipment manufacturer [OEN] supplier). In Rajkot, leading computer numerical control (CNC) machine tool manufacturers – now reportedly competing with leading Asian firms in the global market – trace their origins as humble workshops and foundries established in the 1960s.

In the automobile industry, post-2010, there is an increase in research and development (R&D) intensity across both the OEMs and the component sector. R&D has moved from adaptive to product development, especially application engineering and engineering research, such as reliability engineering for safety. Even so, the lack of basic research and product development capability in India is an essential reason for the high import intensity of automobile components.

In Tirupur, as is widely acknowledged, the standard route for success in the knitted garments industry is to start by making men's innerwear for the local market, then for the national market and then to move to make outerwear for exports. The final stage is competitive for sure, with reportedly small and shrinking profit margins. Yet small enterprises seem eager to get into it, as it enables them to produce a large volume of standardised products (the 'volumes game', to use the industry jargon), with a reasonable scope for learning by doing.

However, beyond a point, most firms reportedly face the difficulty of competing with international brands, as foreign buying agents hold monopsony power, that is, they operate in a market with a single buyer and a large number of sellers. A way out for small suppliers is to diversify to different brands and geographical markets. We came across a compelling case of a Tirupur-based buying agent (on behalf of leading global brands) managing to acquire a fashion design studio in London. The entrepreneur's business strategy was to get his designs approved by the leading brands and get the garments manufactured in the cluster at competitive rates (on the strength of the supply chain that the buying agent can command).

In Jalandhar, one noticed a few firms moving from producing unbranded products to branded ones, but the progression seems too modest and localised to be discernible.

Poor Infrastructure

In most industrial locations, infrastructure facilities – that is, roads, water supply, street lighting, common service facilities and road connectivity to the nearest railhead or highway (or local public goods) – appeared frozen in time, of the early 1990s. Notwithstanding the changes in the official terminology or nomenclature – from industrial estates to clusters or parks, small industry service institutes to MSME Development Institutes, and so on – there seems to be little practical difference in the extent and quality of state support.

However, well-performing locations such as Morbi, Rajkot and Tirupur have perceptibly superior infrastructure provided by state-level promotional agencies. Morbi, for instance, has excellent road connectivity to Kandla port (about 130 kilometres away), permitting the quick import of raw materials and export of finished goods. A natural gas pipeline and uninterrupted power supply reportedly laid the foundation of Morbi's re-taking of the ceramic tile industry from Chinese imports and rising exports to the Middle East.[14]

State-level industrial promotional agencies seem to have played a vital role in Tirupur's growth. For instance, the Tamil Nadu small industries corporation has set up a training school and a design centre in one its industrial estates, in partnership with the local industry association and leading garment producers to train local youth in critical skills. The design centre reportedly works in collaboration with the National Institute of Fashion Design, New Delhi, to impart design capabilities to Tirupur firms and technically qualified youth.[15]

Reportedly, the industry association, together with state-level promotional agencies, are setting up a modern convention centre to hold international exhibitions and buyer–seller meets to showcase Tirupur's textile products. Thus, one could discern a close association between infrastructure support and cluster-level performance and a shared vision of the cluster's future.

Active Industry Association

In well-performing clusters, local industry associations played an active role in promoting their collective interests with state- and national-level promotional agencies. In Morbi, for example, the association lobbied for obtaining the state support similar to what the Chinese government offers to its enterprises (that is, some measure of 'level-playing field'). In Tirupur, the industry association has been active in obtaining the support of state-level agencies to invest in pollution control equipment to overcome the Supreme Court's mandate to shut down the cluster (as discussed in the next section). In Rajkot, the industry association not only does lobbying work with the government for the industry but it also – in association with Saurashtra University's management department – promotes business development by holding lectures and conducting short courses on management subjects, such as quality control. The Lodhika Industrial Association in the Gujarat Industrial Development Corporation (GIDC) estate in Rajkot has set up a skill development centre to train up to 300 technicians at a time.

In contrast, in Howrah, the association seems to carry little heft with the state-level agencies. Exporters, reportedly doing a flourishing business, though formally members, seem to have little interaction with the industry association. Surprisingly, even the industry association's office-bearers seem to have little knowledge about the export-oriented firms and their performance.

Lessons from Comparative Analysis

Role of the local state

Until about 15 years ago, Morbi mostly manufactured cement tiles for the national market. As India's construction industry boomed during the 2000s,

Chinese ceramic tiles displaced Morbi's cement tiles, despite the product's natural protection of low value-to-weight ratio. However, Morbi was able to overcome the import competition, through (*a*) anti-dumping duties, (*b*) assured electric supply, (*c*) a natural gas pipeline from Kandla and (*d*) concessional tariff to import tile-making machines from Italy and China.

Not only has the industry grown in size but the variety and complexity of tiles manufactured have gone up perceptibly. The cluster now reportedly exports up to 50 per cent (and rising) of its output, though not to the top end of the global market, but slightly less demanding customers in the Middle Eastern and East Africa, the local industry association claims. With the rise in technical capabilities, Chinese firms have reportedly become eager to collaborate with firms in Morbi to access the Middle Eastern markets, says the association.

Leading domestic brands of tiles and sanitary fittings, such as Parryware and Kajaria, subcontract a sizeable share of their output to the Morbi manufacturers (though no quantitative information is available). Here is a case study of an industry threatened by imports that overcame it through technological modernisation with specific state support.

In contrast, Jalandhar's sports goods industry continues to focus on wood- and leather-based traditional sports goods for football and cricket, whose share in the sports and fitness goods market has diminished, relative to the overall size of the sports goods market. The Jalandhar cluster has mostly failed to modernise to produce newer products with high-income elasticity of demand, such as badminton and tennis rackets. Such products made using more modern materials (such as aluminium alloys) are mostly imported. Though sports goods were de-reserved in the 1990s – that is, taken off the list of products meant for exclusive production under MSMEs under the erstwhile industrial policy – the industry has failed to attract new investments or technology, or expand scales of production. Similarly, the booming business of fitness equipment or sports garments (complementary goods with overlapping brands) has bypassed Jalandhar, which is stuck to producing low value-added cast-iron items such as weights used in gymnasiums.

Historically, Jalandhar's sports goods industry was an offshoot of Sialkot, now in Pakistan, when entrepreneurs and skilled workers moved across the border after the subcontinent's partition in 1947. Both the locations were thriving centres of hand-stitched footballs, though Sialkot is said to be a much bigger and sophisticated industry. About a decade ago, China edged out Sialkot and Jalandhar in the international market. However, reportedly, Sialkot has recovered its global presence through active state support for modernisation, while Jalandhar has not. The Industry association and prominent entrepreneurs were quite unanimous that the state government has neglected the industrial sector. Its primary focus remains agriculture.[16]

Environmental issues in Tirupur

Rising environmental concerns – heightened by judicial strictures – have lately affected many labour-intensive industries. However, it is interesting to discern how the legal strictures were dealt with in different clusters with varying responses from the local industry and state-level agencies.

In 2011, as per a court order, the Tirupur garment cluster was shut down for over a year as its waste water was polluting the local river, adversely affecting the drinking water sources of villages downstream. The Tirupur garment manufacturers association, however, managed to overcome the ban by making investments in common (or shared) water treatment plants. The Tamil Nadu Pollution Control Board and state-level industrial promotional agencies have collectively provided technical and financial assistance to get over the ban to resume production and regain its markets.

At the time of the survey, going a step further, the industry association was actively engaged in promoting (via advertisement campaign) Tirupur's textiles as 'green products' to overcome the stigma of the court order and to improve its international image.

In contrast, against somewhat similar strictures for the foundry industry in 1995, the West Bengal government responded by setting up a foundry park in 2009 at Ranihati-Amta Road, in Howrah district, at about 40 kilometres away from the existing cluster location. The park reportedly has poor infrastructure, and most enterprises have refused to move their foundries there (though many have acquired plots of industrial land, probably as a safe real estate bet). A foundry owner candidly admitted that the costs of daily commute to the new location would outweigh his profit margin. As a result, the foundry cluster in Howrah remains stagnant, if not declining (though hard to ascertain the claims in the absence of reliable data). One could hazard a guess that the entrepreneurs are probably waiting for changes in urban land-use regulations to reap windfall gains from converting the large industrial plots of land – the average size of the foundry plots is 2–3 *bigha*s, that is, over an acre of land – for property development, as has happened in many industrial cities after the reforms.

Another interesting comparison is possible between Howrah's outdated and polluting foundry industry with Rajkot, which produces advanced automotive-grade casting using electric arc furnaces. The puzzling question is: why did the nation's oldest and reportedly the largest foundry cluster fail to modernise (after losing its principal customer, the railways, decades ago)? West Bengal's history of industrial strife and lack of state-level institutional support explain the differential outcomes. Similarly, why is it that there are some thriving export-oriented foundries in the same location, while the majority of them are languishing. It probably calls for a more in-depth inquiry.

III

Conclusion

India's industrialisation has stagnated, as the manufacturing sector's shares in domestic output and employment have not shown measurable improvement for nearly three decades. It is a setback, as India has lost the advantages of potential externalities of productivity gains in manufacturing for the rest of the economy, following the Kaldorian stylised facts of development. Historically, no large country has become a developed nation without traversing the path of industrialisation. Moreover, for rapid industrial growth, it is needed to meet the Make in India goal. The research reported in this volume asks how to reindustrialise for growth and employment in labour-intensive industries.

The volume addresses the question based on a nation-wide nine case studies of industries/locations and clusters. As they were carried out in parallel, in 2018, a comparison of their performance offers analytical insights and policy lessons. The volume also includes a study offering a nuanced understanding of the potential threat of automation for labour-intensive industries based on an analysis of a unique database of industrial robot usage in Indian manufacturing.

The studies report, expectedly, a wide variation in output, employment and export performance. If the Morbi tile, Rajkot engineering, Kolkata garment and Tirupur knitwear clusters have done well, sports goods in Jalandhar, lock manufacturing in Aligarh and the foundry industry in Howrah appeared to have just about managing to survive. Demonetisation and the introduction of an ill-designed GST seem to have hurt the smaller enterprises in most locations. Imports from China appear to have adversely affected sports goods and locks. However, if the Morbi ceramic cluster has managed to reverse the trend of rising import to get into exports aggressively, it is by modernising and expanding its production capabilities. Auto-ancillary firms were not affected by imports, as they are part of tightly knit global supply chains, tied to their 'parent' automotive assemblers.

The well-performing clusters are those that have benefitted from considerable state support, a close working relationship between entrepreneurs, local industry associations, and the state- and district-level promotional agencies. Morbi's case study, for example, demonstrates how carefully tailored state support helped increase domestic production to reduce imports. The lessons concerning the growth of the global automobile industry suggest the need for an employment-intensive export-oriented strategy with access to free trade zones and redefining the local-content rules. In contrast, the Aligarh cluster has made limited progress in diversifying to produce newer kinds of locks to meet modern demands like automobile locks, which are primarily imported. What is perhaps required is focussed assistance at the cluster level, tailored to meet its specific needs.

Infrastructure in most industrial locations appeared frozen in time, with little changes in the state-level promotional institutions and the kinds of support offered by the government – changes in the nomenclature and designations of promotional agencies and administrative positions are only cosmetic makeovers. It is necessary to reiterate (yet one more time) that access to timely credit, especially for fixed investment, remains a formidable constraint for the small enterprises.

Lack of skills does not appear to be a significant hurdle in most locations; the modernisation of MSME institutes and NSIC training facilities would be helpful in many cases. Improving middle-school education with better designed skill-oriented courses would perhaps help prospective workers to read technical drawings, maps and written instructions more generally.

Labour-intensive industries come into conflict with environmental regulations, with increasing legal strictures. They are nevertheless not insurmountable. In Tirupur, the conflict was collectively resolved by the industry association and state-level regulatory and promotional agencies. In Howrah, in contrast, with poor state support, the problem has barely been resolved, with the foundry industry seemingly remaining in a stagnant state or in decline. The lessons for policy are instructive.

Another discernible conflict is between skill-based labour-intensive clusters with proven export potential and urban land use, for example, in Dharavi, located in the heart of Mumbai city. A strictly financial consideration would suggest displacing the cluster, to use Dharavi's prime land for commercial purposes. However, such a decision would conflict with the cluster's proven export-earning potential and the livelihood of skilled workers, eking out a living directly or indirectly through such production.

Alternatively, one could visualise Dharavi being transformed into a high-end leather goods development centre, including design studios, prototype making facilities, and trade and exhibition centres, with suitable state support that could sustain the livelihood of the leather industry workers. Could the scarce land be creatively used for dual purpose, to meet commercial demand as well as a socially inclusive and economically productive application? Such imaginative solutions perhaps call for thoughtful state support, aided by the active engagement with city planners and the civil society, to re-configure the city spaces.

Where suitable state support is forthcoming, import threat is on the retreat; it is not an argument for naïve infant industry protection (without a sunset clause), but to secure collective efficiency of the skilled workers in Dharavi, as suggested in the global evidence on industrial clusters. Similarly, environmental regulations can be overcome, depending on the nature and quality of state government support. Industry associations were quite explicit in expressing the need for localised state support for modernising the infrastructure; finance for capital investment and the close working of state-level agencies with the entrepreneurs could help expand the clusters and generate employment, both directly and indirectly.

In other words, to reindustrialise for employment generation, and to meet the national goals of Make in India, it is imperative to reimagine the industrial policy in its nitty-gritty. It has to be national in scope and local, context-specific in its implementation, and flexible and agile. Local public goods for facilitating production and their movement to highways, railheads or ports need to get special attention.

Notes

1. The evidence is based on a comparison of the employment–unemployment survey (EUS) of 2011–12 and PLFS of 2017–18, conducted by the National Sample Survey Organisation (NSSO).
2. A news report in the *Economic Times* (dated 29 August 2017) titled 'Government in a Huddle as the Fragrance of Chinese Agarbattis Spreads Far and Wide' provides an example of Chinese import penetration in India's light manufacturing.
3. Its coverage is as follows: 'All economic activities (agricultural and non-agricultural), except those involved in crop production and plantation, public administration, defense

and compulsory social security, related to production and/or distribution of goods and/or services other than for the sole purpose of own consumption were covered' (available at http://www.icssrdataservice.in/datarepository/index.php/catalog/148, accessed on 29 December 2020).

4. On 13 May 2020, the Union finance minister changed the definitions of MSMEs: The distinction between manufacturing and services enterprises was abolished. They are now defined by two criteria: (*a*) investment in plant and machinery and (*b*) turnover, with the following cut-offs. Micro enterprise: investment of less than ₹1 crore, and turnover of less than ₹5 crore; small enterprise: investment of less than ₹10 crore and turnover of less than ₹50 crore; medium enterprise: investment of less than ₹20 crore and turnover of less than ₹100 crore (1 crore = 10 million). These changes will take effect after the MSME Development Act is amended accordingly.

5. Available at https://msme.gov.in/sites/default/files/Annualrprt.pdf, accessed on 8 February 2021.

6. NSSO, *Operational Characteristics of Unincorporated Non-agricultural Enterprises (Excluding Construction) in India*, Report no. 581 (73/2.34/1), NSS 73rd Round, July 2015–June 2016, Ministry of Statistics and Programme Implementation, Government of India, New Delhi (available at http://mospi.nic.in/sites/default/files/publication_reports/NSS_581.pdf, accessed on 29 December 2020).

7. 'Entrepreneurs Memorandum (Part-II) Data on MSME Sector', Ministry of Micro, Small and Medium Enterprises, New Delhi, available at http://www.dcmsme.gov.in/publications/EMII-2014-15.pdf, accessed on 29 December 2020 (p. 1) (emphasis added).

8. For a glimpse of the practical difficulties in researching an industrial setting in India, social anthropologist, Streefkerk's (2006) account of his fieldwork in Udhana, Surat, in Gujarat, is instructive.

9. To illustrate, a (reportedly) successful exporter of castings in the Howrah cluster refused to grant us an interview after giving an appointment and making us wait for an entire day at the factory premises. We experienced this after obtaining a letter of introduction from the concerned government officials and the local industry association.

10. An entrepreneur in Morbi put it succinctly: 'On a qualitative scale, if Italian tiles are at 100, Morbi is at 5 … but we are on a path to reach 25 soon.'

11. In 2008, BBC News reported an article titled 'Indian slum hit by New York woes' which stated: 'So, if you go to Macy's or Marks and Spencer and buy a leather jacket, the chances are that it might have been manufactured here in this one room factory in Dharavi. It exports leather items, jewellery, accessories and textile largely to the US, Europe and the Middle East. However, the current credit crunch crisis has nearly crippled the $1bn (£577.8m) industry' (Ahmed 2008).

12. In 2014, lamenting Dharavi losing its business edge, Reuters reported, 'Global luxury brands such as Louis Vuitton and Burberry fight for a slice of the leather goods pie in luxury Indian malls. Merchants such as Raja, however, manufacture goods that are cheaper and have mass appeal – a leather wallet costs about $4' (Kalra 2014).

13. There are a few exceptional stories from Rajkot, where a handful of very successful entrepreneurs started as daily-wage workers.
14. On the downside, Morbi has a visibly high level of air pollution and poor housing for workers, mostly migrants from the eastern Indian states.
15. At the training centre, we noticed a unique model of public–private partnership in skill development. Each classroom has a banner of a Tirupur textile firm, which reportedly meets the expense of running the classes. In return, the firm gets to pick the students for entry-level jobs.
16. State institutional support for industry set up in the 1970s reportedly remains in disuse. The leading entrepreneurs and local industry association seem to have a tenuous connection with the state-level promotional agencies.

References

Ahmed, Zubair. 2008. 'Indian Slum Hit by New York Woes'. BBC News, Mumbai, 20 October.

Amsden, Alice. 2001. *The Rise of 'The Rest': Challenges to the West from Late-Industrializing Economies*. New York: Oxford University Press.

Chaudhuri, Sudip. 2013. 'Manufacturing Trade Deficit and Industrial Policy in India'. *Economic and Political Weekly* 48 (8): 42–50.

Dasgupta, Sukti and Ajit Singh. 2015. 'Will Services Be the New Engine of Indian Economic Growth?' *Development and Change* 36 (6): 1035–57.

Felipe, Jesus. 2018. 'Asia's Industrial Transformation: The Role of Manufacturing and Global Value Chains (Part 1)'. ADB Economics Working Paper Series, No. 549, July.

Frey, Carl Benedikt. 2019. *The Technology Trap: Capital, Labor, and Power in the Age of Automation*. Princeton: Princeton University Press.

Frey, Carl Benedikt and Michael Osborne. 2013. 'The Future of Employment, How Susceptible Are Jobs to Computerisation?' Working paper, published by the Oxford Martin Programme on Technology and Employment, Oxford Martin School.

Kalra, Aditya. 2014. 'Dharavi's Once-Booming Leather Industry Losing Its Edge'. Reuters, 1 April.

Manna, G. C. 2010. 'Current Status of Industrial Statistics in India: Strengths and Weaknesses'. *Economic and Political Weekly* (13 November): 67–76.

Mani, Sunil. 2018. 'What Is Happening to India's R&D Funding?' *Economic and Political Weekly* 53 (14): 12–14.

Mehrotra, Santosh and J. Parida. 2019. 'India's Employment Crisis: Rising Education Levels and Falling Non-agricultural Job Growth'. CSE Working Paper 2019-04, Centre for Sustainable Employment, Bengaluru. Available at cse.azimpremjiuniversity.edu.in

Nagaraj, R. 2007. 'Industrial Growth in China and India'. In *Institutions and Markets in India's Development: Essays for KN Raj*, edited by A. Vaidyanathan and K.L. Krishna, 178–204. Delhi: Oxford University Press.

————. 2017. 'Economic Reforms and Manufacturing Sector Growth: Need for Reconfiguring the Industrialisation Model'. *Economic and Political Weekly* 52 (2): 61–68.

Nagaraj, R. and T. N. Srinivasan. 2017. 'Measuring India's GDP Growth: Unpacking the Analytics and Data Issues behind a Controversy That Has Refused to Go Away'. In *India Policy Forum, 2016–17*, Vol. 13, edited by Shekhar Shah, Barry Bosworth and Karthik Muralidharan, 73–128. New Delhi: Sage, for National Council for Applied Economic Research.

Perkins, Dwight H. and Moshe Syrquin. 1989. 'Large Countries: The Influence of Size'. In *Handbook of Development Economics*, Vol. 2, edited by Hollis Chenery and T. N. Srinivasan, 1691–753. Amsterdam: North-Holland Elsevier.

RBI. 2019. 'Report of the Expert Committee on Micro, Small and Medium Enterprises'. Available at https://www.rbi.org.in/Scripts/PublicationReportDetails.aspx?UrlPage=&ID=924#CH1, accessed on 10 June 2020.

Streefkerk, Hein. 2006. *Tools and Ideas: The Beginnings of Local Industrialisation in India*. New Delhi: Manohar.

The Economist. 2005. 'Inside the Slums: Light in the Darkness'. 27 January.

Wade, Robert. 1990. *Governing the Markets: Economic Theory and the Role of Government in East Asian Industrialization*. Princeton: Princeton University Press.

CHAPTER 2

Garment Cluster in Kolkata

The Untold Story of Expansion Relying on Low-end Domestic Demand

SATYAKI ROY[*]

A persistent delinking of growth and employment during the high-growth phase of the Indian economy followed by sluggish growth and eventually episodes of absolute decline in employment in the aftermath of the 2008 global financial crisis is the pretext for a quest towards a growth trajectory that facilitates gainful employment. The macro indicators of growth slowdown, decline in the growth of corporate capital formation, persistently low capacity utilisation at 70 per cent and simultaneously declining absorption capacity of agriculture resulting in a shift of employment from agriculture to the non-farm sector to the tune of 20 percentage points in the past three decades raise serious doubts about the possibility of mending the widening gap between the growth of output and employment. The relative stagnation of manufacturing in terms of share in gross domestic product (GDP) for the past few decades have been the cause of concern for policymakers. Given the assumed advantages of manufacturing in terms of relatively faster growth in productivity, higher backward and forward linkages and spillover effects as well as the potential to create gainful employment, this sector had attracted policy attention by successive governments (Kaldor 1966, 1967). However, the production structure within manufacturing is undergoing major changes with rising capital intensity and declining employment elasticities. Additionally, in a liberalised regime, the dichotomy between the domestic and the global market is largely attenuated. Erstwhile local monopolies face a competitive market as price takers, and hence are increasingly inclined to introduce technologies borrowed

[*] The author would like to thank R. Nagaraj, Padmini Swaminathan, Keshab Das and Srinivasan Iyer for their invaluable comments and suggestions on the earlier draft. The author also thanks Suriya Tewari for drawing the map of the cluster.

from the global shelf which are expectedly labour displacing in nature. In such a milieu, the dominant mode of industrialisation, namely export-oriented growth strategies with hardly any choice of technologies left and reliance on inserting domestic production structures into global networks as the shortcut towards industrialisation, is unlikely to proffer necessary solutions.

The problem, however, cannot be resolved by a straightforward solution of promoting labour-intensive industries. It is not only about employing labour but employing them gainfully. Interestingly, industries that are relatively more labour intensive show a low share in manufacturing value-added in India, and also the share of labour in value-added in these industries is much lower compared to other industries (Roy 2016). In that context, apart from the question of just how much employment is being created, what becomes important in a dynamic context is how labour is employed vis-à-vis other factors of production. The overwhelming dominance of a particular industrial strategy with uniform parameters and performance indicators imposed across the world, independent of the composition of factors and possible heterogeneity in objective functions, might have blinded us from various industrial strategies of latecomers in Asia, Latin America and parts of Europe. In many of these countries, 'partial-proletarianisation' of the labour force, unlike those who were in the forefront of the industrial revolution, was a major feature, where multiple occupations and disguised unemployment having roots in agriculture were rampant (Sugihara 2013). The industrial strategy was calibrated to maximise the ratio of labour input to other cooperating factors in the initial phase, followed by a gradual decline in labour use and enhancing skill and capability orchestrated by micro-level interventions in terms of choice of technology and related institutional arrangements.

On the question of appropriate industrial organisation, one also needs to take note of the fact of the 'swelling middle' (Zenger and Hesterly 1997), receding of vertical rigid structures and a possible breeding of an industrial network which is far more diffused and grounded in the local. Neoclassical production functions assume zero transaction costs, and hence preclude any advantage of proximity. Furthermore, the assumption of constant returns to scale implies that production is highly divisible and the optimal size of the firm is given by the technology of production and determined at the minimum point of the long-run average cost curve. In this framework, space can hardly be modelled as a choice variable. Space is considered as synthetic and uniform containers with different factor productivities at the initial point, but factor productivities eventually equalise through the free movement of factors mediated through the market. It is only with the advent of endogenous growth theory that the region is conceptualised as stylised space instead of uniform space; introducing increasing returns to factor productivities and non-linear transportation costs and viewing technological progress as an endogenous response to economic actors. The creation of a dynamic comparative advantage through the cumulative accumulation of industry-specific knowledge and a horizontal structure that is less rigid and amenable to flexible technology showing greater resilience to a crisis is the hallmark of success stories of industrial clusters, particularly of Italy, Spain and Brazil. It is essentially a supply-side response, an industrial strategy based on cooperative competition that diffuses knowledge and capabilities and evolves as an organic entity, a cluster, an open-ended industrial organisation rooted in the history, culture and institutions of the local.

This chapter focusses on an industrial cluster producing ready-made garments in West Bengal. It hardly attracted attention hitherto by policymakers and was mostly unnoticed in the huge gamut of cluster studies, possibly because this cluster has a low share of exports in the total output, the largest share being ready-made garments sold in the domestic market (Mezzadri 2017). It employs a huge workforce in different layers; products of this cluster are sold across India, and, more importantly, the producers hardly face any constraint in demand barring discrete episodes of short-term shocks. It primarily offers a case that once again reasserts the importance of the domestic market, particularly in the context of large countries such as India. Even though it emerged as an artisanal cluster, largely populated by small and tiny producers, mostly job workers, we find contesting trends of fragmentation on the one hand and vertical growth on the other. The chapter argues that entrepreneurial skills, capabilities of labour and institutions that emerged from within the cluster gave rise to a production organisation that showed immense capability of responding to changing demand over time, but it largely remained confined to the low end of the garments market. There are signs of a disconnect between the two segments of the market: one essentially low end, rural or semi-urban, and the other supermarket-driven standardised branded products, destined for urban middle-class customers and the export market. The traditional cluster does not see any challenge in this rift, nor do the artisans think that relatively high-end products require higher levels of skill which they are not capable of offering, but carries a deep sense of deprivation, as institutional supports are largely designed for producers and exporters who cater to the middle-class market.

The next section briefly discusses the essential pointers for cluster analyses and the methodology adopted in the current study using those pointers. In this regard, instead of clinging to rigid notions of sampling, identifying the significant nodes of dynamic growth of the cluster was duly given greater importance. The third section describes the cluster as a static space. The fourth and fifth sections focus on the dynamic aspects of the production process and labour process, respectively. The next section focuses on trade and the domestic market, the rise of new industries, and exports. The final section concludes the chapter.

Industrial Cluster Study and Methodology

Problematising space and the spatial dimension of economic activity was hardly intelligible in economic theory as the movement of factors and information has been assumed to be free and cost less. Sometimes, even if the geography of production is considered to be a choice variable, it is comprehended by minimising transportation cost as a component of transaction costs, and, hence, space is conceived to be linear in mainstream theory. Endogenous growth theory while modelling increasing returns to scale and non-linear transportation costs brings to the fore the question of innovation and spillover of knowledge in conceptualising geography as stylised space (Abdel-Rahman 1988; Gianmarco, Ottaviano and Thisse 2001; Fujita, Krugman and Venables 1999). Paul Krugman (1991) introduced a model involving economies of scale and labour mobility to capture the geography of production. The model reinterprets the Marshallian notion of externalities originating from a localised pool of labour and specialised demand for non-traded inputs. A related body of literature originating from the new growth theory argues that when individuals or firms accumulate new capital, both physical and human, they contribute to the productivity of capital held by others. As Romer (1990) demonstrated, if the spillover effects are strong enough, the private marginal product of physical or human capital can remain permanently above the discount rate, even if individual investments suffered diminishing returns in the absence of external boost to productivity. Therefore, space becomes endogenous to the process of growth rather than being seen as a neutral container transforming vector of inputs into outputs. However, the creation of knowledge and the firm's endogenous decisions to appropriate spillovers resulting in higher productivity had not turned out to be an automatic outcome as assumed in the new growth theory. Knowledge spillover theory further suggests that there is a gap between the creation of opportunities and their appropriation. It precisely suggests that entrepreneurship and the creation of collective knowledge are necessary conditions but not sufficient enough to ensure cognitive capabilities (Acs et al. 2006; Audretsch, Keilbach and Lehmann 2006). Therefore, the dynamics of knowledge and productivity gains that generate increasing returns to factors could not be explained adequately by individual responses to a certain flow of inputs.

This brings us close to a related strand of literature that captures the geography of production more realistically. Based on the success stories of European clusters, 'industry district'[1] literature within the genre of flexible specialisation paradigm provides a marked shift in understanding small and medium enterprise (SME) clusters. Mainstream theories may appreciate the possibility of positive externalities created through knowledge spillover effects but such externalities cannot be a deliberate creation of the firm since the firm cannot capture in the price the full benefits of investment. Therefore, even though investment in new technology and learning affect capabilities of other firms within its proximity, such initiatives could be incidental and involuntary rather than expected as a conscious effort from a profit-maximising firm. Hubert Schmitz (1999) goes beyond the conventional perception of external economies and argues that in the case of the interlinked production environment as in clusters, firms are both recipients and producers of external economics and, hence, underinvestment may not be the dominant outcome. The notion of 'collective efficiency', which is the crux of industry district literature, foregrounds the fact that successes of clusters depend not only on the externalities of incidental individual action but also on the sufficient condition, that is, a conscious process of perpetual joint action at different levels. The idea of 'cooperative efficiency', however, does not pit cooperation as against competition, but rather acknowledges the need for both in a dynamic trajectory. It works through maintaining a fine balance between horizontal and vertical relations between firms in a cluster. Firms within the cluster are not assigned a unique role through planned cooperation. Some are vertically integrated but many produce similar products and compete with each other. Similarly placed firms would be supplying components and products differentiated by specifications given by buyers but they may also be competing with each other. However, even if they are fiercely competing within themselves, at another level they may come together to procure collective indivisible inputs, negotiate with the government for infrastructure or for facilitating and accessing 'service centres' or 'training centres', as a collective entity can interact with universities or knowledge centres to initiate innovations, may develop a brand with common facilities for quality control, and so on. All these joint actions in various levels and with varying degrees impact upon the capabilities of individual producers. F. Belussi and L. Pilotti (2002) define industrial district in a broader sense as a cognitive system, a socio-productive system in which knowledge, social experiences, mental models and collective beliefs are accumulated in a specific space through time. Cluster is viewed in this perspective as a complex network of vertical and horizontal linkages and the field of relational power. Competition among similarly placed firms in terms of roles on the one hand and cooperation among various size categories of firms sharing the same cultural and social milieu on the other hand defines the flow of relational power. In such a scenario, the clusters often tend to freeze certain vertical exchanges as norms flowing from the winners. This has to be continuously destabilised by facilitating competition through new entry and promoting collective capabilities to face the external challenges of competition. It is the equilibrium–disequilibrium dynamics of vertical and horizontal relationships that define the dynamics of a growing cluster. Regional policies facilitating growth and employment in a cluster are to be designed to keep these dynamics alive.

Such pointers are efficacious in designing an appropriate methodology to understand the functioning of a cluster. In the particular case study on the garment cluster in Kolkata, we primarily identified the structures that may cause differentiated outcomes and tried to locate the interactions between economic agents and their roles defined according to various layers within the cluster. Many were located in and around the original space where the artisanal cluster emerged, whereas the new breed of firms were relocated to garment parks. In each of these segments, there were exporting firms and those who cater to the domestic market. It is also important to identify linkages in the production process within and between these two broad segments. Also, there were producers of the different sizes involved in different phases of the production chain. Apart from producers in each of these segments, we found various categories of financers, formal or informal, as well as suppliers of inputs and accessories. There were different categories of workers with varying skills and various modes of outsourcing existing within the cluster. In the first phase of the survey, we met a few small producers, some big manufacturers and one or two traders. From detailed interviews of these key informants, we mapped the interaction of various economic agents acting at different levels and identified the major nodes of this economic space. In the second phase, we chose selective samples that could capture the exchanges and linkages in the two broad segments. It was not a representative sample chosen randomly from a defined population; rather owners who were relatively known in a locality, as well as accessible, were interviewed. In this regard, we ensured that all phases of production were covered. In the case of choosing smaller units, the geographical distribution according to product specialisation was kept in mind to capture the division of labour in the study. Waged and salaried workers were interviewed outside their respective units, mostly in nearby tea stalls during their break time, while self-employed workers were interviewed in their respective home-based units. During several visits to garment parks, we randomly selected firms within the group of exporters as well as from those who primarily sold to the domestic market. Apart from these, some manufacturers that emerged as big brands were interviewed in detail to get some insights from their success stories. Industry associations and various government departments linked to the garment industry in Kolkata were interviewed to understand the institutional ecosystem around the cluster.

Geographical Coverage: Specialisation and Key Players

The garment cluster in and around Kolkata covers an area of related activity spanning mainly four southern districts of West Bengal, namely Kolkata, Howrah, South 24 Parganas and North 24 Parganas, and partly Midnapore (Map 2.1). The two major centres of this garment cluster are Metiabruz in Kolkata and the area centred around Howrah *haat* (market). As the history goes, the last *nawab* of Oudh, Nawab Wajid Ali Shah, was deposed by the British when the princely state of Oudh was annexed to British India in 1856 by Lord Dalhousie. The *nawab* with 500 men had to leave Lucknow and they reached Bichali Ghat in Calcutta via Varanasi on 13 May 1856. He tried to recreate a mini Lucknow (*chota Lucknou*) at Metiabruz located on the bank of the River Hoogly at the south-western fringe of Kolkata (Mitra 2017). The deposed king still had faith in the British sense of justice and believed that he could get back his kingdom if he could plead his case before the queen and the British parliament in London. By that time, the revolt of 1857 had broke out, and Wajid Ali Shah was imprisoned and then freed after 25 months. He lost all hopes of reinstatement but, later on, he was given a financial allowance by the British and allowed to hold the title 'King of Oudh'. In the process of replicating Lucknow, he brought along with him musicians, cooks, tailors, kite makers and the wide and rich culture of Lucknow which constituted and continued to influence the life of Metiabruz through time. There is hardly any historical evidence that shows that they all stayed back at Kolkata over

Map 2.1 Kolkata garment cluster: location of places

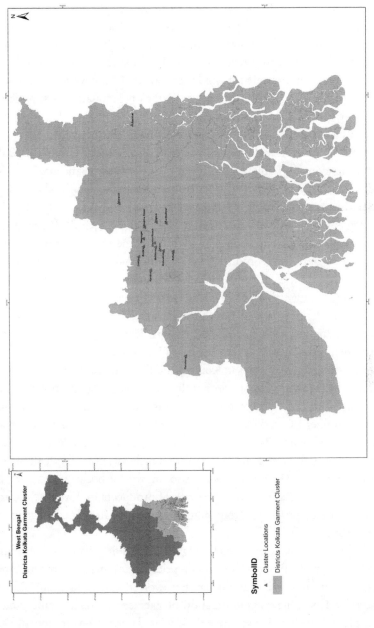

Source: Author, in collaboration with Suriya Tewari.

Note: Map not to scale and does not represent authentic international boundaries.

generations. Some might have remained, and others, particularly musicians and poets, might have left the place after the death of Wajid Ali, who was a great patron of art and culture. The tailors who might have stayed on and those who arrived later for the same profession as the city grew had to find tailoring jobs that were not dependent on the royal family anymore. Many of them survived by taking recourse to repair jobs producing 'second-hand clothes', particularly trousers for the local market. Many were dependent on job works of repairing and tailoring and later on graduated as suppliers of low-end garments for the Howrah *haat*.

According to officials of the Bangla Readymade Garments Manufacturers and Traders Welfare Association, currently in and around Metiabruz, 20,000 units are employing 500,000 workers in the organised sector, and another 5,000 entrepreneurs involving 25,000 artisanal units of manufacturing and trading are located in this area. With time, Metiabruz has grown and expanded its activities and linkages to the adjacent districts of North and South 24 Parganas and Midnapore. Within this area, one can identify a broad distribution of regions specialising in particular product lines. Chota, Ashuti, Manimubbar Hat, Khundin, Nischindipur, Chandanpur and Parashar are some of the villages close to Budge Budge that are involved in the production of jeans trousers. Akra and Santoshpur area in South 24 Parganas are primarily known for tailors producing gents' shirts. The other significant concentration of ready-made garment producers in West Bengal is located in Howrah district. The Metiabruz—Garden reach area in Kolkata and Domjur, Bankra, Dasnagar and Ranihati in Howrah are famous for children's and ladies' garments. Stitching and sewing work largely outsourced by units from Metiabruz provide jobs to a large number of workers in home-based units located in Basirhat and Barasaat area of North 24 Parganas extending further to adjacent villages near the Sunderbans bordering 24 Parganas. Producers in Howrah along with those in Shobhabazar in Kolkata were also known for hosiery garments, but that activity largely declined with the rise of producers in Tirupur in Tamil Nadu, where many producers from Bengal shifted to after repeated strikes in the 1980s (Sen 2013).

The Kolkata garment cluster, including its surrounding districts, is primarily involved in the production of low-end low-priced ready-made garments. Apart from this traditional artisanal cluster that evolved and grew manifold over the years, we find a new agglomeration of garment producers emerging in garment parks. Paridhan is a garment park created by the Government of West Bengal at Topsia in the eastern fringe of Kolkata where the tanneries were earlier located. The other garment park, the Regent Garment Park located in Barasat of North 24 Parganas, was constructed by a private developer. Apart from these two dedicated garment parks, there are dyeing and processing units at the Dhulagarh Industrial Park in Howrah.

There are roughly three layers of units: the bigger units may be employing more than 100 workers, the medium layer consists of units employing 25–100 workers and the lowest rung in the value chain are home-based units primarily involving unpaid family labour. For fabric, the Kolkata cluster is dependent on traders since almost all fabric is brought from other states or from abroad. Some local traders supply processed fabric to tailoring units. Since the cluster's activity is largely confined to making garments with processed fabric, its leverage to increase the share in value-added in the entire value chain is relatively limited. It is primarily cutting and stitching and related works that are required to make the final product that defines the scope of activity of this cluster. The *ustagar*, or the master tailor, generally shares the responsibility of designing and cutting, followed by sewing and stitching of various kinds depending on the degree of complexity of the work. This part of the work is followed by washing, dyeing and processing, particularly for jeans, and then accessories are attached, followed by the final packaging of the product ready for the market. Some of the stages, particularly washing and processing, are usually outsourced to those units who specialise in these job. But the core job of sewing, stitching, trimming and attaching accessories and finally packaging are undertaken by the *ustagar* and his family-based unit. The other important actors are traders who supply raw materials and accessories to producers and also transporters who carry final products to destination states. Most of the bigger units that specialise in a particular genre of garment and have evolved as brand names, local or national, have trained designers, and most of the manufacturing process is undertaken in-house. Big manufacturers and exporters are mainly located in garment parks. But the numerous home-based units that are linked with the cluster and provide huge employment depend on a wide network of similar smaller units thatdo job works at various levels.

Production Processes

The production of ready-made garments is constituted of various phases, and the number of phases depends on the degree of sophistication and the nature of garment demanded by the buyer. A stylised typology can only be derived for an average garment, although phases vary for children's and ladies' garments from those of gents' garments, and the former involve more intricate work. The core raw material, namely the fabric, is sourced from Ahmedabad, Surat, Bhilwara, Bhiwandi, Pali, Erode, China and Bangladesh. The big suppliers, primarily traders located in Borabazar in Kolkata, are the bulk suppliers from where small local traders buy fabric depending on the specialisation of the local producers. Dyeing and washing require various chemicals, which are sourced from Mumbai and Surat. The local dealers in Metiabruz procure these chemicals and fabric and sell them to manufacturers in the local market. The design of the garment assumes great importance with regard to the marketability of a product. The average shelf life of a design is not more than two weeks. In some cases, particularly for children's and ladies' garments, it could be even less. Big manufacturers mainly source designs from Mumbai, Singapore and Dubai. They regularly visit these places and procure design and develop accordingly. Small producers copy new designs from garments procured from Delhi or Mumbai and sold at shops located in Esplanade and New Market in Kolkata. Most producers face an asymmetry in the two sides of the transaction. The manufacturers generally receive trade credit from suppliers for a period not exceeding 15 days, while the credit they are supposed to give to buyers of the final product usually extends up to three months. In other words, manufacturers are supposed to have enough cash to produce successive cycles of production and wait to realise the sale proceeds of delivered orders.

The production process is simple, and the scale of operation in core manufacturing is primarily a function of the number of sewing machines involved. Most of these units, big or small, use Chinese multilayer cutting machines for making trousers. Once the design is finalised, rough patterns are prepared using soft paper boards. These templates are used in the bulk cutting of fabric at multiple layers. Either a home-based unit or a relatively bigger unit uses cutter machines that can shape 10–50 layers of cloth at one go. Earlier, small home-based units were using sewing machines of local Indian companies having brand names such as Sandeep, Gopal and Brother. Now, almost all the producers use second-hand Juki machines or Chinese machines for sewing. Single-stitch second-hand machines cost ₹15,000 as against Indian brands sold at ₹6,000. Multiple-stitching Chinese machines can do three to five stitches simultaneously, and most of the garments require multiple stitching. Such a machine costs ₹75,000 to ₹90,000 on average. To attain a certain quality of stitching, even the home-based units use these imported machines, the second-hand versions of which are available at the local market named Banerjee Haat market near Metiabruz. The modern units in garment parks that cater to the high-end middle-class market for branded products use German Turret, Japanese Fukuhara machines and also machines imported from Taiwan. Many of these units produce 6,000–7,000 pieces of garments a day. Some of the manufacturers in the Regent Garment Park also use Austrian printing machines that can print 2,000–3,000 multi-colour impressions per day.

In the case of bigger units, manufacturers have to develop designs and produce samples accordingly. Those samples are then floated to the buyer for approval, and once the samples are finalised, processed fabrics are bought and then the usual phases of cutting, stitching, washing, finishing and packaging follow. In the case of Metiabruz, the cycle of production spans hardly a week. The orders are booked at one Friday market to be delivered by the next Saturday to the buyers. For big producers who supply to retailers such as Big Bazaar, Flipkart, Pantaloons and Amazon, the process of ordering, approval based on inspection and finally selling the product to the buyer may involve 60–120 days. This is primarily because of bulk orders and for meeting the requisite parameters of standardisation. Sometimes, more improved qualities of washing, dyeing and printing are required, and the manufacturers get it done from Jodhpur, Jaipur or Ahmedabad. The washing units in South 24 Parganas and Howrah report that because of the high degree of humidity and the nature of water used, washing involves additional methods of curing fabric, which increases the cost of washing. After being washed at various phases using six to seven types of chemicals, an ordinary pair of jeans trousers are dried either using machine drying or, as in the case of smaller units in Chota, one can see jeans trousers spread over rooftops where they are dried using natural sunlight. Because of hard water and climate-specific reasons, many respondents reported that often big manufacturers rely on washing units located in Bangalore or Jodhpur so that they can get the requisite quality at a relatively lower cost. An ordinary wash can be of five to six types depending on the nature of the garment, and stone-wash mainly used in the case of jeans can be of six to eight varieties. An organised washing unit washes 6,000–7,000 pieces of jeans garments per day.

The Metiabruz–Garden Reach and Howrah garment cluster is primarily known for low-end low-priced garments mainly catering to rural and semi-urban consumers of India. This does not, however, mean that producers and tailors are not capable of making high-end products. In fact, in the Kolkata cluster, one can find a traditionally evolved skilled labour pool, primarily tailors who are capable of producing gents' shirts and children's trousers priced at ₹120–₹250 per piece and at the same time skilled tailors producing *lehanga*

Table 2.1   Accounts of a simple pair of jeans trousers produced in home-based units

Stages of production	Cost per piece in ₹
Cloth	115–20
Cutting	2
All stitches	55
Washing	26
Accessories + packaging	20
Transport to *haat*	25
Total cost	228
Sale price	240

Source: Author's field survey.

supplied at a price of ₹10,000 to showrooms of big brands. But the major volume of the sale is accounted for low-priced garments sometimes sold at road-side temporary shops in the weekly market or in permanent shops located at Metiabruz or Howrah *haat*. We can have a glimpse of the cost structure of an average pair of jeans trousers of modal quality produced in Chota, South 24 Parganas, that can provide an idea of how the home-based units make both ends meet (Table 2.1).

This is a typical cost structure of a jeans garment produced in a home-based unit. Bigger units produce garments of higher quality using better quality of fabric, and the cost of production increases depending on the design and complexity and skill involved in the process of production. Higher-order products involve more sophisticated modes of washing and dyeing and treatment of the fabric and respond to a higher frequency of changing urban styles. It may require improved stitching machines, but the basic skills required to produce a garment do not differ proportionally to the price differences.

Labour Processes

Garment production is labour intensive and creates employment in various phases of production as well as in allied activities. In the three adjacent districts that the Kolkata garment cluster covers, the garment industry is the second largest employer after agriculture. A labour force comprised of a huge number of young and old is engaged as waged workers or as self-employed in own home-based units. Two forms of labour contracting are involved in various stages of production: One is product subcontracting, where one or more units are engaged by a trader or a brand owner who is subcontracted to produce the required final product. Big retailers usually depend on manufacturers to procure and produce the garments with stipulated quantity, design and quality. These manufacturers may enter into labour subcontracting with various smaller firms and can get the work done or may produce the entire order in-house. The dominant form of contracting is labour subcontracting where units in various stages engage with a network of firms both vertically and horizontally and get various stages of intermediate jobs done through layers of units. The order given by a producer or *ustagar* includes all specifications of designs and the raw material that has to be worked upon. There is hardly any formal transaction between various units, but informal communication and trust within economic agents is the crux of the functioning networks. Since the designs last hardly for a week and changes are incremental, copying designs is not a big threat. However, one who develops the design first reaps the greatest premium over others.

The workers are mainly traditional Muslim tailors who have acquired skills through generations. In the survey villages and semi-urban blocks, one would hardly find young men unemployed in the area. In some way or the other, the local youth are involved in garment industry-related activities. One respondent from a high school at Maheshtala, near Chota, reported that the number of dropouts is very high from the ninth and tenth standards. In other words, in an average household, children are exposed to various kinds of tasks related to garments as casual observers at home and at a later age start helping their parents and family members in various activities (Figure 2.1). A certain level of primary education helps in counting numbers and understanding measurements but beyond that education carries no extra pay-off for these young people. Hence, they drop out of schools and join the family profession aspiring to become an *ustagar*, which fetches higher earning.

As it happens in the case of an average agricultural household, the number of hands joining the production process actually reduces the dependence on hired workers. This perhaps explains why the average number of family members in these households is relatively high. Hence, in a family of six, all adult members, men and women, join hands in performing the assigned tasks. Women are mainly involved in stitching accessories, finishing and packaging. Although women work at home as unpaid labour, because of the entrenched patriarchy and low levels of education one can hardly find females moving out of the home for doing waged work in somebody else's unit. Hence, women's labour is almost invisible although they play a significant role in the production and reproduction of the labour process that sustains the cluster. The low levels

Figure 2.1   An *ustagar* with his son in a home-based unit in Chota, South 24 Parganas

Source: Author.

of education create a vicious circle for the individual, meaning they have hardly any opportunity to opt for other jobs and, as a result, ensures a steady supply of skilled workers in the cluster over generations. It is almost as if the fate of the child is decided before he/she is grown up enough to think of any alternative source of income. The religious kinship also helps in reproducing the trust among economic agents; it reduces transaction costs and encourages cooperation as collective practices emerge in procuring raw materials and particularly in carrying finished products to the local market. Mostly four–five producers make an arrangement among themselves for carrying their products jointly to the market. Many big manufacturers and retailers acknowledge the skill of these workers in copying and reproducing designs. The other important quality of tailors of Metiabruz as mentioned by various buyers is that they are very committed to putting all efforts in delivering orders on time.

The self-employed in home-based units and the waged workers receive income against labour. It is visible from Table 2.1 that the margin which the self-employed workers consider to be their profit is the amount they and their families would have received as wages if they had worked for others. Hence, it is part of the cost, essentially an imputed wage that appears to be profit. It may also be the case that if we considered all the family labour involved in the process and priced them according to market rate, the return per person could be less than what a wage worker receives as net earnings. However, the self-employed considers his position as better-off than working as a wage worker in some other unit because it is believed that he is his own master and enjoy the discretion of distributing his own time and his family members' time according to their convenience. Therefore, he does not have to depend on others and can manage other household work along with producing goods for the market. On average, a garment worker works 10–12 hours a day, irrespective of whether working in own unit or for others as wage worker. The garment-related work time of other family members varies according to the requirements of other compelling household work.

The wage structure is more or less uniform across the cluster. There is also not much difference in wages between workers working in the traditional units in Metiabruz–Garden Reach and those working as factory workers at the Regent Garment Park or at Paridhan. The supervisors and quality checkers in bigger firms get monthly wages, while all other workers in various stages of production receive wages on a piece-rate basis. It is difficult to qualify each work and compare within themselves based on wage. It is rather meaningful to convert piece-rate wages of different occupational grades into average monthly income (Table 2.2).

Table 2.2 shows that workers barely eke out a living. According to unofficial sources, there is huge in-migration of undocumented workers from Bangladesh, which further allows the employers to depress wages. One of the factory owners in the Regent Garment Park who owns a similar factory in Bangladesh reported that, in Indian currency, a garment worker in Bangladesh roughly earns ₹5,000–₹5,500 a month and in India, on an average, garment workers receive ₹8,000–₹8,500 a month. The low wage is the key to the competitiveness of the

Table 2.2 Average monthly occupational wages

Occupational grade	Monthly income (in ₹)
Home-based *ustagar*	10,000–12,000
Stitching job (single)	7,000–8,000
Stitching (multiple)	12,000–15,000
Washing job	7,000–8,000
Helper	5,000–5,500
Button fixing and ironing	6,000 (1.5–2 per piece)
Trainee	1,500–2,000 (and food)
Line supervisor (RGP)	9,000–11,000
Line supervisor (Paridhan)	10,000–11,000
Helper (RGP)	5,000–5,500
Helper (Paridhan)	4,000–5,000

Source: Author's field survey.

cluster. It is the 'sweatshop' regime (Mezzadri 2017) that is reproduced that help in retaining the larger share of the low-waged low-priced garment market. Production and reproduction are intertwined in the sense that informality, social oppression and patriarchy reinforce each other towards a self-exploitative fragmentation (Roy 2013). This is the existing form of a dense network of free and unfree labour that is increasingly giving rise to a collation of the site of production and consumption. Every activity within the home is increasingly conditioned by the imperative of the circuit of capital.

Market and Trade

Garments produced in the cluster in and around Kolkata are marketed across India. Those produced in the original space of the artisanal cluster that evolved naturally and historically primarily cater to the demand for low-end low-quality garments sold at rural and semi-urban segments of India. Garments produced in garment parks where big brands usually house their manufacturing units are marketed through malls and supermarkets and branded shops mainly targeting the middle-class market of urban India. The two most important trade centres that historically evolved as mass market for garments are located in Howrah and Metiabruz. A *haat*, meaning weekly market in Bengali, in case of garments is usually a multi-storeyed building where, on each floor, traders sell their products in shops which are permanent establishments; but a *haat* also includes a large number of temporary stalls that are put up on particular days in a week in and around that building. The Howrah *haat* is the oldest garment market in Bengal. It is close to the Howrah railway station and currently there are 11 such buildings named as Mimani Mongola, Ganesh and Mahesh, Modern, Nabeen, and so on. In and around these 11 *haat*s on both sides of the road, there are numerous small stalls that sell their merchandise in weekly markets on Mondays and Tuesdays. In the Metiabruz *haat*, which is currently the biggest garment market in Bengal, there are 42 permanent multi-storeyed buildings or *haat*s, and the somewhat bigger and popular *haat*s among them are ABM, Jobber, Kohinoor, Baba, Janata, Quality, Shakila, Masoom, Shopping *haat* and Express *haat*. Only ABM *haat*, which is the biggest *haat* in Metiabruz, have three floors each of 110,000 square feet and houses 4,500 stalls (Figure 2.2). The weekly garment market in Metiabruz is put up every week on Saturday and Sunday. Metiabruz came up in a big way since early 1990s, and before that producers of Kolkata used to depend largely on the Howrah wholesale garment market.

Figure 2.2 Metiabruz: inside ABM *haat* in a weekly market, Kolkata

Source: Author.

Buyers from various states come to Metiyabruz mainly on Friday to trade on Saturday and Sunday. The traders have rented spaces as *gaddi* in the market, and they also hire rooms in nearby guest houses where buyers can stay. Some of these guest houses are named as VIP and New VIP, which are privately owned guesthouses located in Metiabruz. Buyers visit the shops in markets, choose garments which they want to buy and place orders. It is the responsibility of the traders to ensure the delivery of the garments through transporters within the stipulated time. This arrangement works based on mutual trust. The manufacturer sells the goods mainly to traders against cash payment; it is the responsibility of the traders to get the orders delivered and receive payment from buyers. The trader receive a premium for facilitating the exchange as well as for bearing the risks involved. The transporters who deal with garments are mainly located in the Tarachand Street area opposite Muhammad Ali Park in Kolkata. Trucks loaded with bales of ready-made garments are sent to the respective buyers of different states every week. According to the transporters, the volume of the sale every week from the Metiabruz area amounts to roughly ₹3 billion. In some cases, transporters evolve into traders who connect buyers from different states to producers, bear the responsibility of actualising the trade and receive a 4–5 per cent cut on price.

According to the manufacturers of Metiabruz, cheap labour and low establishment cost are the key to producing goods for the mass market which are relatively low priced, and that seems to be the prime attraction for traders coming from various states. As reported by almost all producers, there is no dearth of demand; rather, buyers sometimes do not get enough time to interact with various producers or do not get the required quantity as there are a large number of buyers. It seems that because of its low share in exports, the cluster has not drawn much attention compared to other garment-producing clusters. Perhaps the extent of exports has become the most important metrics of industrial performance in the era of globally integrated markets. But most of the respondents of Metiabruz are reluctant about focusing on export possibilities. The simple argument that came out quite interestingly in various conversations with big manufacturers is that if 'low margin with huge turnover' is a good enough strategy for their expansion in the domestic market, why bother about exports? In other words, the Kolkata garment cluster relies on the domestic mass market and has been able to expand its activities both in terms of turnover and employment. Figures on district-level employment derived from census data of various years suggest that employment in South 24 Paraganas and Howrah has increased in the past decades. Since the garment industry records a high share in employment in these districts, it is obvious that employment in this sector has increased in the past decade. This also emerges from industry-level distribution of employment (Charaborty 2017). The producers reported that only two months in the year, namely July and August, are the relatively lean period; otherwise demand in the garment market rises steeply around festivals of various states, namely Durga Puja, Diwali, Eid, Raja and Pongal. Some garment producers of Kolkata, including of Metiabruz, could develop their own brands which are well known in national and local markets. Some of the popular jeans brands are Moustache, Pilot and Dolphin; shirt brands include Hyphen and Turtle; and some other well-known brands originating from Metiabruz are Happy, Dynax, Tina Dresses, Kalam Dresses, and so on. Trade fairs are organised annually by the traders' and manufacturers' associations at various levels. The trade fair organised by the Bangla Readymade Garments Manufacturers and Traders Welfare Association primarily showcase ready-made garments produced by 95 local brands of Metiabruz.

As mentioned earlier, apart from the traditional space of the industrial cluster, a new space has emerged that houses relatively bigger and modern enterprises, including exporters. One such space is the Regent Garment Park located near Barasat in North 24 Parganas (Figure 2.3). This is a park developed by a private developer offering space to roughly 300 factories with an average space of 5,000–7,000 square feet each. Exporters such as JPM Exports, SAR

International, Bali Export, Hopman and Dollar have their manufacturing units within this park. Roughly 15,000 workers work in this garment park, mainly coming from the adjacent districts of North 24 Parganas, Howrah and Hoogly. The exporters in this garment park cater to companies located in Italy, Spain, Germany, UK, Denmark, Switzerland, France, Portugal, Japan, New Zealand and the Middle East. The main export product is industrial garments. Companies generally abide by AC 8000 social standard norms as stipulated by importing companies. The second important garment park is Paridhan developed by the West Bengal Industrial Development Corporation in 2008. About 90 companies have their manufacturing facilities here, including renowned brands such as Manyavaar, Rupa and Moustache. Manyavaar has in total 450 outlets across the country and also in Dubai, USA, Bangladesh and Nepal. The number of workers working in this garment park would be roughly 4,000 in total, mainly coming from the adjacent districts. It is worth noting that the skills required to work in these factories do not have great variance from those working in traditional clusters.

There are of course some differences in machines, standards, materials and in terms of greater division of jobs, but in terms of individual skills acquired it is hard to say if workers in exporting firms as well as in bigger firms are endowed with higher skills. The exporting firms produce industrial garments that have some standard specifications, and it is very much possible that

Figure 2.3 Regent Garment Park at Barasat, North 24 Paraganas

Source: Author.

such goods might not require the multiple skills that a garment producer in Metiabruz might possess. Similarly, an interaction with one of the renowned brands producing wedding garments in India suggests that the products are defined by their designs and fabric. They have their in-house design units where professional designers are employed, but the stitching and other related production jobs are done by workers who primarily work with traditional skills. Some big companies outsource job works to producers located in traditional clusters. Therefore, it is not always the case that exporting firms are leaders in fashion, technology or design in the cluster, which has been assumed to be true in most case studies on industrial clusters. A leading Indian brand sells *kurta* with a price ranging from ₹800 to ₹25,000 and *lehenga*s having modal range from ₹25,000 to ₹30,000 each. They also offer an exclusive collection of *lehenga*s with a price range of ₹100,000–₹150,000 per piece. This huge range of products and variations in design and quality is the hallmark of the Kolkata garment cluster. Some companies deal with big retailers supplying low-end garments to Reliance, Zabong, Flipkart and Amazon. They supply multiple products such as salwar suits, leggings and palazzo pants for the ladies' segment on the one hand and gents' shirts and jeans for children on the other. Serving such big orders require various sets of machines that cater to a particular operation required for a particular type of garment. This involves large investments and long turnaround time but not necessarily higher-order technology and skills. Some initiatives have been undertaken by the Government of West Bengal in response to the demands of the garment manufacturers in and around Kolkata. New garment parks are being set up with the help of private players at Ankurhati, Jagadishpur, Gorubathan, Nungi, Belur and Barasat. The government provides space to global buyers such as Triberg and Impulse at Paridhan so that manufacturers are exposed to global fashions and standards. The Apparel Export Promotion Council has a plan to set up a knowledge centre at Paridhan where designing skills and other training facilities would be provided to workers.

Concluding Remarks

The garment cluster in Kolkata is expanding in terms of both the number of units and employment. But the growth in the number of units may not always be considered as a healthy sign for an industrial cluster, particularly when it is because of increasing fragmentation of production. There seems to be two contradictory tendencies emerging, which may not always be in conflict with each other. One is the increasing fragmentation of family units, which is primarily because most of these household enterprises rely on family labour and families fragment for economic and non-economic reasons, resulting in new household enterprises. Since most of these workers are landless and do not have any other asset to fall back upon, there is no common ownership of a family asset to bind large families together as it happens in agricultural communities. The process of fragmentation divides resources and capital as well, and hence most of these units are stuck to a subsistence level of making both ends meet. They cannot think of moving up the value chain or increasing their scale of operation. But there are amazing success stories of individuals who started as petty tailors and emerged as the owners of many garment factories as well as of one of the biggest *haat*s in Metiabruz.

The other process, which is relatively new but distinctly observable, is the process of consolidation through agglomeration. Large space with easy access to other production facilities allows firms to increase their scale of operation and plan for multi-plant arrangements in close vicinity. It also integrates several operations performed by the independent units. It is worth noting that these tendencies also manifest in some geographical patterns. The process of fragmentation is dominant in the artisanal cluster, and the garment parks seem to epitomise the organised as well as consolidated face of the emerging garment hubs of Bengal. However, there is hardly any shift taking place, in the sense that none of the producers of Metiabruz or of the adjacent areas of the traditional cluster have relocated their production sites to the new garment parks. There seems to be a clear divide also in terms of target buyers of these two sets of producers. Producers at Metiabruz mainly rely on traditional rural and semi-urban customers, continuously innovating as well as copying new designs at a cheaper price to bridge the gap between rural and urban styles. The manufacturers at the garment parks mainly cater to the middle and upper segments of the urban market. The divide continues, and in terms of infrastructure or other allied service facilities, the age-old traditional cluster has largely been neglected by successive state governments.

During the survey, most of the respondents reported that they had to undergo a very tough time for about three months just after demonetisation when all production and business transactions were brought to a halt. Since most of the home-based units work with very little working capital and transactions take place in cash, the whole system was jeopardised by the sudden shock that hit the small producers the most. Most of them were able to come out of that trying time but were left with very little resources to expand. Later, since the goods and services tax (GST) was introduced, it has been the smaller firms who have been sharing the larger burden of tax incidence at the end of the value chain. Most of the small producers, who are largely exempted from GST themselves, have to share the effect of GST in purchasing raw materials and accessories. Since competition in the relevant segment of the market is largely based on price, the small producers are facing a contraction of orders as a result of rising costs. What happened in this process is not a destruction of small producers and traders; they did withstand both demonetisation and the change in tax structure, but of course through huge income losses in the entire process. The coercion involved in the margin of a transaction between the large and the small has increased and has gone further in favour of the relatively powerful in the value chain who can easily pass the burden of reducing costs to the lowest end.

The supply of cheap labour is what makes this cluster competitive in the domestic market. A huge number of school dropouts of the locality enter the labour force at a very early age. Internalising the discipline of work as well as skills required in various phases of production is learnt from parents and relatives at home. The supply of skills and its diffusion is almost costless. Having very low educational attainments, people have hardly any opportunity to move out and think of better jobs. This keeps the supply of low-waged and unwaged workers going, and the worker is more or less trapped in the same work forever. Moreover, weighing the costs and benefits of education, particularly the wait time and a very low chance of getting a formal job, further discourages parents from investing time and money on formal education. Indeed, hardly any young people are sitting idle at home in these areas. Everyone has some work, howsoever little earning it fetches. But the flip side of this low-educated workforce and entrepreneurs is that many a time even these producers are capable of producing garments of higher quality and accumulate substantial wealth and experience over the years, but they are hesitant and often fearful to interact with beyond their relatives and kinship networks. Only because of the lack of exposure and a minimum level of education, the producers of Metiabruz are sometimes forced to rely on traders and other sorts of middlemen for sourcing materials and designs from abroad or for marketing products.

The strength of the Kolkata garment cluster lies in its capability to produce a wide range of products and at different price levels. Even though the cluster is known to buyers across the country for cheap low-end products, that does not mean that they are not capable of producing high-end products. None of the producers is looking for export markets, as they are flooded with orders every week from buyers of different states. But one important fact reveals that, given the changes happening in the demand for garments and their marketing, the Kolkata cluster has not yet been futuristic in terms of responses to such changes. One of the biggest retail chains in the country sources garments worth only ₹10 million from West Bengal out of its annual total purchase of garments amounting to ₹200 million. It seems there is a growing disconnect between the rural and urban markets, and the cluster is not yet prepared to produce standardised garments in huge quantities with proper specifications. Factory production with an organised structure could provide scale advantages in this regard, and public policies and initiatives should be aimed at creating infrastructure and facilities for such a vertical growth. Within the traditional cluster, training and service centres providing industry-specific focused knowledge might increase the capability of workers and entrepreneurs. The cluster is gradually facing competition from products originating in Ahmedabad, the only reason being that the producers there have an integrated backward linkage of making and processing fabric. So, fabric producers entering into the business of producing ready-made garments are gradually becoming more competitive than those who purchase raw materials from other states. There have to be state-level interventions to initiate and facilitate internalisation of some of the backward linkages such as providing common facilities for good quality dyeing, processing and washing. Since this is one of the largest employment-generating sectors for the low- and medium-skilled workforce in the southern part of the state, it deserves far greater policy attention and support from the state government in triggering a virtuous growth path of higher value addition together with greater employment.

Note

1. Alfred Marshall first used the term in Marshall (1920). For a detailed discussion on the literature, see Roy (2012).

References

Abdel-Rahman, H. 1988. 'Product Differentiation, Monopolistic Competition and City Size'. *Journal of Urban Economics* 18 (1): 69–86.

Acs, J. Zoltan David B. Audretsch, Pontus Braunerhjelm and Bo Carlsson. 2006. 'The Knowledge Spillover Theory of Entrepreneurship'. CESIS, Electronic Working Paper Series No. 77.

Audretsch, B. David, Max C. Keilbach and Erik E. Lehmann. 2006. *Entrepreneurship and Economic Growth*. Oxford: Oxford University Press.

Belussi, F. and L. Pilotti. 2002. 'Knowledge Creation, Learning and Innovation in Italian Industrial Districts'. *Human Geography*, Special Issue 84 (2): 125–39.

Charaborty, Judhajit. 2017.'Employment in the Manufacturing Sector: A Disaggregated Level Analysis'. Chapter 1 of M. Phil thesis titled 'Has India Deindustrialised? Disaggregated Employment Trends and a Case Study', IGIDR.

Fujita, M., P. Krugman and A. Venables. 1999. *Economics of Agglomeration: Cities, Industrial Location and Industrial Growth*. Cambridge: Cambridge University Press.

Gianmarco, I., P. Ottaviano and J. F. Thisse. 2001. 'On Economic Geography in Economic Theory: Increasing Returns and Pecuniary Externalities'. *Journal of Economic Geography* 1 (2): 153–79.

Kaldor, N. 1966. *Causes of the Slow Rate of Economic Growth of the United Kingdom*. London: Cambridge University Press.

———. 1967. *Strategic Factors in Economic Development*. Ithaca: New York State School of Industrial and Labour Relations, Cornell University.

Krugman, P. 1991. 'Increasing Returns and Economic Geography'. *Journal of Political Economy* 99 (3): 483–99.

Marshall, A. 1920. *Principles of Economics*, 8th ed. New York: Macmillan.

Mezzadri, Alessandra. 2017. *The Sweatshop Regime: Labouring Bodies, Exploitation and Garments Made in India*. New York: Cambridge University Press.

Mitra, Sudipta. 2017. *Pearl by the River*. New Delhi: Rupa.

Romer, P. M. 1990. 'Endogenous Technological Change'. *Journal of Political Economy* 98 (5) : S71–S102.

Roy, Satyaki. 2012. 'Spatial Organization of Production in India: Contesting Themes and Conflicting Evidence'. *Journal of Regional Development and Planning* 1 (1): 1–16.

———. 2013. *Small and Medium Enterprises in India: Infirmities and Asymmetries in Industrial Clusters*. London and New York: Routledge.

———. 2016. 'Faltering Manufacturing Growth and Employment: Is "Making" the Answer?'. *Economic and Political Weekly* 51 (13): 35–42.

Schmitz, Hubert. 1999. 'Collective Efficiency and Increasing Return'. *Cambridge Journal of Economics* 23 (4): 465–83.

Sen, Ratna. 2013. 'West Bengal Garment Industry and the Informalisation Process'. *The Indian Journal of Industrial Relations* 48 (4): 563–81.

Sugihara, Kaoru. 2013. 'Labour-intensive Industrialisation in Global History': An Interpretation of East Asian Experiences'. In *Labour-Intensive Industrialisation in Global History*, edited by G. Austin and K. Sugihara, 20–64. London and New York: Routledge.

Zenger, Todd R. and William S. Hesterly. 1997. 'The Disaggregation of Corporations: Selective Intervention, High-powered Incentives, and Molecular Units'. *Organization Science* 8 (3): 209–22.

CHAPTER 3

Constraints to Upgrading and Employment Expansion in the Tiruppur Knitwear Cluster

M. Vijayabaskar

Introduction

When the quota system for the global garment trade came to an end with the expiry of the multi-fibre arrangement (MFA) in 2005, questions arose on how the removal of quantitative restrictions on exports will impact different countries (Joshi 2002; Vijayabaskar 2002). China and, to a lesser extent, India were expected to be the biggest gainers in the new global trading regime given their better production capabilities. After more than a decade, while China has indeed gained considerably with a global market share of 37 per cent in 2015, India's share has only marginally increased from around 3.5 per cent to 4.2 per cent in 2015 (Ministry of Textiles 2018b). As garment manufacturing is the most labour-intensive segment within textiles, this stagnation in market has implications for expanding manufacturing employment in India. There are two dimensions of such employment generation. An increase in global market shares for garments through improved competitiveness can translate into expansion of employment opportunities. Second, literature suggests that it is important for producers to upgrade, that is, to move into more value-adding segments rather than to compete merely on the basis of low wage costs to ensure better returns to production (Gereffi 1999). Appropriation of more value also enables producers to improve the quality of employment, which is particularly important in the context of countries such as India characterised by a substantial presence of the 'working poor'. This upgrading, particularly functional upgrading into downstream and upstream segments and diversification into related industries (Neffke, Henning and Boschma 2011), also generates additional employment linkages.

Despite stagnation in global market shares, expansion in output has been accompanied by shifts in product composition of garment production in India. Within apparels, there has been an increase in the share of knitted garments from about 17 per cent to 21 per cent during 2006–16 (Indian Institute of Foreign Trade 2018). Tiruppur, a cluster in southern India comprised of a dense network of over 5,000 small and medium firms specialising in different stages of garment production, is the biggest centre of the country's cotton knitwear exports. Firms in the cluster cater to several leading retail chains and supermarkets, particularly in Europe and USA. Based on secondary material and detailed interviews with key stakeholders in the Tiruppur cluster, this chapter seeks to identify (*a*) the extent to which exporters have been able to respond proactively to global market trends and 'upgrade' to enable better value realisation, (*b*) multiple aspects of governance failures to further upgrade to avoid prospects of 'immiserising growth' and (*c*) implications for employment generation in terms of quantity and quality.

I adopt the 'upgrading' schemata proposed by the global value chain theorists (Gereffi 1999; Gibbon 2000) for this exercise. The literature, in addressing the way power is dispersed along the value chain, points to the constraints and opportunities available for clusters in peripheral economies to undertake such upgrading. The chapter will focus on constraints to expansion into new markets and to upgrade within the value chain in terms of processes or movement into value-added products and functions. I shall then explain such constraints in terms of gaps in institutional support. Here I draw attention to issues of institutional governance within the apparel value chain and also to policy institutions external to the value chain such as those governing social infrastructure. I highlight the role of institutions at the cluster-level, subnational institutions governing infrastructure (soft and physical) provisioning and macro-economic policies such as trade and exchange rate policies. The chapter also draws attention to how shifts in the structure and the governance of the value chain interact with governance regimes across all the three scales to generate barriers to upgrading.

Method

Apart from the use of secondary data from the Ministry of Textiles, the Apparel Export Promotion Council (AEPC), the Tiruppur Exporters' Association (TEA) – a producer organisation in the town – and newspaper reports, the chapter draws substantially from primary information collected from detailed interviews with key stakeholders in firms differentiated by size, specialisation and market orientation. According to officials in the TEA, out of the 800 odd exporters, 25 are in the ₹100 crore-plus[1] annual turnover (TO) category, around 50 firms in the ₹50–100 crore category, 100 firms in the ₹10–50 crore category, 50 in the ₹5–10 crore category and around 150 firms in the ₹1–5 crore category. Together, the 800 odd exporters have about 3,600 factories for sewing, 1,000 dyeing and bleaching units, and 600 printing and embroidery units. The chapter draws from detailed interviews conducted with 5 large exporters (annual TO of >₹50 crores), 5 medium exporters (annual TO of ₹10–50 crores), 6 small exporters (annual TO of <₹5 crores), 5 domestic producers (out of which 3 produce for both export and domestic markets), and owners/managers of 10 ancillary units such as dyeing, printing and embroidery. In addition, I conducted interviews with 3 key managers in buying houses/ agents, 1 mid-level employee in a quality audit firm, 2 office bearers of the TEA, 1 office bearer of the Dyers' Association, 3 officials associated with the AEPC and the Ministry of Textiles and 2 members of faculty at the National Institute of Fashion Technology-TEA (NIFT-TEA), Tiruppur. Given the informal nature of the bulk of the economic activity in the cluster, it is impossible to map exact shifts in the quantum of employment. Instead, I have tried to capture segments where employment intensity has declined and segments where new employment opportunities have opened up. In the next section, I locate the cluster's trajectory within the development of textiles and clothing (T&C) sector at the national level.

Indian Garment Sector: Trends and Specifities

The T&C sector is clearly one of the most important segments within manufacturing, accounting for 2 per cent of gross domestic product (GDP), 7 per cent of industrial output and 15 per cent of India's export earnings, and is one of the largest sources of employment, employing more than 45 million workers (Ministry of Textiles 2018a). India is also one of the largest producers of cotton and the second largest producer of man-made fibres (MMF). Despite the growing share of MMF garments in the global market, Indian output of garments, particularly exports, continues to be dominated by cotton, though the share of MMF and blended garments has increased in the export profile (Table 3.1).

Table 3.1 Share of fabrics in ready-made garment (RMG) exports of India (in %)

S.No	Type of fabric	2013–14	2014–15	2015–16	2016–17
1	Cotton	54.5	48.4	47.6	43.9
2	Man-made fabric (MMF)	9.6	12.3	12	13.3
3	Silk	0.2	0.1	0.1	0.2
4	Wool	2	1.5	1.6	1.3
5	Other/blends	33.7	37.7	38.7	41.4
	Total RMG exports	100	100	100	100

Source: Data provided by the Tiruppur Exporters' Association.

Though garment and textile production is relatively more widespread, export capacities tend to be agglomerated in specific clusters such as the National Capital Region (NCR), Ludhiana, Bangalore and Tiruppur. There are some differences across these clusters as well, with the older ones such as Tiruppur and Ludhiana tending to be more vertically disintegrated and with higher levels of subcontracting. Even at the all-India level, subcontracting levels are higher than the global average (Kathuria, Martin and Bharadwaj 2000).

This organisational peculiarity is largely due to the national policy of reserving garment-making for the 'small scale' sector until the 2000s, which is believed to have prevented firms from taking advantage of scale economies. Firms with a capital investment below a limit (which was revised over time)[2] were categorised as 'small', and any firm with greater investment needed to commit to export more than 75 per cent of its output. Firms, therefore, split up or vertically disintegrated into smaller units to remain 'small'. As a result, a multi-tiered garment production structure dominated in India, with only 25 per cent of the total garment output accounted for by firms registered under the Factories Act, 1948, until 2005 (Bedi and Cororaton 2008). This decentralised production structure meant that Indian garment producers tend to be relatively more competitive in the low-volume casual-wear and semi-fashion segments of the market as compared to, say, China or Bangladesh where the minimum efficient scale of operation is much higher due to larger factories. The policy of reservation for the small-scale sector, however, allowed for the entry of entrepreneurs from economically less privileged backgrounds (Damodaran 2008), some of whom since then have managed to consolidate and expand in response to the growing market demand. The competitive edge for the Tiruppur cluster was largely through the cluster's ability to cater to order lots of varying sizes and involving relatively more design content than standardised garments that are produced on a large scale.

This is in contrast to the considerable role played by foreign direct investment (FDI) in competing countries such as China and Vietnam and, to an extent, Bangladesh. In Tiruppur too, larger firms have begun to take advantage of scale economies through expansion of capacities and also through vertical integration after de-reservation in 2005. Even large firms in Tiruppur, however, are smaller compared to factories in China. Another significant aspect of India's garment sector is the continued significance of the domestic market despite increase in exports. While domestic demand amounted to 70 per cent of demand since the mid-1990s, it has gone up to 82 per cent in 2010–11, reflecting partly the effect of global recession in 2009. This domestic market orientation has been fuelled by an increase in per capita apparel consumption in India in the post-reform period (Oberoi 2017).

Apart from de-reservation, there have been several initiatives to enhance capabilities in the sector. The government launched the Technology Upgradation Fund (TUF) scheme that allowed firms to access cheap credit to buy frontier technologies, which has helped the spinning segment to upgrade and India to be a global leader in production and export of cotton yarn. Regional governments have also supported the creation of physical infrastructure through the creation/promotion of export zones/parks with subsidised land, power and water supply apart from tax subsidies for exports. To improve the competitiveness of MMF-based textiles, both the National Textile Policy of 2000 and the National Fibre Policy of 2010 encouraged shifting fibre consumption and production in line with global trends. It has also been argued by the producers' lobby that Indian manufacturers are losing their competitiveness due to labour market rigidity forced through legislation. Given the seasonality of global demand for cotton garments, exporters are of the view that their wage costs become uncompetitive because they cannot adjust the quantum of labour hired in line with shifts in product demand. Following this, the union government has recommended labour law reform to cope with seasonality.

Despite such interventions, exports of value-added segments continue to stagnate. As Oberoi (2017) points out, the share of finished products has fallen from 76.9 per cent in 2005–06 to 64.3 per cent in 2013–14, a period when India was expected to actually take advantage of the emerging market opportunities in the wake of the expiry of the MFA (Oberoi 2017: 87, Table 3.3). Further, as stated earlier, India's share in the global apparel market has only marginally increased. Respondents believe that Indian policymakers did not make enough efforts to restructure the industry to take advantage of possible market opportunities. According to a long-term exporter, a big difference in the ability of China and India to take advantage of the reduced entry barriers in the post-quota phase is the absence of long-term planning in India. While China started investing in capacity right from 2000, and built large factories, there were hardly any comparable efforts in India, with exporters more interested in buying quotas than in investing in capital equipment. In the next section, I focus on the shifts in the global garment value chain that are likely to have had an impact on the cluster.

Dynamics of the Global Garment Value Chain and the Route to Upgrading

An important shift over the second half of the twentieth century is the taking over of control of the chain by retailers (buyers) from manufacturers in the advanced capitalist countries. Large retail chains and supermarkets use branding, fashion and design to generate market differentiation. Studies also point to a growing concentration, over time, in the retailing segment, though recent innovations in e-retail are believed to have undermined this to an extent. The ability of the advanced capitalist economies to sustain their presence in the global apparel value chain is generally attributed to the differentiation of the sector on the basis of fashion, design and quality. Production for mass markets characterised by stable designs and not subject to fashion trends can be moved to distant locations where cost of production can be minimised. Fashion-sensitive markets, however, require quicker responses to shifts in demand and hence production closer to the point of consumption to ensure timely delivery. Further, with the intensification of fashion-based marketing and consumption, there has been a decline in lead times, that is, the time that buyers give producers to deliver their output from the time of placing of orders. In this regard, a major trend is the increase in the number of seasons from two, that is, summer and winterwear, to up to six and even eight fashion cycles in a year (interview with leading exporter, Tiruppur, 14 March 2018). The declining lead times are also driven by buyers holding on to lesser inventory and moving towards placing orders closer to the time of consumption.

Along with declining lead times, attention to design and quality has led to an increase in transaction costs of coordinating the value chain. This has led to two tendencies in the chain. One, the higher transaction costs work against dispersion and buyers prefer to source from established suppliers/locations to minimise losses due to delays and defects. The higher transaction costs have also led to the emergence of new levels of intermediation. Merk (2014) points to the emergence of a layer of tier 1 suppliers who coordinate sourcing across disparate locations and even products across sectors. The emergence of such intermediaries forces new firms into becoming tier 2 or 3 suppliers. The upshot of such developments is, therefore, the emergence of new barriers for upgrading among new or smaller producers. Since buyers prefer to engage with such tier 1 suppliers, suppliers at lower tiers have to surmount this tier 1 intermediary if they want to appropriate more value.

Another dimension shaping the geography of the value chain is the persistence of regional, bilateral and preferential trade arrangements that undermine market access for countries that are not part of such agreements (Wazir Advisors India 2016). For example, the Trans-Pacific Partnership Agreement, a preferential trade agreement between 12 countries bordering the Pacific Ocean, played an important role in aiding Vietnam's access to US markets through lower tariffs. Exporters also believe that the lower wage rates, particularly in Bangladesh, and poorer adherence to labour and environmental standards in competing countries have all contributed to the inability of Indian exporters to compete with such countries. Further, in most competing countries, exports are dominated by large firms, often with FDIs. For example, Korean and Japanese firms have moved to China and Vietnam in the last two–three decades to take advantage of the lower costs and have better access to capital, markets and technologies. Finally, innovations in MMFs and blends that not only mimic the properties of natural fibres but also put them to novel uses such as in medical or technical textiles are becoming important sources of rents in the value chain.

Based on these global trends, it is, therefore, possible to identify the various routes to upgrading open to producers in Tiruppur. To begin with, they can aim to upgrade functionally by bypassing intermediaries to appropriate margins accruing to the latter. Alternatively, they can create brands and/or enter into direct retailing. With regard to product upgrading, producers can move into production for fashion/high-value segments or move more into MMF/blends/technical textiles. At the level of processes, they may also improve quality and productivity of processes and thereby cut down costs. Firms may also choose to cut costs by backward integration into spinning and into garment machinery making. The latter may also be important to ensure employment generation through the development of new manufacturing linkages. Given these possibilities, in the upcoming sections, I map the constraints that firms face with regard to specific types of upgrading, beginning with the prospects of branding and design upgrading.

Constraints to Upgrading into Branding and Design

There are instances where producers from Asian countries have managed to launch their own brands. 'Crocodile' is an example of a successful brand launched from Hong Kong. The biggest constraint to movement into branding stems from the fact that branding, especially international branding, costs a lot of money, particularly given the smaller size of firms in India. To overcome this constraint in Tiruppur, the idea of a common brand was mooted by the textiles ministry, and the Tiruppur brand was launched under which different exporters could export (Gurumurthy 2002). However, issues such as the modalities of sharing of orders and apportioning of losses incurred due to quality defects began to crop up. Further, since the market for Tiruppur's products was highly differentiated, it was not easy for the margins to be fixed across different styles. There were also complaints about domination by four–five major players in the cluster. As a result of such coordination failures, the common branding proved to be a failed effort.

The emergence of online retailing has, however, opened some possibilities in recent years. While it may not allow for high margins, it allows producers to build a brand over time which can then be leveraged. For example, the brand 'Guru T-Shirts' is being sold on Redbubble in the European Union (EU). Branding also, however, requires design capabilities, which are not well developed in the Tiruppur cluster. A home-grown buying house has bought a design studio in the UK, but few firms actually venture into design. A design studio launched with the help of the textiles ministry actually failed to take off in Tiruppur. A concern expressed by some of the informants is that designs developed by them are often leaked to competitors within the cluster through intermediary actors. A few firms do employ designers, but a common refrain among exporters is that designing can generate high returns only when it is tied to branding. At present, designing is confined to working with variations of designs launched in the destination markets. This is in contrast, according to industry experts, to the presence of design studios in many firms in China and Vietnam as well as warehouses close to buyers.

Constraints to Product Upgrading

High fashion generates more value added per piece and can also potentially contribute to better quality employment as it involves more skilled work. Respondents point to constraints of geography and capital to move into such segments. To begin with, shorter fashion cycles make it difficult for firms in Tiruppur to respond in time. Given that firms from Tiruppur export largely to the EU and USA, exporters cannot supply fast enough compared to producers located closer to these countries, such as those in Eastern Europe or Mexico. This has become particularly tough with the proliferation of fashion cycles in a year (Lutz 2012), which reduces the turnaround time, that is, time between when an order is placed and when the finished garments reach the buyers. While earlier retailers launched fashions well ahead of the season, at present firms increasingly use real-time information on buying trends and launch styles or buy more in line with such demand. Such temporalities of design and fashion production generate spatial barriers and make it difficult for firms in Tiruppur to enter into such segments.

Exporters may instead move into segments where fabric and quality of stitching and processing become important. An important factor which greatly constrains exporters from taking on large-scale orders that are of relatively high value is the considerable risks posed by both currency and yarn price fluctuations. At about 65 per cent of the total cost of production, yarn accounts for the bulk of the production cost for exporters. Since contracts and prices are fixed before the commencement of production, any increase in yarn prices after signing the contract is likely to undermine profit margins. The same holds good for exchange rates. Tiruppur's growth and expansion of exports was in good measure made possible by the devaluation of the Indian rupee, making exports steadily cheaper in dollar terms, since the early 1990s. Since then, fluctuations due to the strengthening of the rupee after finalisation of contracts have been posing considerable risk to exporters. In recent years, though insurance instruments are available to address this risk, the high transaction costs of utilising such mechanisms deter several small firms from accessing such instruments for risk mitigation and hence the possibility of entering into newer product markets. Such barriers notwithstanding, firms in Tiruppur have managed to not only expand production but also undertake both product and process upgrading.

Upgrading Initiatives in Tiruppur Cluster

Though, on an average, the sales price per garment has not gone beyond $2.5 for more than a decade, different kinds of upgrading can be observed at the firm level. To begin with, there is evidence of both capacity expansion and vertical integration among a few lead firms, accompanied by the emergence of 'line production' capable of producing thousands of pieces in a day. While individual plants have expanded, firms have also increased the number of plants or factories owned. In the case of leading exporters, there are separate factories to produce for export and domestic markets, for innerwear and outerwear and also for semi-fashion and standardised products. While this expansion of capacity cannot be called upgrading as defined in literature, such expansion is often accompanied by innovations in organising production such as line engineering and process upgrading.

Firms have also moved from outsourcing processes such as dyeing, printing and embroidery to build capacities internally, and to that extent there has been an increase in vertical integration. Given the emerging quality requirements, such vertical integration is often accompanied by investments in new process machinery. Open winch dyeing, which was common until the early 2000s, has practically disappeared from the cluster and soft flow dyeing is routinely used, which increases the quality of dyeing. Open drying has now been replaced with drying using machines. Digital printing technologies and computerised embroidery have diffused into the cluster as well. To be sure, all these technologies displace labour. However, the reduction in time taken to process and the better quality ensured allow firms to expand production and thus employment. Processing has become increasingly capital intensive, and though smaller firms do have access to high-quality processing in clusters like Tiruppur through networking with large firms that own such technologies, they also simultaneously rely on non-frontier technologies when the orders they receive do not impose stringent restrictions on the nature of processing to be undertaken.

Many large firms also have set up spinning mills that not only feed their requirements but also operate independently as sellers and exporters of yarn. Spinning mills are equipped with the latest automated machines with auto-doffing, auto-packing and auto-piercing that once again have not only dramatically reduced the need for labour on the shop floor but also ensure better quality. Apart from scale-induced process innovation, a few firms have also moved into the use of organic cotton and other natural fibres such as banana which fetch better value realisation though market size for such garments is much smaller. There are several domains where firms have invested in process upgrading. Internal testing has become mandatory for processes like shrinkage, colour bleeding and azo dyes. Most buyers insist on mandatory auditing and certifications. In terms of work processes, about 20–25 lead firms in the cluster have also introduced in-house training for workers. Apart from such firm-level upgrading initiatives, there have been several efforts undertaken by producer associations and policy institutions to improve the competitiveness of the cluster through cluster-level initiatives.

Since the early 2000s, the exporters' association has been instrumental in conducting yearly international trade fairs in Tiruppur where buyers, machinery suppliers and exporters can interact and learn. The government also supported the setting up of an inland container depot in the town which helped firms to reduce transaction costs of securing bureaucratic clearances for exports as well as that of logistics involved in transporting goods from Tiruppur to the ports. Institutional efforts have also enabled the development of zero liquid discharge (ZLD) technology in the cluster, though the extent of its diffusion is far from what is desired given the high costs involved and the inability of the producers to pass on the higher costs of such ecologically sensitive production to buyers. According to the respondents, per garment cost goes up by 4 per cent ZLD technology is used and hence renders them uncompetitive. They are, however, also optimistic over its technological potential as the costs of effluent treatment are falling steadily from 30 paise per litre a few years ago to 18 paise per litre at present. More recently, NIFT-TEA initiated research towards improving the quality of fabrics, for example, the anti-microbial properties fabric project and research to address spirality, a common defect in cotton fabric-based garments. NIFT-TEA has also established a design centre, but there are few takers for this at present. There is also a cluster-level emphasis on renewable energy plants such as solar and wind with a few large exporters having invested in them. Despite such upgrading with regard to processes, key informants are of the opinion that ecological and other process upgrading is inadequate.

Gaps in Process Upgrading Capabilities

Though about 300 units are linked to a Common Effluent Treatment Plant (CETP) and another 100 to individual effluent treatment plants (IETPs), it is seen to be insufficient with existing CETPs functioning at low capacity utilisation. A few large exporters do perceive the importance of value creation through eco-labelling, but there has not been much progress as they feel that there is not enough demand from their buyers. Technologies for recycling of sludge have also been developed. While chemical sludge can be used in the cement industry, bio-sludge has higher calorific value and can be used as compost. Despite such advances, association representatives do not think that policy measures are adequate to showcase such ecological upgrading in the cluster to realise better values. Compounded by the absence of support from within the value chain, producers have little incentive to actually adopt such processes. There are other gaps in process upgrading as well.

Established exporters and buying agents concede that Tiruppur continues to possess relatively weak capabilities in machinery for processing, weaving and knitting. Seamless knitting machines, which are necessary to move into sportswear, are inadequate. Technology for dyeing polyester through a tie-up with Reliance and Gwalior Rayons at NIFT-TEA is yet to diffuse widely. Importantly, as stated earlier, even the extant process upgrading in the cluster has not translated into higher prices. The average value realised per garment continues to be around \$2.4. Apart from factors that we discuss later, a major bottleneck is the inability of the cluster to diversify into markets for MMF-based products.

Constraints to Upgrading to MMF and Blended Garment Exports

Traditionally, India's textile policy framework is seen to be biased towards cotton. Despite the country having emerged as a major producer of synthetic fibres, exporters are of the opinion that monopoly or oligopolistic control over fibre production has led to higher domestic fibre prices than that prevailing in the global market. Studies on the textile industry too confirm this observation (Nair and Dhanuraj 2016). Even after taking on board transit costs, imported yarn is reported to be cheaper by 3–5 per cent. Some respondents also cite lack of access to duty-free imports of synthetic fibres due to lobbying by domestic producers. Antidumping duty within the range of \$23.75 and \$117.09 was imposed on the imports of purified terephthalic acid (PTA) from China, Korea and Thailand, thereby increasing the cost of raw material (Nair and Dhanuraj 2016). Further, while cotton invites an optional excise duty of only 6 per cent, a mandatory duty of 12.5 per cent is levied on MMF and yarn (Oberoi 2017). In addition, customs duty is also levied on some raw materials and additives used for producing MMF. A 5 per cent duty is imposed on rayon-grade wood pulp used for manufacturing viscose and PTA as well as monoethylene glycol (MEG) used for manufacturing polyester and 8 per cent duty on caprolactam used for manufacturing nylon (Nair and Dhanuraj 2016). However, in competing countries, tax equality is reported to be established between cotton and MMF along with duty free or lower duty imports of required raw material. Apart from such governance failures, there are also gaps with regard to skill formation in the cluster.

Governance of Skill Upgrading

Respondents cite better labour productivity in competing countries because of better skill formation. Recently, a skill gap study conducted by NIFT-TEA in collaboration with a private agency showed that while in Tiruppur, stitching a collar cotton T-shirt takes 12 minutes to be completed, it takes only 8 minutes for the same in China and Vietnam (interview with faculty, NIFT-TEA, Tiruppur, 19 April 2018). Given the smaller firm size in India and the frequent turnover of labour, there are fewer incentives for firms to invest in training as they cannot appropriate all the gains from such investments at the firm level (Vijayabaskar and Jeyaranjan 2011). Cluster-level training initiatives are, therefore, essential. Though many such initiatives have been launched in Tiruppur since the early 2000s, the extent to which such training initiatives have contributed to improved labour productivity is not clear. A major issue is the standards of training. For instance, though the National Skill Development Corporation (NSDC) generated 15,000 skilled workers in two years, the skill assessment is not good enough and key actors in the cluster do not perceive it to be a success. There are efforts to address the issue of poor standards through developing national-level skill accreditation – National Skills Qualifications Framework (NSQF) – with different levels. Efforts to grade factories by the Quality Council of India are also being discussed. Identifying and implementing appropriate standards is, therefore, a critical governance gap to ensure upgrading. Also, while training is essentially meant for basic tailoring skills, they do not contribute to improving and diversifying skill sets. Another constraint is that since firms in Tiruppur specialise in multiple kinds of garments, they require multi-skilled workers as opposed to specialisation in competing countries.

Forward Upgrading

Apart from issues in launching a common brand or moving into design, exporters also face barriers to bypassing intermediaries and thereby appropriating more values within the firm and/or the cluster. Buying agents tend to make a margin of 5–10 per cent and few buyers have managed to bypass them. The emergence of tier 1 supplier-intermediaries increase the barriers to such forward upgrading. This trend has been accompanied by a decline in the number of suppliers with increasing supplier capacity on the one hand and decreasing number of buyers/buying agents on the other. Firms, therefore, find it more difficult to reduce the loss in margins due to such intermediation. Apart from such issues within the value chain, there are other institutional gaps at the cluster, regional and national levels as well.

Absence of User–Producer Networks

A key mechanism that facilitates upgrading in clusters is non-market horizontal and vertical networks of collaboration and learning among firms and other actors in the chain (Gibbon 2000). While there are horizontal networks between sets of firms rooted in social and kinship ties between exporters, processors and subcontracting firms within the cluster, there is an absence of vertical collaborative networks such as between material suppliers and users and between textile machinery producers and users. These networks transcend cluster-level ties, and exporter firms are less equipped to forge such ties as their social networks seldom go beyond the scale of the cluster. Cotton yarn trade and exports are controlled by a traders' lobby that seldom interacts with garment producers. Respondents point out that traders are a strong lobbying body and prevent policymakers from intervening to regulate prices. Stable prices are crucial for garment exporters to reduce risk, but traders are likely to gain from speculation around price fluctuations. Producers of synthetic raw materials again tend to view their output as a commodity, not as an input for value-addition. Hence, they have stronger incentives to gain through monopoly pricing and import restrictions than through investment in innovations to improve fibre properties. Declining public investments and attention to public research and development (R&D) infrastructure is another major factor affecting upgrading prospects in the cluster.

Constraints to Innovation: Institutional Failures in R&D

Discussions with officials at the South Indian Textile Research Association (SITRA) reveal that there has been a steady decline in public R&D support for textiles. At present, the government support for SITRA is only 10 per cent of its budget, and the association is expected to mobilise its own resources. The number of scientists employed in SITRA has declined from around 300 in the 1980s to less than 50 at present. Further, there seems to be a policy bias against long-term R&D investments and a preference for short-term research projects that have immediate but not substantial results. This decline in public support has not been accompanied by any step up in R&D investments by large private actors. To quote a key informant, 'Reliance can do the work that DuPont does, but sees this merely as a commodity' (interview with a senior official in SITRA, Coimbatore, 17 April 2018). Experts also cite the absence of active university–industry collaborations with regard to innovations. The relative neglect of the sector by the state also manifests itself through the absence of a full-time textiles minister and a less than active bureaucracy. Emerging requirements, such as a separate R&D support centre for knitwear given its growth and expansion, hardly figure in policy discussions. Even the provision of subsidies for process upgrading through the TUF is reported to be misused in the case of knitting and weaving. Apart from chain-level and national-level governance institutions, regional policies also play an important role in shaping the upgrading prospects of the cluster, particularly with regard to social and physical infrastructure.

Regional Institutions and Provisioning of Infrastructure

Though it has improved at present, erratic supply of electricity has pushed most firms to invest in diesel power generators that not only require additional capital costs but also add to the cost of production as diesel-generated electricity is three times more expensive than what is supplied by the state government. Even the move to solar or wind energy is not sufficiently incentivised, as there is no support for energy credit, according to respondents. The second constraint with regard to infrastructure is the spiralling costs of land. In early 2018, the monthly rent for a small factory space in the town was about ₹ 1.8 lakhs[3] for 30,000 square feet. Given that such firms have an annual TO of less than ₹5 crores per month, firms spend substantially on rents. This spiralling land costs in fact came in the way of efforts by the state government to set up hostels for migrant workers on a public–private partnership with the exporters' association. The cost of land acquisition for this purpose proved to be unaffordable. Apart from big firms housing workers in dormitories, several small firms provide basic accommodation for their workers at subsidised rates. Bigger firms also spend on transporting workers from nearby villages, which according to respondents works out to about ₹50 per day per worker. There are other non-sectoral policy issues as well.

Shocks of New Policy Implementation

Given the small size of most firms, economic shocks brought about by global market shifts or national or regional policies are likely to adversely impact them more than large firms, as their resilience and ability to recover are lower. Two recent policy shocks, demonetisation and implementation of the goods and services tax (GST), are reported to have led to losses for the small producers in Tiruppur (Kumaramangalam 2018). The implementation of the GST without proper infrastructural support has burdened their working capital requirements, as refunds that were promised within a period of two weeks had not materialised even three months after the launch of the new tax regime. This has generated a huge liquidity crunch. Further, the new tax regime imposes additional transaction costs of compliance on small firms, as it has to be done online, such as E-way bills for every process. Given that many exporters are semi-literate, compliance requires them to employ tax consultants, contributing to operating costs. The squeeze on working capital translates into delayed payments for their suppliers and additional interest payments for informal borrowing. Demonetisation was another policy shock that wiped out liquid currency in the system, which again imposed undue burdens on small firms, as they all survive on a cash and carry system. The inability to pay workers their salaries or make payments to their suppliers for the work completed all meant freezing of work flows in the cluster and hence loss of incomes. Given such institutional shortfalls within and external to the value chain, how do producers cope and sustain?

Coping Strategies by Exporters

A few larger firms are beginning to move factories to lower cost locations, including other districts in the state and in Odisha to a limited extent. A firm has also set up factories in Ethiopia and Sri Lanka. The success of such moves is, however, not clear at present. Other strategies include cutting down on dyeing costs by shifting production to areas like Mysuru where pollution control norms are not stringent and hence costs of dyeing are lower (Rajasekaran 2018). A more common coping strategy is diversification into the domestic market.

Studies point to a rapid expansion in consumption of textiles in the last two decades with economic growth (Oberoi 2017). This expansion in demand has also been accompanied by change in patterns of consumption, with knitwear casuals becoming a popular garment across income groups. This increase has led to the diversification of production for the domestic market, albeit segmented. In the case of lower-end segments for innerwear and outerwear, a separate set of firms are involved in production. There is, however, a middle- and upper-end segment where organised retailing has emerged and has sought to use branding to create markets. Organised retail stores such as Reliance, Lifestyle or Big Bazaar all source garments from Tiruppur, and many have their own brands. While in the past, export firms rarely combined production for exports and the domestic market, at present several firms have diversified even as they continue to cater to global markets.

The capability acquired through production for global markets has definitely served firms to expand into the domestic market. Apart from better margins and faster payments, the absence of certification requirements also implies lower costs of compliance with social and environmental standards. Producers also report to have less stringent turnaround times and hence face less pressure. While industry observers claim that this also encourages firms to indulge in cost cutting through violation of pollution norms, this could not be verified. This expansion has above all contributed substantially to employment generation, particularly in the context of stagnant market shares in the global market and the inability to realise higher values in export production. Employment generation, however, may not be sustainable if policy emphasis does not shift towards upgrading of the cluster.

From Labour Intensity to Economic/Social/ Ecological Upgrading

Due to growing levels of automation, labour absorption per unit of output has reduced considerably in the spinning, knitting and processing segments such as dyeing, bleaching, printing and embroidery. According to respondents, employment generation would have fallen by two-thirds in these segments on an average. In garment making, however, the fall in labour intensity is much less. While cutting machines do reduce per unit labour requirements, garment making continues to be labour intensive. Introduction of line production has, however, involved greater task fragmentation, an increase in labour productivity and a slight decline in employment required per unit. Further, the need for certifications and standards adherence has led to the emergence of new sets of jobs in quality control and monitoring. Growth in size of firms has led to the emergence of human resource (HR) departments and managerial staff, which constitute new employment avenues. Overall, though employment intensity has decreased with time, the expansion in output has ensured an increase in demand for labour, which is also accompanied by fluctuations due to global market trends and domestic policies discussed earlier.

Importantly, this expansion has not been accompanied by the formation of economic linkages through related diversification that could have contributed to better employment generation. The growth in garment exports over nearly three decades has been accompanied by a steady replacement of domestically produced machines with imported ones, largely on account of quality and productivity requirements. Development of a robust domestic machinery base could have led to the creation of additional employment linkages in both machinery and component production, which are absent now. Similarly, entry into MMF segments could have opened an additional set of employment linkages. Fibre and material science and production of accessories such as buttons and zippers are other avenues that are not available for employment generation at present.

Apart from the quantum of employment, there are issues with the quality of employment as well (Vijayabaskar 2001). Though the cluster has witnessed a degree of vertical integration and increase in firm size compared to the previous years, there are still no long-term career paths for entry-level workers. Low salary levels and mobility prospects deter students from taking up the study of textile engineering as an option. Cost pressures and demands of flexibility in global markets have led to the bulk of the firms taking the 'low road' marked by outsourcing to smaller units and lower incentives for spending on pollution control. While the insistence on certifications has led to a decline in such practices, the absence of a long-term career path undermines incentives for workers to make claims for better conditions for work and employment. To be sure, such issues are not unique to the Tiruppur cluster and resemble working conditions globally in many ways. In fact, wage rates for skilled tailors in the cluster are higher than that paid to tailors in the NCR region.

The expansion in output and an inability to upgrade by firms and the use of labour market flexibility to sustain cost competitiveness are suggestive of the phenomenon of 'immiserising growth' despite some evidence of upgrading and value realisation among a handful of firms. If increases in nominal wages are indeed undermining the competitiveness of firms, improvements in labour productivity and attention to real wages through provisioning of subsidised housing, healthcare and education become essential. Though registered workers are eligible for subsidised healthcare through the employee state insurance

(ESI), perceived poor quality of healthcare provisioning in ESI hospitals force workers to seek expensive private healthcare. Worker households also tend to prefer expensive private schooling for their children for similar reasons.

Literature on social and economic upgrading has also begun to draw attention to the environmental externalities posed by segments of the value chain. In the context of Tiruppur, increasing water extraction for processing and pollution of groundwater and water bodies around the cluster has undermined water security in nearby areas. While legal strictures on pollution has led to the shifting of dyeing and other processing operations to Perundurai, a nearby town, and further to Mysuru, there are gaps in governance with regard to enforcing compliance across all firm types in this regard.

Concluding Observations

Some of the explanations offered initially for India's ability to take advantage of new market opportunities such as reservation for the small-scale sector and labour regulations are less sustainable at present. Large-scale garment manufacturing has emerged following de-reservation of the sector, and de facto labour practices characterised by considerable flexibility render explanations based on labour market rigidity unconvincing (Sood, Nath and Ghosh 2014). However, even the 'large' firms in Tiruppur continue to be smaller in size compared to factories in competing countries such as Vietnam and Bangladesh. While this allows them to compete in the semi-fashion segment, they face constraints in terms of moving into mass market segments. In this regard, support for provision of real services at the cluster level appears inadequate. The raw material base of apparel production and exports continues to be dominated by cotton fibre, though the global market share of MMF garments is expanding. The inability to penetrate the MMF market is attributed to the import duties imposed on raw material and the oligopolistic manipulation of pricing by Indian producers. Even in the case of cotton, fluctuations in yarn prices pose a high degree of risk for firms in negotiating viable prices. Exporters are of the opinion that policies around cotton yarn pricing and trade are shaped by strong lobbying by big traders.

Smaller exporters cite high transaction costs of availing and accessing insurance against global market risks. Though there was an increase in the average value realised per garment in Tiruppur, especially among the bigger exporters until 2009, there has been stagnation in prices received since then. Importantly, this is happening despite considerable investments in process upgrading. Imported machinery has replaced the local machinery used earlier for stitching. Ancillary firms such as those involved in dyeing, printing and embroidery increasingly use latest technologies based on computerised control and monitoring systems. Some export firms have moved into new high-value-added garments, and many have integrated cotton spinning with garment production. A few firms have also moved from exports to production for the domestic market. Nevertheless, the fact remains that such upgrading has not become widespread across the cluster.

In this context, I would like to highlight the absence of institutional support for innovation and, importantly, how emphasis on cost reduction undermines incentives to innovate and upgrade. Rising cost of land also undermines the margins of small firms operating from rented premises as well as their ability to expand capacity. Other disruptions by the government such as demonetisation and the introduction of the GST regime without adequate infrastructure have also contributed to increasing the transaction costs, particularly for the smaller players. This has had an adverse impact, particularly in the context of stagnation in the global apparel market and an inability to bargain for better prices. The diversification of firms into the expanding domestic market, while generating considerable employment opportunities, has been accompanied by the absence of any need to adhere to social and environmental standards. While this 'short-termist' approach is a rational response on the part of small and medium firms confronted with declining margins in the global market, national and regional policy governance should generate disincentives for such an approach to growth and expansion.

The chapter also highlights the absence of adequate investments in public healthcare and housing that may help workers improve their real incomes. Strategies that privilege competitiveness or product market behaviour are less capable of understanding labour market outcomes, and hence less useful to improve working conditions. A better strategy would be to simultaneously focus upon labour markets and product markets. Labour market outcomes are an outcome of a number of other structural factors rooted in the local economy. Competitiveness in product markets, be it of the low road or the high road, seldom lead to improved working conditions without effective intervention. The cluster lacks in social infrastructure such as quality healthcare and housing. An important entry point for ensuring better conditions for labour, therefore, involves recognising the distinction between real and nominal wages. While for capital it is the nominal wage level that influences profit levels, it is the real wages that affect workers' livelihoods. Intervention by the state in the area of provisioning quality education, healthcare and housing can go a long way in improving the real wages of workers. Good quality and affordable public transport systems would be another service that requires attention of policymakers. This distinction between nominal and real wages ought to be critical for any policy intervention that seeks to simultaneously emphasise employment expansion and worker welfare in globalising sectors.

Finally, policy emphasis on manufacturing as a route to employment expansion is driven crucially by the greater economic linkages that manufacturing has with other sectors. However, in the case of apparel exports, the chapter points to a reduction of domestic linkages with reliance on imported machinery, ancillaries and even fabric over time due to demands of quality in global markets. Knitting machines, which were largely made in Ludhiana, for example, are completely imported at present. The inability to foster such local linkages lies in a larger shift in macro-policy that allowed for market-based incentives to guide economic actions without active public interventions to build capabilities. This becomes particularly important in a context where the use of automated machines in several segments of garment processing has reduced employment intensity considerably in such segments. The decline in public support for research in textiles and the absence of support for developing effluent treatment technologies are institutional failures in this regard. The inability to regulate yarn prices or ensure competitive access to MMF also suggests that policy reforms may be embedded in certain business interests that may not contribute to efforts at industrial upgrading and employment expansion.

Notes

1. 1 crore = 10 million.
2. It was revised to ₹3 crores since 1998, before which the limit was ₹1 crore.
3. 1 lakh = 100,000.

References

Bedi, Jatinder S. and Caesar B. Cororaton. 2008. 'Cotton Textile Apparel Sectors of India: Situations and Challenges Faced'. International Food Policy Research Institute Discussion Paper No.00801, Washington, DC.

Damodaran, Harish. 2008. *India's New Capitalists: Caste Business and Industry in a Modern Nation*. New Delhi: Permanent Black

Gereffi, G. 1999. 'International Trade and Industrial Upgrading in the Apparel Commodity Chain'. *Journal of International Economics* 48 (1): 37–70.

Gibbon, P. 2000. 'Global Commodity Chains and Economic Upgrading in Less Developed Countries'. Working Paper: No. 2, Centre for Development Research, Copenhagen.

Gurumurthy, G. 2002. 'Tirupur Cluster Development: Textiles Committee May Take Over from Unido'. *Hindu BusinessLine*, 16 April. Available at https://www.thehindubusinessline.com/2002/04/16/stories/2002041602331700.htm, accessed on 24 November 2018.

Indian Institute of Foreign Trade. 2018. 'Challenges and Strategies to Promote India as a Sourcing Destination'. Submitted to Ministry of Textiles, Government of India, New Delhi.

Joshi, Gopal, ed. 2002. *Garment Industry in South Asia–Rags or Riches? Competitiveness, Productivity and Job Quality in the Post-MFA Environment*. New Delhi: South Asia Multidisciplinary Advisory Team, New Delhi: International Labour Organization.

Kathuria, Sanjay, Will Martin and Anjali Bharadwaj. 2000. 'Implications of MFA Abolition for South Asian Countries'. Paper presented at the NCAER-World Bank WTO 2000 South Asia Workshop, 20–21 December, New Delhi.

Kumaramangalam, R. Mohan. 2018. 'Unmade in India: The Story of Tirupur's Decline'. *The Hindu*, 25 March. Available at https://www.thehindu.com/business/Industry/unmade-in-india-the-story-of-tirupurs-decline/article23349892.ece, accessed on 7 July 2019.

Lutz, Ashley. 2012. 'Zara Has Fundamentally Changed Fashion and There's No Going Back'. *Business Insider*, 10 November. Available at https://www.businessinsider.com/how-zara-is-changing-fashion-forever-2012-11?IR=T, accessed on 30 November 2018.

Merk, Jeroen. 2014. 'The Rise of Tier 1 Firms in the Global Garment Industry: Challenges for Labour Rights Advocates'. *Oxford Development Studies* 42 (2): 259–77.

Ministry of Textiles. (2018a), *Annual Report 2017–18*. New Delhi: Ministry of Textiles, Government of India.

———. 2018b. *Study on 'Garment Sector to Understand their Requirement for Capacity Building*. New Delhi: Ministry of Textiles, Government of India. Available at http://texmin.nic.in/sites/default/files/Garment%20Study%20-%20Final%20Report%20-%2026.02.2018.pdf, accessed on 26 June 2019.

Nair, Lakshmi R and D. Dhanuraj. 2016. *Common Man's Clothing: Effects of Taxes and Tariffs*. Elamkulam: Centre for Public Policy Research, 2016. Available at www.cppr.in, accessed on 25 June 2019.

Neffke, F., M. Henning and R. Boschma. 2011. 'How Do Regions Diversify Over Time? Industry Relatedness and the Development of New Growth Paths in Regions'. *Economic Geography* 87 (3): 237–65.

Rajasekaran, R. K. 2018. 'Tirupur Garment Makers Shift Fabric Dyeing to Mysuru'. *Times of India*, 27 January. Available at https://timesofindia.indiatimes.com/city/coimbatore/tirupur-garment-makers-shift-fabric-dyeing-to-mysuru/articleshow/62666741.cms, accessed on 30 November 2018.

Vijayabaskar, M. 2001 'Industrial Formation under Conditions of Flexible Accumulation: The Case of a Global Knitwear Node in Southern India'. Unpublished Ph.D. dissertation, Centre for Development Studies, Jawaharlal Nehru University, New Delhi.

————. 2002. 'The Indian Garment Industry'. In *Garment Industry in South Asia-Rags or Riches? Competitiveness, Productivity and Job Quality in the Post-MFA Environment*, edited by G. Joshi, 39–81. New Delhi: South Asia Multidisciplinary Advisory Team, International Labour Organization (ILO).

Vijayabaskar, M. and J. Jeyaranjan. 2011. 'The Institutional Milieu of Skill Formation: A Comparative Study of Two Textile Regions in Ohara'. In *India and China Industrial Dynamics in China and India: Firms, Clusters, and Different Growth Paths*, edited by M. Vijayabaskar and Hong Lin, 135–56. New York: Palgrave McMillan.

Wazir Advisors India. 2016. 'Existing and Prospective FTAs and Their Impact on Indian Textiles Exports: Final Study Report'. Submitted to Ministry of Textiles, Government of India.

Chapter 4

Determinants of Employment in the Indian Automobile Industry

Madhuri Saripalle

Introduction

Employment generation in India has been skewed in favour of services since early 2000 (GOI 2018), reflecting the sectoral gross domestic product (GDP) shares of manufacturing and services at 17 per cent and services at 53 per cent, respectively. But as the employment growth in services tapers off, one needs to re-examine the role of the manufacturing sector in creating jobs. To be specific, labour-intensive industrialisation is a term that needs elaboration to understand the role of specific sectors and their interlinkages to the local and global economies. In a sense, one needs to reimagine labour-intensive industrialisation in the manufacturing sector and the possible strategies for the same.

Historically, industrialisation strategies depend on factor endowments. A country's direction of trade also signifies its nature of industrialisation. If a country exports labour-intensive goods and imports capital-intensive goods, it follows labour-intensive industrialisation. Over time, as the quality of skill and education improves, the character of exports also improves qualitatively with an improvement in living standards. This is the transition that is targeted by emerging economies with abundant labour endowment. The definition of labour intensive, however, can be relative. For example, despite being more capital intensive than traditional industries such as textiles, the automotive industry is relatively labour intensive in comparison to its counterparts in developed countries. Further, only specific processes such as transfer presses, paint shop and welding operations are capital intensive whereas assembly operations and parts manufacturing are outsourced to the upstream section of the value chain consisting of structured suppliers in the automotive ancillary industries. The contribution of the global automotive industry to GDP ranges between 3 and 7 per cent while the employment share ranges between 5 and 15 per cent in the developed and emerging economies,[1] respectively.

The present chapter analyses the employment potential of the Indian automobile industry, which is a technology-intensive industry with extensive backward and forward linkages. The automobile industry is composed of the original equipment manufacturers (OEMs) and the auto component manufacturers, which come under different National Industrial Classification (NIC) codes. The component industry is organised into subsegments or tiers based on tasks or activities. For example, an auto manufacturer contracts to a tier 1 supplier of automobile system, such as the seating or the exhaust system; the tier 1 supplier assigns the sub tasks to a tier 2 supplier, and so on. The component sector can be further categorised into the organised and unorganised segments depending on the size and nature of employment. Tier 1 and tier 2 component suppliers come under the organised segment, whereas firms further upstream (tiers 3 and 4) fall under the unorganised segment.[2]

The share of direct employment generation in the economy is 7 per cent, as per the annual survey of industries (ASI) in 2015–16. However, because of its extensive inter-firm linkages, the extent of indirect employment generation is huge and, overall, it is estimated at 10 per cent of the total employment in the economy. Direct employment includes personnel working with automobile OEMs and auto component manufacturers (about 30 per cent to 40 per cent). Indirect employment includes personnel working in enabling industries, such as vehicle finance and insurance, vehicle repair, vehicle service stations, vehicle maintenance, vehicle and component dealers, drivers and cleaners (about 60 to 70 per cent) (PwC 2013). However, in recent times, the growth rate of direct employment in this sector is falling. Hence, it is important to understand the reasons for this decline and critically examine the future potential of this sector in employment generation.

Structurally, in the auto component segment, the majority of the sales is now accounted for by the domestic auto industry, followed by aftermarket and exports. Since the auto ancillary sector's contribution to employment is higher, a total of 45 firms (15 tier 1 and 30 tiers 2 and 3) were interviewed across Chennai, Hosur and Gurgaon. The firms are involved in the manufacture of engine components,[3] namely cylinder heads, blocks, springs, valves, pumps, clutch systems, die casting, pistons and pulleys. To complement the qualitative findings, a quantitative analysis is done based on secondary sources – the Prowess database of the Center for Monitoring Indian Economy (CMIE) – to analyse the determinants of labour demand as a function of trade and technology acquisition (R&D effort) in the automobile industry. As a contrast in industrial policy, the results from the automobile industry are used to compare with the electronics industry. Hardware electronics is also a technology-intensive industry but was not able to develop indigenous technological capabilities because of historical policy factors. Using a panel data on 555 firms in the automobile industry and 628 firms in the electronics and electrical industries from 2000–2016, the chapter estimates an econometric model for determinants of employment generation.

The chapter is organised as follows. The second section discusses growth of the industry in terms of turnover, employment and trade. It also discusses the role of R&D, skill gaps and the impact of automation on the industry. The third section presents a case study of the automobile cluster in Tamil Nadu and the challenges in the unorganised segment of the automobile industry. This is followed by a model of labour demand as a function of trade and technology variables in the organised segment of the automobile industry in the fourth section. The final section concludes with policy suggestions.

The Indian Automobile Industry

Automobile Industry Growth and Global Footprint

The Indian automobile industry has been growing at a compound average annual rate of 15 per cent per annum (Figure 4.1) and is the fourth largest (excluding two wheelers) in the world as per the International Organization for Vehicle Manufacturers (OICA 2018). The growth in turnover has been higher for the component sector during this period at 17 per cent per annum compared to 10 per cent for the OEMs or the assemblers (Figure 4A.1 in Appendix 4A). Despite an impressive growth in production during the period 2000–2017, growth in direct employment has been approximately only 5 per cent (Table 4.1). Within the auto component sector (NIC code 293), which is the major employer across all categories of employment, the share of contract workers is very high at roughly 50 per cent, as opposed to the OEMs who employ roughly 30 per cent of contract workers.

Post 2000, with the entry of multinational corporations (MNCs) and intensified competition, automobile manufacturers have changed the employment structure, giving rise to a regional contract labour system that

Table 4.1   Employment by 3-digit NIC categories in the automobile industry

Employment (numbers) in NIC codes 291–93 and 309 (motor vehicles, coaches and trailers; components, motor bikes and other transport equipment)						
Year	Total direct	Total contract	Total managerial	Total other admin	Total	% of contract
2011–12	**416,725**	**355,592**	108,150	100,684	981,151	36
2012–13	**448,748**	**309,074**	107,758	102,956	968,536	32
2013–14	**416,455**	**341,702**	119,309	111,535	989,001	35
2014–15	**467,515**	**405,060**	120,164	127,142	1,119,881	36
2015–16	**465,512**	**452,448**	126,198	137,251	1,181,409	38
2016–17	**458,143**	**480,293**	131,160	139,674	1,209,270	40

Source: Annual Survey of Industries, Government of India.

relies heavily on contract workers.[4] Findings from primary survey support these facts (Table 4A.2 in Appendix 4A). A recent study (Kapoor and Krishnapriya 2019) reveals that not only has the share of contract labour increased, especially in capital-intensive industries, it has coincided with the years in which the growth rate of wages of contract workers surpassed that of direct workers, the increase seen mainly as a need to reduce the bargaining power of direct workers and reduce the wage differential over time.

Figure 4.1   Growth in total vehicle production

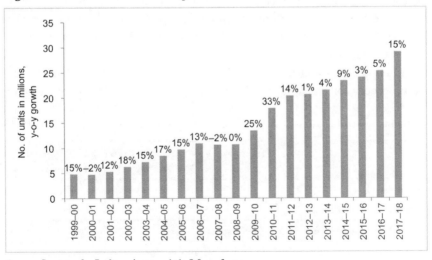

Source: Society for Indian Automobile Manufacturers.

Export and Import

Vehicle exports constitute 57 per cent of the total automotive exports while component exports constitute the rest (Table 4.2). Of the total production of vehicles, exports comprise 15 per cent as on 2018–19, of which 50 per cent is compact cars. India has emerged as a global base for small and compact cars as its share in world exports of compact cars increased from 0.01 per cent in 2000 to 3.7 per cent in 2015 (Athukorala and Veeramani 2017). Component exports still consist of traditional mechanical parts for engines, such as gearboxes and brakes, with electronics comprising a low share in the export basket. Component exports by Indian firms to their affiliates abroad is a rising trend. As Table 4.2 shows, there is an increasing import intensity of exports indicative of integration with global production networks. During 2000–18, exports of auto components have grown at a compound annual growth rate (CAGR) of 26 per cent while imports have grown at a rate of 29 per cent (Figure 4.2).

The direction of exports has also shifted from European countries in 2005–06 to the US market in 2017–18, while China and Germany have emerged as the major import sources for the industry (PwC 2018). Among exports, the share of engine, transmission and steering parts and body/chassis/BiW (body in white) is the highest at 70 per cent in 2015–16, while the rest 46 per cent is contributed by segments such as bumpers and rubber products. The stringent quality requirements and inventory challenges make it difficult for many domestic firms to break through to export markets. For example, because of high transit times, companies maintain one month's stock for exports compared to OEMs, which maintain much less inventory. This proves risky in case of defects, as the entire stock consisting of three months' inventory must be contained.

Among imports, engine, transmission, steering and suspension and electronic parts account for greater than 60 per cent of overall auto components being

Table 4.2   Export and import shares of vehicles and component manufacturers in 2018–19

	Share in total automotive imports (%)	Share in total automotive exports (%)
Vehicles (HS code 8703) #	5	57
Components (HS code 8708)	95	43

Source: Ministry of Commerce, EXIM database.

Note: #Automotive vehicles include only three and four wheelers. Components include tractor parts.

Figure 4.2   Exports and imports from 2000–18

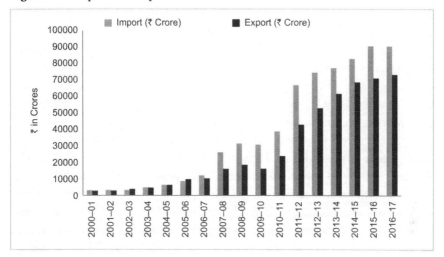

Source: ACMA annual reports

imported; the major source of imports include China, Japan and Germany. Imports are driven by proprietary technology, free trade agreements, quality requirements, lack of domestic capability in such components (electronics) and shift to new technologies. Indian firms lack the capability to manufacture some basic parts because of low R&D. For example, a belt manufacturer in Chennai imports components for manufacturing rubber timing belts, such as additives, fibres, chemicals, silica and basic rubber. In general, the import content of new generation pumps is 10–15 per cent of raw material cost as compared to 1 per cent in conventional pumps.

Automation, new technology and future mobility solutions

A recent study by Sunil Mani (2018) finds that, in India, the automobile sector accounts for the majority share of robot installations in tasks which are inhospitable and require precision, such as arc and spot welding, soldering, handling and machine tending. This is supported by the fact that the auto industry is dominated by subsidiaries of MNC affiliates with a history and experience in usage of industrial robots. According to a tier 1 supplier of engine systems, robots are cost-effective and take 28 seconds per product for running a big assembly line and reduce the requirement of nine workers (three workers across three shifts). According to a senior executive from the company, as the share of new generation product has increased in total production, from 13 per cent to 50 per cent from 2007 to 2017, share of manpower has fallen from 87 per cent to 50 per cent. In general, low-cost automation was found to be more feasible in the component sector because of high sunk costs and the requirement of high precision. Examples include substituting manual shifting of components with a conveyor belt system, the use of automated programmable logic controller (PLC) machine that takes care of the entire assembly line with just two persons, and automation in foundry for pressure die casting.

The restructuring in the industry may result in a gradual fall in direct employment in the industry. However, with changing mobility preferences, demand will move towards logistics service providers, fleet managers and urban mobility solution providers, such as car aggregators. Future demand for employment will come from the entire eco-system of the automobile industry covering the entire gamut of finance, mobility and driving, repair and maintenance. For example, the Ford Technology Center in Chennai employs 11,000 people across four centres, from commerce, information technology (IT) and engineering backgrounds. They provide the back office for accounting, IT infrastructure and global manufacturing services. Bosch also has a separate back offices in Bangalore, Hyderabad and Coimbatore for software services for the global market, in which employment has increased from 9,000 in 2010 to 23,000 in 2018.

Employment Generation through Exports: Role of Free Trade Agreements (FTAs)

Indian exporting firms are primarily exporting through their affiliates or to tier 1 multinational suppliers who are members of free trade zones. For example, Indian suppliers such as Sunbeam Auto export directly to overseas suppliers (Continental Automotives) in the USA, which supplies to its Mexico plant through the North American Free Trade Agreement (NAFTA). VW India exports cars to Mexico because it offers exemption of duties on imported cars for a number equivalent to 10 per cent of the total production of cars done by the brand in Mexico. Multinational tier 1 suppliers to Ford India export cylinder heads and blocks and semi-finished aluminum blanks to their own plants in China. Other tier 1 suppliers such as SSS Springs, TVS Autolec, JBM Kanemitsu and Luk India export directly to tier 1 suppliers (for example, Standardine and John Deere) as well as OEMs in the USA, Europe and Russia. A recent study (Veeramani 2016) finds that between 1999–2000 and 2012–13, export-related jobs grew significantly faster than that of the country's total employment during 1999–2012, from 9 per cent to 14.5 per cent.

A recent study identifies three generations of auto exporting countries based on the nature of competition faced by them. While the first two generations of exporters – USA., Germany, Japan and South Korea – faced open competition in the world market, the third generation of exporting nations – Mexico and the East European countries – primarily export within economic trade zones. Export-oriented strategy requires breaking into these trade barriers and negotiating agreements that favour employment generation, as can be seen from the third-generation exporters such as Slovakia and Mexico. The share of employment in Slovakia is quite high at 15 per cent (ACEA 2020) of the total manufacturing employment.

> Without membership of a large economic zone in which duty-free internal-market trade exists, no third-generation country has yet succeeded in entering export markets for cars on a significant level. (Rudolf 2017)

Foreign direct investment (FDI) is an integral part of the automobile industry in any country and can be oriented towards domestic or export markets. However, in the absence of local content regulation, exports will have a high import content without domestic value addition. A study (Ghosh and Roy 2015) in the context of Indian manufacturing finds that foreign ownership does not have any significant impact on employment generation in the Indian manufacturing sector, except for food and beverages on account of growing exports and diversification of the export basket into higher value-added items such as marine and processed food items.[5] In the automobile industry, local content regulation in some form should be encouraged for exporting firms in order to generate inter-firm linkages and employment opportunities.

Research and Development (R&D) and Skill Gaps

In the past decade, the R&D capabilities of the Indian auto industry have increased significantly. Interviews with senior R&D executives bring out the changing nature of R&D in India from adaptive to application engineering and product development. There are, however, no incentives to undertake basic research activities in the Indian auto industry, as there is no market demand for the same. Prior to 2000, R&D intensity (R&D as percentage of sales) was negligible among the OEM and component categories, gradually increasing to around 1 per cent of turnover in 2010 and 6 per cent in 2016 among the OEMs (Table 4.3). R&D was mostly adaptive and process oriented (Narayanan and Vashisht 2008); however, it has moved towards product development post 2000. R&D activities in India are targeted towards engineering research activities such as application engineering (applying/modifying the design to local conditions) and reliability engineering (using optimisation methods to improve the reliability of auto components).[6] Quality standards have gone beyond parts per million to zero defects. With increase in warranty time frame to three years, the ability of component to withstand wear and tear has gone up from 0.1–0.3 million kilometres, requiring training on topics such as reliability engineering.

Application engineering includes skills that require metal composition analysis, testing parameters, mould analysis and adapting design to customer requirements. One of the firms has established eight R&D centres across India and employs 13 per cent of its engineers for R&D. A tier 1 system supplier (a US–Japan joint venture established in 1986) is a market leader in transmission timing belts and industrial belts globally and currently holds 150 active and

Table 4.3   Research and development intensity

Year	Auto components (%)	OEM (%)
2000	0.04	0.9
2001	0.02	0.3
2002	0.35	4.8
2003	0.33	0.7
2004	0.47	0.6
2005	0.34	0.6
2006	0.19	0.6
2007	0.16	0.6
2008	0.23	0.6
2009	0.24	1.1
2010	0.22	1.1
2011	0.22	1.1
2012	0.39	1.7
2013	0.39	7.3
2014	0.46	3.5
2015	0.69	3.8
2016	0.62	6.4

Source: Prowess database, CMIE.

600 past patents. An example of application engineering is the development of the belt system for e-bikes in India for Ather Energy, the producer of e-bikes in India. While the carbon belt was imported, the sprocket for the bike was developed in-house. Specialised suppliers for thermal spray coating and powder coating were sourced from Jaipur and Chennai. The 22 engineers as well as a few operators at the Chennai plant undergo rigorous training programmes, which include online in-house developed personalised courses, field trips to factory locations abroad. To develop skills in the industry, the firm also collaborated with colleges on research projects worth up to ₹500,000 and allowed use of their lab equipment for application engineering.

In general, skill gap as a constraint was not reported across all firms in Tamil Nadu and Hosur. Some of the major skill gaps discussed by the auto component firm included specialised skills such as rubber technologists, pressure die casting, material sciences, welding and machining, and practical knowledge of sheet metal operations. Firms get around the skill gaps by tying up with local engineering colleges for internships, and instating practical training rooms to impart knowledge on fine motor skills, measurement equipment, hydraulic, pneumatic and lubrication systems for machines. Some firms also reported sending their production workers abroad for training in the affiliate firms. There is a need to introduce quality and safety as behavioural attitudes in the course curriculum and not as a mere checklist to be followed.

Unorganised Sector: Auto Component Cluster

With the entry of large multinational players, the supplier base has become more concentrated and spread across a few regional clusters. Regional clusters are important, as they are the catalysts for employment and innovation, especially in the automobile industry, and the pattern of their spread reflects policy factors such as FDI and education (Okada and Siddharthan 2008). Changes in clusters can follow different paths, as summarised by Belussi (1999) in the case of Italy. These can be (*a*) a general decline in employment and output because of loss of competitiveness, (*b*) a partial de-localisation of activities to low labour cost countries, (*c*) a strong internal restructuring with more hierarchy among enterprises because of mergers and acquisitions and (*d*) a shift of the local system towards new production or productive diversification such as transformation of transport firms into logistic operators. In the case of Tamil Nadu's automotive cluster, there seems to be evidence for (*c*) and (*d*). Auto component suppliers are concentrated in the northern region, followed by western and southern regions, and within each region, the companies are concentrated only in states that have proximity to port and infrastructure facilities (ACMA 2017). Post 2000, with the entry of foreign players, the number of new companies incorporated fell drastically as barriers to entry have increased.

Tamil Nadu Auto Cluster

Automotive clusters in south India are concentrated in Karnataka and Tamil Nadu. Within Tamil Nadu, Chennai accounts for the majority of firms because of locational advantages. The Chennai automotive cluster is spread around three main areas: the Ambattur, Sriperumbudur and Orgadam industrial estates. Of these, Ambattur, which was established in 1964, is the oldest and largest in terms of number of small and medium firms. It is comprised of 500-plus auto component firms that include tier 1 domestic firms, tier 2 and tier 3 small and medium firms, followed by a cluster of 2,000 odd tiny jobbing and repair units which provide support to these firms. Figure 4.3 shows the key actors in the industrial estate and their interlinkages.

Post 2000, the eco-system has evolved with the emergence of many supporting firms catering to the broad engineering segment such as steel

Figure 4.3 Ambattur automotive cluster

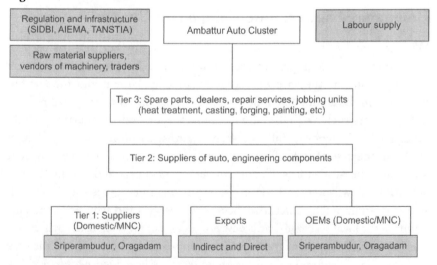

Source: Field survey.

and fabrication, heat treatment units and automotive after-sale services. The Ambattur estate has a strong network of jobbing units which are used as shop floor extensions by the tier 1 and tier 2 suppliers. This is a unique feature which is not present in the other two auto clusters. Besides the eco-system of the automobile industry, there are other firms form the food industry, IT, and garments and textiles as well. The labour pool of the industrial estate is localised and consists of a floating population of workers who seek employment through word of mouth and referrals, mostly temporary and contractual in nature.

A sample of 30 auto component firms was surveyed with turnovers ranging from less than ₹1 million to greater than ₹100 million, and it was found that while there was growth in turnover across all sizes, only the bigger firms with turnover greater than ₹100 million created more employment (Table 4.7). Many small firms have grown organically over the years and gained access to export markets through repeated customer interactions.

To summarise, the employment in tier 3 and tier 4 segments of the automobile industry is growing but is highly unorganised and temporary in nature. The growth of the auto industry has augmented the growth of the Ambattur automobile cluster by promoting a large number of enterprises with engineering skills. With tougher quality standards and changing technologies, this section of the workers is most vulnerable to any policy or technology shocks.

Impact of Technology Acquisition Strategies on Employment

There is extensive literature that supports trade liberalisation as a positive factor for employment generation. According to trade theory, in labour-abundant countries, after trade liberalisation, demand for labour in export-oriented industries should increase and that in import-competing sectors should decrease. However, if imports are not the substitutes of domestically produced goods but mostly complementary input goods that are not being produced domestically, then they can have a positive impact on employment. Furthermore, imports can have a positive impact on demand for labour in medium- to high-skilled industries, while the positive impact of exports on labour demand can be low if exporting firms engage in labour-saving innovations in high-skill industries (Aydiner-Avsar and Onaran 2010). A recent study in the Indian context (Raju, Chaudhuri and Mishra 2016) finds that exports have a positive impact on labour demand while import penetration is found to be negative, though less robust across estimation specifications. As the discussion indicates, the results offer a mixed perspective, as the studies have been conducted at various time periods, using different data sets and variables. There is a need to conduct specific firm-level studies which would give policy insights for specific industries. The present study estimates a labour demand equation for the Indian automobile and electronics/electrical industry, both of which have followed very different policy trajectories. The study uses data for the period 2000–2016 from the Prowess database that covers almost 10,000 listed and unlisted firms in the Indian industry. The next section explains the model and estimation approach.

A Model of Determinants of Labour Demand in the Organised Sector

The study uses the standard production function approach whereby output is expressed as a function of inputs in an augmented Cobb–Douglas production function for firm i at time t:

$$Y_{it} = A^{\gamma} C_{it}^{\alpha} L_{it}^{\beta} e^{\varepsilon it} \tag{1}$$

where Y is expressed as value added (output less expenditure on raw material, power and fuel); L is labour; C is physical capital; α, β and γ are output elasticities with respect to physical capital, labour and technical efficiency, respectively; and ε is the stochastic error term, representing productivity shocks. Following Hine and Wright (1999), a profit maximising firm will employ labour at the real wage rate (w) and capital at its user cost (r) and at the optimum, the capital–labour ratio is equal to the input–price ratio. So, substituting for capital, we rewrite equation 1 as

$$Y_{it} = A^{\gamma} (\alpha w L_{it}/\beta r)^{\alpha} L_{it}^{\beta} e^{\varepsilon it} \tag{2}$$

Taking logs and rearranging the above equation in terms of labour demand, we get the following, where letters in small case denote logs of the variables.

$$l_{it} = \emptyset_0 - \frac{\emptyset_1 w_1}{r} + \emptyset_2 y_{it} + \varepsilon_{it} \tag{3}$$

$$\phi_0 = -(\gamma \ln A + \alpha \ln \alpha - \alpha \ln \beta)/(\alpha + \beta);$$

$$\phi_1 = \alpha/(\alpha + \beta)$$

and
$$\phi_2 = 1/(\alpha + \beta)$$

First differencing the above equation, we get the growth in labour demand equation:

$$\Delta l_{it} = \Delta \emptyset_0 - \frac{\emptyset_1 \Delta w_i}{r} + \emptyset_2 \Delta y_{it} + \Delta \varepsilon_{it} \tag{4}$$

where, $\phi_0 = -(\gamma \Delta \ln A + \alpha \Delta \ln \alpha - \alpha \Delta \ln \beta) / (\alpha + \beta)$

Change in technical efficiency parameter Δa as a function of technology acquisition

In equation 2, changes in technical efficiency ΔA_{it} can result from technology adoption and can be modelled as a function of variables that reflect the means of technology acquisition by the firm. These include R&D expenditures, technology imports in the embodied form of raw material and capital imports and disembodied form of royalty expenditures and, finally, exports of goods and services. This also captures the trade-induced effects of technical change and its impact on labour intensity and employment.

$$\Delta A_{it} = e^{\delta 0 Ti} M^{\delta 1}, X^{\delta 2} RD^{\delta 3}, \delta_0, \delta_1, \delta_2, \delta_3 > 0,$$

where M = imports, X = exports, RD = R&D expenditures and T_i = time trend

$$\Delta l_{it} = \emptyset_0 - \frac{\emptyset_1 \Delta w_i}{r} + \emptyset_2 \Delta y_{it} - \mu_0 T_i - \mu_1 \Delta m_{it} - \mu_2 x_{it} - \mu_3 rd_{it} - \Delta \varepsilon_{it} \tag{5}$$

Change in error term is assumed to be a function of firm-specific fixed effects μ_i and year-specific intercepts λ_t in addition to serially uncorrelated measurement errors v_{it}.

$$\Delta \varepsilon_{it} = \mu_i + \lambda_t + v_{it} \tag{6}$$

At the level of the firm or industry, the demand for labour is expected to be negatively affected by real wages and positively by real output. An interesting question is which effect is stronger in absolute terms. For the sake of simplicity, the cost of capital is supposed to vary only over time, assuming perfect capital markets; thus, its variation is captured by time dummies at the stage of estimation (Milner and Wright 1998).

Empirically, the equation to be estimated is as follows:

$$l_{it} = \alpha + \beta_0 l_{it-1} + \beta_1 \Delta yit - \frac{\beta_2 \Delta w}{r} - \beta_3 R\&Dint - \beta_4 \text{ Royaltyint}$$

$$- \beta_5 \text{ Impint} - \beta_6 \text{ Imports*RD} - \beta_7 \text{ Expint} - eit \tag{7}$$

where l is log employment, Δyit is log growth in real output, Δw is the real average wage rate, R&D is research and development expenditures, royalty is expenditure on royalty payments and technology licence fees and Imp is import of raw materials and capital goods. All variables in equation 7 are divided by total income to arrive at R&D intensity, royalty intensity, import and export intensity. Imports are further divided into raw material and capital goods imports.

The next section explains the data sources and descriptive statistics.

Data Description

The study uses data on 555 automobile firms, of which 513 are tier 1 and tier 2 auto component firms and the rest are OEMs, from the Prowess database. Prowess is a subscription-based database offered by the CMIE and consists of financial data from the audited annual reports of more than 27,000 listed and unlisted Indian companies. Time series data from profit and loss and balance sheets are collected from 1998–99 onwards and updated annually.

The auto component firms include those who manufacture engine, electrical, suspension, transmission and other equipment. The OEMs include commercial vehicles, cars and two- and three-wheeler manufacturers. The study also includes 628 firms in the electronics and electrical industry segments to understand inter-industry differences in the impact of trade. The Indian hardware electronics industry consists of firms that are technology oriented as well as assembly oriented. The category of other electronics and electrical equipment includes battery manufacturers, consumer and industrial electrical appliances, electrical transmission equipment and telecom product manufacturers.

The study uses data of gross value of the firms' sales as a measure of output, and it is deflated by industry-specific wholesale price indices (WPI). This deflator is obtained from the Office of the Economic Adviser, the Ministry of Commerce and Industry of India. Table 4.4 provides the descriptive statistics.

The Prowess database does not provide information on the number of workers but only salaries and wages. Information from the ASI database is used to compute the firm-level employment figures, in line with other studies (Saxena 2011; Ghosh and Roy 2015). The number of workers is computed for each firm by dividing the salaries and wages reported in the Prowess database by the average wage rate for the electronics industry for various years. The average wage rate is obtained from the industry ASI database computed as

Table 4.4 Descriptive statistics

Variable	Obs	Mean	SD	Min	Max
			Automobile		
Ln Employment	5,525	6.2	1.7	−0.9	10.9
Ln Real Output	5,669	6.9	1.9	−2.4	13.1
Ln Real Wage	5,732	−0.1	0.2	−0.7	1.0
Ln Import_RM_int	5,669	−4.0	2.2	−6.9	2.9
Ln Import_Capital_int	5,669	−5.5	1.6	−6.9	3.9
Ln Royalty_int	5,669	−6.2	1.1	−6.9	−1.0
Ln R&D Stock_int	5,669	−6.0	1.4	−6.9	1.3
Ln R&D intensity	5,669	−6.3	1.0	−6.9	−1.0
Ln Export_int	5,669	−4.3	2.4	−6.9	1.6
			Electronics/Electrical		
Ln Employment	6,064	4.9	1.8	−1.2	11.7
Ln Real Output	6,203	5.8	2.1	−2.6	11.4
Ln Real Wage	6,298	0.02	0.3	−1.4	1.8
Ln Import_RM_int	6,203	−3.8	2.4	−6.9	4.5
Ln Import_Capital_int	6,203	−6.1	1.4	−6.9	5.4
Ln Royalty_int	6,203	−6.6	0.8	−6.9	−0.7
Ln R&D Stock_int	6,203	−6.2	1.5	−6.9	4.9
Ln R&D intensity	6,203	−6.5	1.1	−6.9	2.1
Ln Export_int	6,203	−4.6	2.5	−6.9	0.2

Source: Prowess database; author's calculations.

total emoluments in the industry divided by employees in the industry.[7] It is deflated by consumer price index (CPI) to arrive at the real wage rate. Figure 4.4 shows the trend in real wage rate during 2000–18 in the auto and electronics/electrical sectors, which is clearly higher in the latter. Because of averaging across skilled and unskilled, the wage rate is underestimated.

Other independent variables used in the study have also been acquired from the Prowess database and include import of raw materials and capital goods (embodied technology), expenditure on royalty payments (disembodied technology) and R&D expenditure on current and capital account and expenditure on royalty payments.[8] The study uses a measure of R&D stock as an indicator of the accumulated R&D effort of the firm. R&D stock is obtained by the perpetual inventory method (PIM) using a depreciation rate of 15 per cent.[9] The R&D stock for the year 2000 is calculated as the cumulative

Figure 4.4   Real wage rate: 2000–16

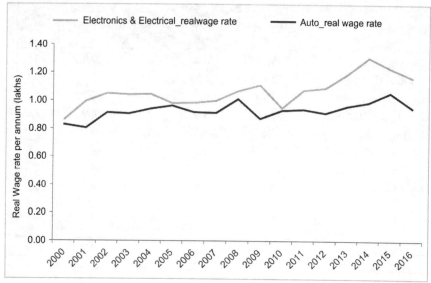

Source: Annual Survey of Industries; author's own calculations

Note: 1 lakh = 100,000.

sum of discounted R&D expenditures for the past three years after deflating them using the wholesale price index for capital goods. R&D stock for the subsequent years is calculated by adding the current R&D expenditures to the initial value of R&D stock thus calculated.

In other words, R&D Stock$_t$ = (1-δ) Stock$_{t-1}$ +R&D exp$_t$.

Since current R&D expenditures have a lag effect and may influence employment decisions through their impact on sales, R&D stock is assumed to be endogenous to the employment decision.

Ownership dummies are also introduced for foreign and private firms, based on equity ownership of more than 25 per cent. A firm having more than 25 per cent equity stake by a foreign affiliate is termed as foreign joint venture, otherwise a private Indian firm. A firm with 100 per cent government ownership is categorised as government owned.

Dynamic Panel Estimation

A dynamic panel data model is adopted to estimate the impact of trade and technology on labour demand, using an augmented production function.

Dynamic panel estimation is most useful in situations where an unobservable (time invariant) factor affects both the dependent variable and the explanatory variables, and some explanatory variables are strongly related to past values of the dependent variable.

For example, a firm's labour demand may be a function of past demand and output and a firm's trade and technology decisions may also be a function of firm's past output. This requires incorporating a lagged dependent variable as one of the explanatory variables in the model. To take care of the simultaneity and endogeneity problems in panel data, the generalised method of moments (GMM) technique has been suggested (Arellano and Bover 1995; Blundell and Bond 1998). In this chapter, results from system GMM estimation are presented, which uses moment conditions in which lagged differences are used as instruments for the level equation in addition to the moment conditions of lagged levels as instruments for the differenced equation. Lagged values of endogenous variables are used as GMM instruments, while all the exogenous explanatory variables are used under instrumental variable (IV) style instruments. In the present chapter, lagged employment and R&D stock are assumed to be endogenous variables. Instruments in system GMM estimation for equations in levels are differenced values of the endogenous variable, that is, twice and thrice lagged change in employment and R&D stock. All the other explanatory variables, including growth in output, wage rate, exports and technology imports, are assumed to be exogenous to the system. Time dummies are also included in the regression.

Results

Results (Table 4.5) from the econometric estimation show that real output growth is positive and significant, while real wage rate is negative and significant for both the automobile and the electronics industry. Employment elasticity of output is higher in the automobile industry (0.4 per cent) compared to electronics/electrical (0.2 per cent). Imported capital goods intensity, royalty intensity and R&D stock intensity are positive and significant for the auto industry. Export intensity is positive but not significant.

In the electronics industry, only imported capital goods intensity and export intensity are positive and significant. This is consistent with the empirical evidence. The electronics industry has one of the highest imports in the country and is engaged in assembly-oriented manufacturing in a big way, especially the production of mobile phones. Hence, the import of embodied technology

Table 4.5 Estimation results

Variables	Auto	Electronics and electrical	All
lnemploy	Coef.	Coef.	Coef.
L. lnEmploy	0.97*** (0.02)	0.91*** (0.04)	0.96*** (0.02)
Dlnout_real	0.42*** (0.06)	0.21*** (0.03)	0.27*** (0.02)
Dlnwage_r	–0.91*** (0.08)	–1*** (0.01)	–1*** (0.02)
lnIMP_RM	–0.001 (0.00)	0.01* (0.01)	0.003 (0.003)
lnIMP_K	0.02*** (0.01)	0.02*** (0.01)	0.03*** (0.005)
Lnroyint	0.02** (0.01)	0.01 (0.01)	0.02** (0.008)
lnRDstock	0.03 ** (0.01)	0.02 (0.01)	0.02*** (0.007)
lnExp	0.003 (0.00)	0.02 ***(0.01)	0.008* (0.004)
Foreign	–0.02 (0.04)	–0.08 (0.06)	–0.005 (.02)
Private	–0.002 (0.04)	–0.13 (0.09)	–0.012 (0.03)
Year			
2001			0.7***
2002	–0.05	0.010	0.7***
2003	–0.14***	–0.2*	0.6***
2004	–0.09***	–0.09***	0.7***
2005	–0.09***	–0.09***	0.7***
2006	–0.06***	–0.04***	0.7***
2007	–0.02	–0.05	0.7***
2008	–0.05*	0.03	0.8***
2009	–0.09	–0.05	0.7***
2010	–0.14***	–0.1	0.7***
2011	–0.04*	–0.03***	0.7***
2012	–0.07**	–0.05**	0.7***
2013	–0.07***	–0.09***	0.7***
2014	–0.01	–0.08***	0.7***
2015	–0.07**	–0.06**	0.7***
2016	–0.04*	–0.04	0.7***
_cons	0.6***	1.1 ***	
N	4758	5211	9969
AR(1) Pr>z	0.00	0.00	0.00
AR(2) Pr>z	0.4	0.6	0.3
Sargan Pr>z	0.00	0.00	0.00
Hansen Pr>z	0.2	0.3	0.2

Source: Author.

Notes: ***, ** and * refer to 1%, 5% and 10% levels of significance. Figures in parenthesis are standard errors.

in the form of capital goods and machinery is complementary to employment growth, as these inputs are not competing with any domestic industry. In the automobile industry, only disembodied technology import intensity and R&D intensity are positive and significant, implying that both disembodied technology transfer and R&D increase the demand for high-skilled workers, thereby having a positive impact on employment growth in this sector. The coefficients on time trend are negative and significant for both industries except during 2007–09.

The analysis of the organised segment of the auto industry shows that R&D and technology imports positively impact employment in the industry. However, this presents only a partial picture of employment. As one goes down the value chain, the majority of the employment in the industry is in the small-scale sector, which is the backbone of the traditional automotive supply chain. The next section explores the challenges faced by this sector.

Conclusion

There are a few key takeaways from the study. One, the study finds that while he Indian automobile industry has been witnessing rapid growth, there is a sluggish growth in direct regular employment and an increasing contractualisation of the labour force. The automobile industry offers a mixed experience with respect to skill development. While skill gap was observed as a constraint in Tamil Nadu, it was not so in Hosur. Many auto ancillary firms have internalised the cost of training and developed in-house tool rooms and personalised online courses to train workers, while some have a close technical association with private engineering colleges in offering internships and job-oriented training to skilled workers to become supervisors. Some multinational suppliers send their managers and operators abroad for on-site training. Firms such as Bosch and JBM Kanemitsu are moving towards new-generation products that require high skill and less manpower. This has resulted in an increase in the demand for high-skill workers and an increase in average wages for white-collared workers. Technological changes and R&D capabilities may have led to increased polarisation of skill levels.

Post 2010, there is a jump in R&D intensity across both the OEMs and the component sector. R&D has moved from adaptive to product development, especially application engineering and engineering research such as reliability engineering for safety. Even so, the lack of basic research and product development capability in India is an important reason for high import intensity of automobile components. Imports of electronic components from China have increased because of the lack of domestic capability in such components. The share of auto components in total imports in the auto industry is as high as 95 per cent, while their share in exports has also increased in the recent years to 43 per cent, indicating a rising import intensity of exports. The study finds that imports are not hurting domestic employment. Imports are driven by the nature of product involving new/proprietary technology, free trade agreements and quality requirements.

Third, results from the econometric estimation of the employment demand model show that disembodied technology and R&D intensity have a positive impact on employment growth, indicative of the rising demand for skilled labour. Embodied technology imports have a positive impact in the electronics sector, which is indicative of the assembly-driven manufacturing with imported components. Post 2012, R&D and technology imports have become important contributors to growth and employment of skilled manpower.

Coming to the role of exports in employment generation, Indian exporting firms are primarily exporting through their affiliates or to tier 1 multinational suppliers who are members of free trade zones. Post 2000, members of free trade zones have been able to follow export-oriented strategy to increase employment. However, India has not been able to strategically make use of FTAs to break through export markets. The study argues that there should be an aggressive strategy to break into export markets through FTAs and local content rules for multinational firms with high import content. The focus of policymakers should be on (*a*) how to make labour competitive in these skills in future and (*b*) how to improve the export competitiveness of auto component companies by developing skills in new technology components and by investing in R&D. Changing mobility preferences require a different eco-system and infrastructure. A detailed study of infrastructure needs should be done, and capabilities for key actors in the electric value chain should be identified and developed. Investment in incubation centres for additive technologies and new generation technologies will also enhance employment opportunities in the future.

Appendix 4A

Table 4A.1 Employment, trade and R&D in sample tier 1 auto component firms

Nature of firm	Component	No. of employees	Shop floor	Contract labour (%)	Location	Import of raw material (%)	Exports turnover (%)	R&D turnover (%)
OEM Engine shop	Cylinder head, block and crankshaft	450	350	20	Chennai	60	40	1
Tier 1_MNC	Cylinder head and block	300	260	40	Chennai	10	own affiliates	0.01
Tier 1_MNC	Piston, piston pins and piston rings	3,500	1,455	48	Hosur	30	own affiliates	0.4
Tier 1_MNC	Cylinder pumps and unit injector system	2,600	1,500	40	Hosur	78	10	2
Tier 2_JV	Engine valve spring	800	700	70	Hosur	25	4	3
Tier 1/2_MNC	Clutch system	1,175	875		Hosur	15	8	0.01
Tier 1/2_Indian	Aluminum die casting	4,000	3,000	50	Gurgaon	1	20	0
Tier1_JV	Pulleys (aluminium)	50	45		Gurgaon	10	8	
Tier1/2_Indian	Pumps	350	290	80	Chennai	25	45	0.01
Tier1/2_JV	Hydraulic assembly	350		40	Chennai	42	0.004	0.01
Tier2_JV	Pressure die casting	2,161	1,900	50	Chennai		32	0.01
Tier 1_JV	Timing belt	300	250	30	Chennai	30	own affiliates	n.a
Tier 1_Jap_MNC	Spark plugs	200	150		Bawal	80	own affiliates	0.001
Tier 1/2_Indian	Fasteners	3,000	2,000	60	Chennai	22	32	0.01

Source: Field survey.

Figure 4A.1 Gross turnover in ₹ millions (deflated by WPI)

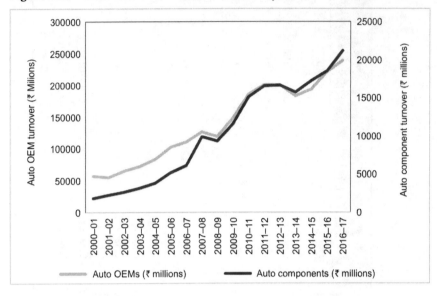

Source: SIAM (2018).

Table 4A.2 Profile of firms interviewed in the Tamil Nadu small-scale auto cluster

Type	Total unit	Yearly turnover <1 mill (INR)	Yearly turnover 1 mill to <10 mill (INR)	Yearly turnover 10 mill–100 mill (INR)	Yearly turnover >100 mill (INR)	Type of product/ service	No. of employees	Percentage of contract labour	Growth in employment and turnover during 2016–18	Out-of-state employees/migrant workers
Tier 1	3	0	0	2	1	Forgings, machining and heat treatment	20–25	0–30	One of the three units reported growth	Yes
Tier 2	18	0	7	6	5	Machining, sheet metal, fuel injection and transmission components, and spares	<50:60 %; <100:40 %	0–70	28% units reported growth	Yes
Tier 3	9	2	6	1	0	Total room, sheet, metal and machining	Less than 20	0–40	No growth	No

Source: Field survey.

Notes

1. As per recent data from the Federal Reserve Bank of St. Louis, USA; European Automobile Manufacturing Association (ACEA); and Mexican Association of Automotive Industry (AMIA).

2. The organised segment of the economy in the national accounting statistics (NAS) broadly includes all large mining enterprises, manufacturing enterprises registered under the Factories Act, 1948, and private and public corporations engaged in non-manufacturing activities. All other units are classified as unorganised units. The unorganised segment of the economy (CSO 1989, 2007) refers to all operating units whose activities are not regulated under any statutory act or legal provision and/or those which do not maintain any regular accounts.

3. Engine system constitutes 31 per cent of the total auto-components in terms of volume, comprising cylinder block, cylinder head, crankshaft, camshaft and connecting rod, of which the first three (3Cs) are made in-house by the OEMs. Camshaft, connecting rod and component parts associated with the main engine system are outsourced.

4. For example, Maruti Suzuki India Limited (MSIL) pioneered the implementation of Japanese management principles of lean management and brought in new work organisation and social relations through workplace productivity and participation by increasing the proportion of wage allowances and bonuses. However, post liberalisation, with change in market conditions, MSIL changed its employment conditions and remuneration policies, which was followed by periods of labour conflicts. By 2004, the size of the regular workforce was reduced by 42 per cent over a three-year period and, to meet the increasing demand, the proportion of contract workers was increased. Post 2012, the company changed its policy of employing company casuals or temps directly at the factory gate or in Industrial Training Institute (ITI) campuses. In March 2016, the company reported 13,259 regular and 10,626 contract or temp workers and 1,276 apprentices (Barnes 2018). Similarly, another study found that 65 per cent of Hyundai Motor India Limited's (HMIL) 16,674 employees in March 2013 were contract workers earning between ₹5,300 and ₹10,000 (Gopalakrishnan and Mirer 2014).

5. Studies have found that FDI had positive impact on both output and employment growth because of productivity and technology spillovers (Kokko, Tansini, and Zejan 1996; Kathuria 2002). In the Indian context, Siddharthan and Pandit (2006) argue that post liberalisation, with the entry of and new investments by foreign firms and joint ventures, new technologies encouraged the use of skilled labour, leading to employment growth, though in some industries, new technology may be labour saving.

6. An example is pedestrian-friendly bumper design, which is a regulatory norm in European countries. The European Enhanced Vehicle-safety Committee (EEVC) Working Group 17 has proposed establishing a series of component tests based on the three most important areas of injury – head, upper leg and lower leg – which

has been accepted as a regulatory norm. However, no such regulations exist in India (Chaudhari and Kharde 2013).

7. If the wage is the same across all firms in the industry, it is problematic and may not be realistic. If R&D-intensive firms pay relatively high wages and employ fewer people, they will have higher productivity; hence, the construction of labour data might bias the estimated R&D coefficient. However, given the data limitation, it is believed that the estimation with such constructed data should be regarded as better than nothing.

8. The R&D expenditures refer to the definition followed by corporate accounting, wherein total R&D expenditures are divided into current and capital accounts. Expenses on current account refer to the expenditure on hiring R&D personnel. Capital account expenses refer to any machinery or capital equipment bought for R&D/designing purposes.

9. See Hall, Mairesse, and Mohnen (2009) for issues related to the measurement of knowledge capital.

References

Athukorala, Prema-chandra and C. Veeramani. 2017. 'Internationalization of Indian Enterprises: Patterns, Determinants, and Policy Issues'. *Asian Economic Papers* 16 (1): 142–66.

ACEA (European Automobile Manufacturers' Association). 2020. 'Share of Direct Automotive Employment in EU, by Country'. 1 August. Available at https://www.acea. be/statistics/article/share-of-direct-automotive-employment-in-the-eu-by-country, accessed on 1 February 2020.

ACMA (Automobile Component Manufacturers Association). 2017. *Member Directory*. Chennai: ACMA.

Aydiner-Avsar, Nursel and Özlem Onaran. 2010. 'The Determinants of Employment: A Sectoral Analysis for Turkey'. *The Developing Economies* 48 (2): 203–31.

Barnes, Tom. 2018. *"Making Cars in New India: Industry, Precarity and Informality.* Cambridge: Cambridge University Press.

Belussi, Fiorenza. 1999. 'Policies for the Development of Knowledge Intensive Local Production Systems'. *Cambridge Journal of Economics* 23 (6): 729–47.

Chaudhari, Mukesh, and B. R. Kharde. 2013. 'Procedure to Obtain the Bonnet Thickness for Adult Pedestrian Head Safety'. *International Journal of Engineering Research & Technology* 2 (7): 1835–40.

Ghosh, Maitri and Saikat Sinha Roy. 2015. 'FDI, Technology Acquisition and Labor Demand in an Emerging Market Economy: A Firm Level Exploration of Indian Manufacturing Industries'. *Journal of Industrial Statistics* 4 (1): 19–36.

GOI (Government of India). 2018. *Key Economic Indicators*. Delhi: Ministry of Statistical and Planning in India. Available at http://eaindustry.nic.in/key_economic_indicators/ Key_Economic_Indicators.pdf, accessed on 1 December 2019.

Gopalakrishnan, R. and J. Mirer. 2014. *Shiny Cars, Shattered Dreams*. New York: International Commission for Labor Rights. Available at http://www.laborcommission. org/files/uploads/2Shattered_Dreams_FINAL_website.pdf, accessed on 1 December 2019.

Hall, Bronwyn H., Jacques Mairesse and Pierre Mohnen. 2010. 'Measuring the Returns to R&D'. In *Handbook of the Economics of Innovation*, Vol. 2, edited by Bronwyn H. Hall and Nathan Rosenberg, 1033–82. Amsterdam: Elsevier.

Hine, Robert C. and Peter W. Wright. 1998. 'Trade with Low Wage Economies, Employment and Productivity in UK Manufacturing'. *The Economic Journal* 108 (450): 1500–10.

Kathuria, Vinish. 2002. 'Liberalization, FDI and Productivity Spillovers: An Analysis of Indian Manufacturing Firms'. *Oxford Economic Papers* 54 (4): 688–718.

Kapoor, Radhicka and P. P. Krishnapriya. 2019. 'Explaining the Contractualisation of India's Workforce'. Indian Council for Research on International Economic Relations (ICRIER), Working Paper 369, New Delhi.

Kokko, Ari, Ruben Tansini, and Mario C. Zejan. 1996. 'Local Technological Capability and Productivity Spillovers from FDI in the Uruguayan Manufacturing Sector'. *Journal of Development Studies* 32 (4): 602–11.

Mani, Sunil. 2018. 'Robot Apocalypse Does It Matter for India's Manufacturing Industry?' Working paper 474, Center for Development Studies, Trivandrum, India.

Narayanan, B. G. and P. Vashisht. 2008. 'Determinants of Competitiveness of the Indian Auto Industry'. Working paper no. 201, Indian Council for Research in International Economic Relations, New Delhi, India.

OICA (Organisation Internationale des Constructeurs d'Automobiles). 2018. '2018 Production Statistics'. OICA, Paris. Available at http://www.oica.net/category/ production-statistics/2018-statistics/, accessed in December 2019.

Okada, A. and Siddharthan N. S. 2007. 'Industrial clusters in India: Evidence from Automobile Clusters in Chennai and the National capital Region'. Discussion paper no. 103, Institute of Developing Economies, JETRO.

PwC (PricewaterhouseCooper). 2013. *Automobiles: Economic Outlook and Employment Situation*. PricewaterhouseCooper, India, August. Available at https://www.pwc.in/ assets/pdfs/publications/2013/automobiles-the-economic-outlook-and-employment-situation.pdf, accessed on 1 December 2019.

———. 2018. *Export–Import Analysis of Indian Auto Component Industry*. PricewaterhouseCooper, India, June. Available at www.pwc.com.

Rudolf, Traub-Merz, ed. 2017. *The Automotive Sector in Emerging Economies: Industrial Policies, Market Dynamics and Trade Unions*. Berlin: Friedrich-Ebert-Stiftung, Global Policy and Development.

Raju, Sunitha, Bibek Ray Chaudhury and Mridula Savitri Mishra. 2016. 'Trade Liberalization and Employment Effects in Indian Manufacturing: An Empirical Assessment'. Working Papers MPIA 2016-19, Partnership for Economic Policy (PEP)–MPIA.

Saxena, Shishir. 2011. 'Technology and Spillovers: Evidence from Indian Manufacturing Microdata'. *Applied Economics* 43 (10): 1271–87.

SIAM (Society for the Indian Automobile Manufacturers Association). 2018. *Statistics*. New Delhi: SIAM.

Veeramani, C. 2016. 'Inter-linkages between Exports and Employment in India'. Occasional Paper No. 179, Export–Import Bank of India.

CHAPTER 5

Upgrading Technology and Space as Collective Strategy
Creation of Jobs and Market Potential in Gujarat's Ceramic Clusters

KESHAB DAS[*]

Introduction

During the period of economic reforms in India, the crisis in manufacturing employment has manifested not only in terms of what is characterised variedly as *jobless* or *job loss* growth (falling labour intensity and even absolute decline in numbers) (Das, Sen and Das 2015; Mehrotra and Parida 2019) but also in certain trends which suggest a decline in the *quality* of employment. These include (*a*) a steady rise in contractual jobs in the so-called organised manufacturing (Srivastava 2016: 10–12), (*b*) a decline in the manufacturing employment elasticity at least since the turn of the century (Giri and Singh 2017: 9) and (*c*) the continued dominance of informality in both production and labour processes across sectors, or the *low road* syndrome, reflecting entrepreneurial immaturity (Tooze 2017; Das 2005, 2017).

Even as, historically, micro, small and medium enterprises (MSMEs) have been recognised as sources of large-scale job generation, accommodating a wide range of skills and age groups, firms adopt strategies that could reduce costs of production and compliance while they continue to identify and access echelons of markets. MSMEs have no intention of effecting numerical changes

[*] For constructive and insightful comments and suggestions, earnest thanks are due to R. Nagaraj, Shuji Uchikawa, Vikas Rawal and Jaya Prakash Pradhan. For their helpful observations, thanks are also due to all the co-researchers and participants of workshops where earlier versions of this chapter had been presented. For fieldwork support, Dipak Nandani and his team deserve appreciation.

to employment, irrespective of what policy expects. MSMEs, even in the face of uncertain market demand and low resources (to invest in the expansion of production and acquiring new technology), have often displayed dynamism and resilience. Unlike integrated large plants constrained by the indivisibility of factors of production, MSMEs in a cluster have been mutually supportive, whether in sharing bulk orders through in-cluster subcontracting or through small-batch production to cater to niche markets or even by using workers from another factory. This has implied that business has thrived through a curious admixture of competition and cooperation in clusters with the munificent role played by the local industry association.

The study, based on both primary and secondary sources of information, aims at understanding what drives the growth and external orientation of MSMEs in the ceramic clusters of Morbi in the western Indian state of Gujarat. This is to unravel the nature of positive transformation, including unleashing the potential to generate jobs, that could be effected through proactive, responsive and symbiotic approaches to policy initiatives, including *rescaling* territory, infusing an innovative ethos and reaching out to wider markets. An attempt has been made to delineate (*a*) strategies of firms in clusters to upgrade the business ecosystem and (*b*) the specific role the provincial state and local industry associations have played to face up to the challenges of imports as well as competing producers outside Morbi. This would, hopefully, inform a more relevant policy strategy.

Current Status of the Ceramic Industry in Morbi and Gujarat

Tiles from Morbi began to enjoy growing demand from the construction sector which took off by the 1980s, and the pace of urbanisation had contributed to it in a big way. The ascendancy of the initial tile cluster in Morbi attracted a large number of entrepreneurs, and the current huge ceramic clusters in and around Morbi is only an advanced phase of what had started as a single factory in the region. From a local economic regeneration perspective, it is instructive to appreciate a constellation of regional factors that contributed to the remarkable growth of this industry here (Government of Gujarat 1965: 380–81; Dave 1972: 97–119; Das 1998).

Over 700 enterprises in and around this small industrial township manufacture a wide range of ceramic tiles and sanitaryware products (ceramic tiles, floor tiles, roofing tiles, lustre wall tiles, glazed wall tiles, vitrified tiles, porcelain tiles, 2D and 4D tiles, mosaic tiles, quartz stone and sanitaryware). This is the largest ceramic tile production region in the country (and the second largest globally, only after Guangdong in China) accounting for above 80 per cent of national production with an estimated cumulative investment of over ₹80 billion. This provides employment – direct and indirect – to over 600,000 people across India.[1] The availability of cheap (and often migrant) labour on contract basis remains a key advantage to the units here; with large-scale automation, factories here do not need to employ skilled labour on a permanent basis. Given that a large part of the production and labour processes operate informally, it is difficult to have a reliable database on various aspects of business here.

Even as Morbi remains the key driver of ceramic production in Gujarat, there are other areas (mainly, Thangadh, Wankaner, Jetpar and Himmatnagar) where this industry has flourished. As summarised in Table 5.1, during the last couple of decades or so, Gujarat's ceramic industry has grown in terms of the number of units, production, net value added and, importantly, employment (although the informal workers are not included here). Interestingly, over the years, with the capital–output ratio on the decline, labour productivity has risen. The share of exports has started to take off after a phase of decline. It

Table 5.1   Aspects of ceramic industry in Gujarat, 1999–2015

Variables	1999–2001	2004–06	2009–11	2013–15
Factories (number)	512	905	1,195	1,601
Fixed capital (₹ million)	3,630.18	13,850.00	34,600.00	57,900.00
Total workers (number)	12,216	28,518	60,822	52,800
Total output (₹ million)	4,515.47	22,681.43	95,200.00	103,600.00
Total input (₹ million)	2,753.45	17,204.62	75,260.00	82,845.00
Net value added (₹ million)	1,762.02	5,476.81	19,940.00	20,755.00
Exports (₹ million)	2,092.55	4,879.65	11,637.08	40,418.52
Share of exports to total output (%)	46.34	21.51	12.22	39.01
Labour productivity (output per worker)	369,611.17	795,337.33	1,565,223.11	1,962,121.21
Capital–output ratio (fixed capital/output)	0.80	0.61	0.36	0.56

Source: Annual Survey of Industries (unit-level data at 4-digit NIC) and, for exports, UN Comtrade.

Notes: Export data relate to all-India total; 2-yearly averages are considered for all variables.

is possible to surmise that the growing industry has contributed to the rising domestic demand as well.

Exports and Imports of Ceramic Products

An important indication of the maturing of the ceramic industry in Morbi has been its continued efforts at enhancing manufacturing competitiveness. A close look at the trade figures in ceramic products suggests significant progress made by enterprises here to participate in global markets.

Figure 5.1 presents the values of Indian exports and imports of ceramic products for a three-decade period. It may be useful to mention here that the data on ceramic products at the all-India level almost entirely represent those of Morbi clusters. After a decade of very low levels of exports from this sector, since around the beginning of 2000s exports have peaked steadily even as the value of exports has typically remained lower than that of imports for several years. The major share of imports is attributable to China which has flooded Indian markets with low-cost ceramic products. What is interesting to note is that these imports from China also included products *for* Indian ceramic makers. However, by 2013, the gap between exports and imports had closed

Figure 5.1   Export and import of ceramic products: India, 1988–2017

(Values in US$)

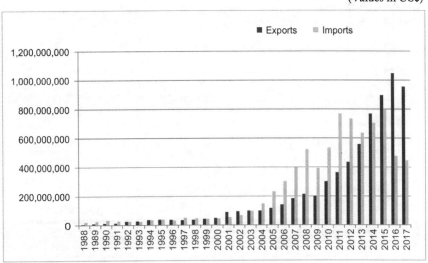

Source: UN Comtrade.

perceptibly. What remains relevant for the analysis is that since 2014, the value of exports from the Indian ceramic sector has overshot the import values, and within a couple of years (by 2016 and 2017), imports had fallen drastically. This is no ordinary achievement for a group of MSME clusters operating from a small Indian urban region.

The worrying aspect was that between 1996 (by when the industry began to shift to ceramic tiles from the previous mosaic and *galicha* tiles) and 2015, the share of Indian imports of ceramic products from China (as compared to that from the rest of the world) had sharply risen from less than 1 per cent in 1996 to 74 per cent in 2015 (Figure 5.2). This, however, has dropped since then, indicating a strengthening of the Morbi ceramics. As corroboration, observable in Figure 5.3, while the trade balance in Chinese ceramic products has risen impressively between 1992 and 2015, the subsequent drop is noteworthy. Similarly, the sharp rise in the trade balance in Indian ceramic products establishes the growing competitiveness of Morbi ceramics since 2011, in more sense than one (Figure 5.4).

In addition to the improving trade balance, it is useful to examine the major types of products being exported from and imported into India over the three-decade period, considering ceramic products at the 4-digit harmonised

Figure 5.2   China's share (%) in India's exports and imports of ceramic products, 1988–2017

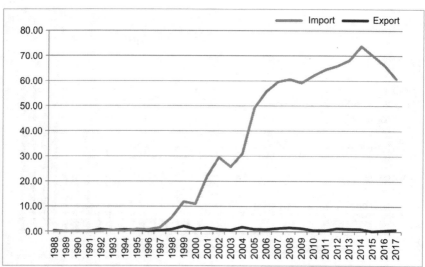

Source: UN Comtrade.

Figure 5.3 Trade balance in ceramic products: China, 1992–2016

(Values in US$)

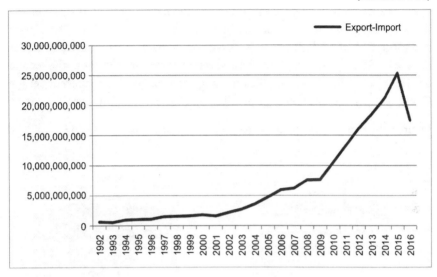

Source: UN Comtrade.

Figure 5.4 Trade balance in ceramic products: India, 1988–2017

(Values in US$)

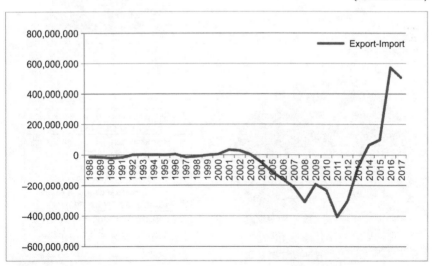

Source: UN Comtrade.

system (HS)–level classification. So far as export figures are concerned, Figure 5.5 exhibits the changing dominance of product groups over the said period. Over the three decades, five product groups have dominated (accounting for over three-fourths of value) the ceramic export basket. From bathroom and sanitaryware and glazed tiles as the top items of export during the first decade (1988–97), refractory bricks and refractory ceramic items in the second decade (1998–2007) to glazed tiles and unglazed wall tiles in the recent decade (2008–17), the ceramic export profile has changed notably over the years.

Figure 5.5   Share of exports of ceramic products by type: India, 1988–2017

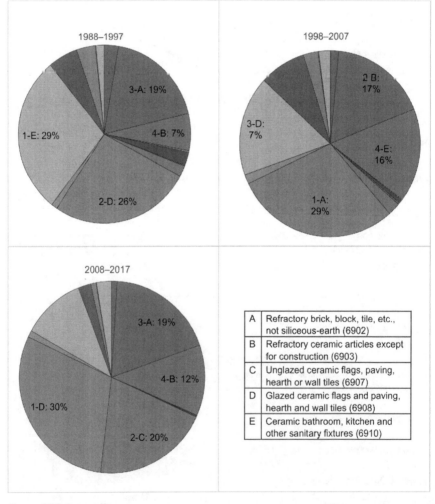

Source: UN Comtrade.

Figure 5.6   Share of imports of ceramic products by type: India, 1988–2017

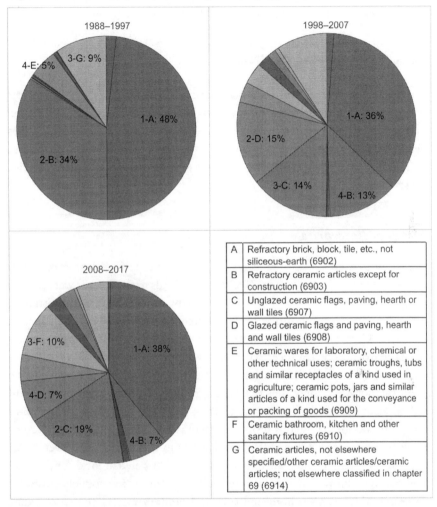

Source: UN Comtrade.

This signals a shift towards high-value items, as superior tiles have emerged as major items of export from, essentially, the Morbi clusters. Similarly, Figure 5.6 suggests that seven product groups have dominated the imports into India. While refractory bricks, blocks and tiles remained the top items of import all through the almost three-decade period, refractory ceramic articles, except for construction and ceramic wares for laboratory, chemical or other technical uses, were relegated to a marginal position over the period; the new product groups those emerged in the import basket included both glazed and unglazed ceramic flags and paving, hearth or wall tiles.

Observations from the Field

In order to understand the functional dynamics of enterprises and constraints facing the clusters, a total of 50 units have been surveyed using a structured questionnaire, and discussions were also held with other stakeholders. Issues engaged with through the survey included aspects of production, employment, technology, marketing, financing, industry associations and interface with the state.

Profile of Enterprises

The study covered a total of 50 ceramic units from the three clusters of Morbi (32), Wankaner (11) and Jetpar (7). Over two-thirds of these units were private limited companies and about one-third were partnership firms. Importantly, not only all the sample units were registered as SMEs with the District Industries Centre, but every sample unit had the International Organization for Standardization (ISO) certification for exports.

The ceramic products in Morbi clusters may be classified under three broad categories, namely tiles (for floors, roofs and walls), sanitaryware and miscellaneous products (cups, saucers, toys, jars, vases, lab flasks, and so on). The aforesaid miscellaneous products are mostly produced in a few micro or home-based units in Thangadh (not included in this survey) and even to an extent in Wankaner; these are of low quality and targeted at local- or district-level markets. However, as shown in Table 5.2, the main products currently being manufactured are high-end tiles and sanitaryware. The predominant item, expectedly, is vitrified tiles in which Morbi units have established their reputation for quality, design and durability. On being asked what products were being manufactured by them (and others in the clusters) in the initial years (until the late 1990s), sanitaryware (both Indian- and western-style commodes, urinals and accessories); small-sized plain tiles (typically, 20 × 20 centimetres, 20 × 10 centimetres and 15 × 15 centimetres) for bathrooms, floors and walls; *naliya* decorative tiles and crockery items were mentioned. What is important to note is that the upgrading and diversification of ceramic products since early 2000 have signalled a transformation of business not usually observed in

Table 5.2 Main products manufactured by sample units

Products	Units (%)
Vitrified	26 (40.0)
Sanitary	10 (15.4)
Bathroom tiles	3 (4.6)
Floor tiles	10 (15.4)
Wall tiles	7 (10.8)
Gels tiles	6 (9.2)
Granito	3 (4.6)
All (MR)	65 (100.0)

Source: Field survey.

Indian MSME clusters. However, such a change has come about through the long experience of entrepreneurs in Morbi and the ceramic sector; a majority (90 per cent) of respondents had over six years of experience in the sector and two-fifths of all respondents had spent over six years in Morbi.

The source of finance for the sample enterprises varied although all had obtained a loan from commercial banks. The supplementary funds came from personal sources (friends and relatives), as indicated by 45 respondents. Financial support has also been sought through various government programmes, as stated by 34 of the respondents.

The transformation of the Morbi ceramic clusters, especially since the mid-1990s, may be attributed to a few 'turning points', as listed by the respondents, the crucial being their growing exposure to export markets which prompted every enterprise to focus on competitiveness, whether through product or process upgradation. The adoption of new technology has yielded positive results for the entrepreneurs. Similarly, the provision of a dedicated gas pipeline by the state government for uninterrupted supply of the key fuel to the units has also been recognised as a favourable factor. Government policies, depending on the context and particular mechanism, have affected business favourably or otherwise; some of the recent policies have been discussed later.

Employment and Skills

With substantial changes in the technological sphere, the ceramic units in Morbi clusters bear no semblance to the labour-intensive factories that one observed in the 1990s. It was quite possible to envisage then that the ceramic industry would remain a huge source for generating jobs that would not involve much formal skills. However, the present sophisticated factories have several automated operations – the conveyor belt, automatic mixers, automatic heavy-duty pressing, glazing liquid spraying, spool-roller-based tunnel firing, and so on – that have transformed the labour process almost entirely. That is not to say that the labour requirement has declined drastically. Newer skills and operations have taken over but still involve human manoeuvring. An idea about workers in the units may be obtained from Table 5.3. It is interesting to note that the units are dominated by male workers who constitute about three-fourths of the workforce and often in large numbers. Women workers are engaged in much smaller numbers, and seven units did not have a single woman worker.

The average per unit size of employment works out to be almost 46. It may be useful to mention here that even during the early 1990s (1990–93) the per unit number of persons engaged in the ceramic industry in Gujarat (as per relevant Annual Survey of Industries data) was about 44. This suggests that despite a rise in capital intensity in ceramic factories, per unit employment has risen; the quality of work and skill requirement would have changed, nevertheless. Assuming that there are about 800 units in Morbi clusters, the total employment in all would come to over 36,000. However, the Morbi Ceramic Association (MCA) website informs that the Morbi clusters provide direct factory-based employment to 350,000 workers and another 1 million jobs in auxiliary and related businesses and professions. While these claims are difficult to verify through our survey, it is important to acknowledge that the actual employment figures could be high. For instance, during the survey, this author interacted with a group of migrant workers from Odisha, and they put

Table 5.3 Number of workers in sample units

Number of workers (range)	Male	Female	Total
Up to 19	101 (8)	363 (43)	464
20–39	667 (26)	192 (7)	859
40–59	367 (7)	–	367
60–79	523 (8)	–	523
80 and above	80 (1)	–	80
Total	1,738 (50)	555 (50)	2,293

Source: Field survey.

Note: Figures in brackets indicate the number of units.

the number of just Odia migrant workers in Morbi ceramic factories at 30,000 to 40,000 depending on the usual or busy season. There are migrant workers in these clusters from Madhya Pradesh, West Bengal, Bihar, Chhattisgarh, Jharkhand, Tamil Nadu and Kerala. That these and other local workers hold mostly casual and temporary status, resulting in high turnover, is common knowledge in the locality.

While most permanent workers receive monthly salaries, most temporary and casual workers are paid on a piece-rate basis. Table 5.4 presents the estimated monthly average income by broad skill category and worker status. However, there were several skilled workers (especially in the sanitaryware segments) who could earn close to ₹100,000 a month, and that is considered a huge income, irrespective of the extremely unhygienic and unhealthy working conditions.

The nature of the production process largely determines labour use schedule and the type of skills required. In the Morbi ceramic units, depending on the order profile, often the production cycle continues for days without a break. The survey found that three shifts a day was quite a common practice in over three-fourths of the units, and in others there were two shifts. Although every shift was usually of 8 hours duration, in certain cases (12 units) these shifts lasted for as long as 12 hours. Except for certain unskilled tasks such as cleaning the premises, dusting racks, and so on, most of the tasks involved skill relating to operating electrical and electronic equipment and constant vigilance over a range of machines, conveyor belts, rollers and firing tunnel.

Table 5.4   Monthly average income by skilled and unskilled workers in sample units

Type	Males	Females
	Skilled workers	
	Amount (₹)	Amount (₹)
Permanent	31,857 (14)	22,000 (1)
Temporary	17,731 (26)	-
Casual	15,000 (49)	14,000 (1)
	Unskilled workers	
Temporary	10,875 (20)	9,333 (3)
Casual	6,250 (49)	5,000 (49)

Source: Field survey.

Note: Bracketed figures indicate the number of units.

Other important tasks included (*a*) unloading and sorting different types of sands, clay and chemicals in the warehouses, (*b*) collecting tiles at the final stages and stacking and packaging those ensuring zero breakage and (*c*) making various moulds, especially for sanitaryware products. While 30 entrepreneurs reported that they provided special training to workers, others were confident that workers often came with some initial acquaintance with certain processes and learnt on-site from older and experienced workers in the unit. However, in the absence of any formal regulations to ensure decent working conditions, firms generally neglected issues of dealing with thick dust pollution inside the factory premises. About 10 to 20 per cent of responses in this connection indicated providing some form of personal kits to workers as sunglasses, masks, hand gloves, helmets, shoes, caps and uniforms.

Similarly, in terms of other facilities offered to workers, the survey came up with these details: first aid (37 units), accident insurance (27 units), staying facility on factory premises (9 units) and food during working hours (26 units). It was interesting to learn through the survey that the entrepreneurs faced absolutely no difficulty in locating or engaging either skilled or unskilled workers in the region. Their unanimous opinion has been that because of the bustling business activity in the clusters, workers – both local and from other states – were available in large numbers.

Production Process and Subcontracting

The annual turnover of Morbi ceramic unit owners, the survey revealed, has mostly been on the rise during at least the last five years; 45 out of 50 respondents confirmed the sustained increase, while five entrepreneurs observed no change in the figures. A sense of the stated turnover values may be obtained from the responses that about 60 per cent of the sample units did business to the tune of around ₹200–₹600 million. There were another 12 units which reported a much higher turnover of above ₹600 million. As regards reasons for a rising turnover in most of the firms surveyed, the major factors cited related to (*a*) an increase in demand within the country (29 firms), (*b*) growing exports (33 firms) and (*c*) increase in production capacity (13 firms). Easy access to loans through public sector banks was also pointed out as a favourable factor that enhanced business (16 firms). Despite high and sustained turnover levels, the real constraint related to high prices of procuring required raw materials and other inputs of good quality in desired quantities and reasonable prices.

A total of five units surveyed had been engaged in taking subcontracting work from top brands from the Morbi clusters. Last year, while three units manufactured for Vermora, the other two worked for Somany and AGL; both tiles and sanitaryware products were being produced. The share of in-contracting work for the concerned units would amount to 10 to 20 per cent of their production, and the total production time ranged between 40 and 90 days depending upon the volume of orders placed. The cost estimates were based on rate fixed per box (of, usually, 12 tiles), typically with a profit margin of 5 per cent (that is, the in-contracting firm would have to supply the required output at a cost 5 per cent higher than what the parent firm would have incurred). In 2017, these five in-contracting firms reported having done business to the tune of ₹3 million to ₹15 million with the parent firms, which were unable to respond to (by producing in their units) the massive surge in demand they are burdened with.

The ceramic manufacturers of Morbi have a keen sense of markets and assign significance to different echelons of the market with varying demand that might exist, whether in rural areas, small towns or large cities or foreign countries. While dependence on exporters and big traders for distant markets is common for local markets, small traders and even subcontractors are taken as the agency for sales. Several of the units (28 sample firms) have set up marketing outlets, showrooms and shops within Gujarat and even outside the state. All the respondents agreed that they have engaged sales representatives within and outside the state and have close links with a huge number of dealers across the country. The dealers are offered as incentives long months of credit, free travel (including airfare to and from Ahmedabad) and concessions for bulk purchase. In terms of prices of similar products (including those imported from China), only 15 firms chargeed higher rates than the market rates, while others stated that their prices were either on par (18 firms) or even below market prices (17 firms).

Technological Upgradation as the 'Game-Changer'

A key factor explaining the ascendancy of Morbi ceramics is the collective preference to build up an innovative ethos in the clusters. Respondents were unanimous in asserting that adoption of new technologies – in manufacturing, processing, fuel use, raw material mix, designs and even sorting and packaging – by most units almost simultaneously was a 'game-changer' in Morbi's ceramic business. An idea about the technologies adopted in the early decades can be obtained from Table 5.5. The process of firing using traditional coal or charcoal-based kilns (*bhattis*) remained a dominant technology, which not only implied a huge dependence on imports of coal (from other Indian states or even from abroad) but also meant that the quality of the output was not comparable to most available in the global markets.

As all ceramic units in the Morbi clusters have gone in for modern types of machinery and new processes, the units look virtually transformed to this researcher who had surveyed units in the clusters way back in 1994–95. A few questions were asked regarding the type and current status of the machinery being used. While 36 units (72 per cent) described most of their main types of machinery as new, 11 units used second-hand machinery and the rest old ones. However, as high as 92 per cent of the respondents insisted that their types of machinery were foreign made, mostly Chinese, Italian, German and Japanese brands. All the respondents stated that the machines were run by electricity and controlled by electronic apparatus. This is a remarkable contrast to the scenario during the early 1990s when the majority of the processes (mixing, pressing, firing, and do on) were done manually. Even those machines using electricity required a large number of skilled and semi-skilled workers to operate those under the constant supervision of the technical staff. While 39 respondents stated that the types of machinery being used were 'modern', the remaining dubbed theirs as 'general' or 'traditional'. The reasons for introducing new (or replacing old) types of machinery were dictated by strong market signals – the need to raise production capacity substantially to cater to a burgeoning demand domestically and also for exports. There was also a reference to being able to make newer designs/sizes with new technology.

The major changes, as indicated by the entrepreneurs, that have been brought about through these changes in technology included the two most-cited ones related to an increase in output and an improvement in quality. The

Table 5.5   Technology used until the mid-1990s in sample units

Technology adopted	Response (%)
Local coal-based *bhattis*	48 (36.9)
Local machinery	32 (24.6)
Highly labour-intensive manual processes	28 (21.5)
Locally available raw material	22 (16.9)
All	130 (100.0)

Source: Field survey.

Note: Multiple responses.

additional investment incurred by firms to upgrade technology was nullified by the extra benefits that bigger business prospects brought. Further, over 90 per cent of the respondents held that the transition to higher forms of technology implied major shop-floor reconfigurations which involved enhanced work intensity but mostly highly skilled personnel.

The sources of new technology, that is, information about or the agency from where it could be purchased, were varied. While purchases were made from machinery dealers from abroad or domestically, local technical expertise was available to modify existing machines by copying from others' machines. Consultants or repair service providers, input suppliers or even job work offering firms were noted as sources of new technology for the Morbi clusters. What is important to recognise is that the firms in the Morbi clusters have made persistent efforts at promoting an innovative ethos in the business which sharpened their acumen to enhance both product and process qualities. As shown in Table 5.6, the most important in-house initiative taken by the sample firms has been the setting up of laboratories to ensure quality checks at various stages of production. Further, there have been initiatives to introduce novel designs and sizes of products. One of the specialities of the Morbi tiles has been the introduction of unusually large sizes which are in great demand in both the Indian and foreign markets. For instance, there are floor tiles with different sizes (300 × 300 millimetres, 400 × 400 millimetres, 600 × 600 millimetres, 800 × 800 millimetres, and 600 × 1,200 millimetres) and wall tiles of varying dimensions (200 × 300 millimetres, 250 × 375 millimetres, 200 × 600 millimetres, 250 × 750 millimetres, 300 × 450 millimetres, and 300 × 600 millimetres). To achieve higher standards of products, the entrepreneurs have engaged skilled professionals, modified processes of manufacturing and tried numerous new designs, colours, textures and finishes.

Table 5.6   In-house changes/innovations undertaken in sample units

Details	*Responses (%)*
Set up a testing laboratory	42 (33.1)
Introduce new products with different sizes, shapes and textures	38 (29.9)
Employ skilled workers	21 (16.5)
Alter processes in manufacturing	14 (11.0)
Introduce new designs	12 (9.4)
All	127 (100.0)

Source: Field survey.

Note: Multiple responses.

The concern about the quality of products is reflected in their pursuing quality testing procedures; 64 per cent of the firms reported that they undertook quality test at all stages until the final product was ready. Only a small proportion mentioned a one-stage quality check at the end of production. Statistical quality control procedures have also been introduced gradually into the clusters. By upgrading technology, entrepreneurs noticed huge possibilities for making innumerable changes in designs, input-mix and sizes of tiles. Similarly, almost all respondents agreed that new technology has considerably expanded their production capacity, enhanced their profit margin due to high-quality products made with cost advantages, reduced administrative or managerial intervention and, importantly, opened up scope for competing in the global market.

Policy Challenges

Anti-Dumping and Morbi Ceramics

Despite the Morbi ceramic industry's sustained efforts at upgrading both technology and marketing towards meeting growing domestic demand for their products, the cataclysmic effect of the import of Chinese ceramic products posed a huge challenge to the local clusters (ASSOCHAM 2013a). A detailed study by ASSOCHAM (2013b) reported that close to two-thirds of Indian imports of ceramics came from China. The inability to compete with the huge Chinese imports mainly on account of prices but also quality and variety of products had led to a situation where several ceramic units in Morbi were under pressure to close down production due to thinned profit margins; a report in October 2016 pegged the number of closed units at about 100. The challenge to compete with the Chinese imports was difficult to meet, the study indicated, due to rise in the costs of transportation (both raw material and finished goods), inputs (mainly sand and other chemicals), electricity and gas. This threat to the very prosperity of the Morbi clusters had not deterred the local entrepreneurs who had initiated collective action to lobby the central government to impose anti-dumping duties to protect domestic firms.

For instance, by around February 2016, the Government of India imposed an anti-dumping duty (of \$1.37 per square metre on all types of vitrified tiles from China), and this was considered effective as it encouraged Morbi's clusters; a contemporary report on Sandesh TV suggested that this step encouraged some 50 new units to be set up within six months of the implementation of the tariff restriction. Interestingly, Indian tile exporters also receive incentives through the provisions of schemes under the foreign trade policy, namely the Merchandise Exports from India Scheme (MEIS) and the Export Promotion Capital Goods (EPCG). While such a supportive mechanism has been lauded by the Morbi clusters, exports have not always been rewarding. However, it is important to note that recently, in December 2018, Morbi ceramic products also faced constraints of accessing the market in Gulf nations – one of its key destinations – where there had been demands by local firms to impose anti-dumping duties on imports from India at the earliest possible time. The MCA had represented to the Director General of Trade Remedies (DGTR) to prevent the move by the Gulf Cooperation Council (GCC) – members of which include Bahrain, Kuwait, Oman, Qatar, Saudi Arabia and the United Arab Emirates – preparing to lay an anti-dumping duty of 15 per cent on tiles imported from India. As per a report, in 2017–18 the value of ceramic exports from Morbi was around ₹80 billion, and approximately 35 per cent of it was accounted for by exports to Gulf nations.

> Indian tiles industry is already reeling under overcapacity situation along with pricing pressure and the latest development on exports front will only aggravate the situation at home. The antidumping duty by GCC will impact exports of Indian tiles to Gulf, part of which may be diverted to (the) domestic market, putting supply glut in the market. (Rao 2018)

Demonetisation and Its Impact

Surmising from media reports and also through the field survey, it may be observed that there have been three major reasons why (or, rather, how) demonetisation (disbanding of ₹500 and ₹1,000 currency notes on 8 November 2016) adversely impacted the enterprises in the Morbi ceramic clusters. First, the ceramic business is deeply a cash-transaction-based activity wherein, as in numerous similar MSMEs, varying credit payment options (whether for paying wages or for raw materials, transportation and several business services) act as 'oil in a machine'. As has been an acknowledged characteristic of industrial clusters, direct cash dealings reflected the mutuality of different stakeholders within an informal sector setting. Second, the ceramic industry, as has been mentioned earlier, is almost entirely dependent on the demand from both the real estate and construction sectors. The nationwide sudden slowdown in these sectors (which are also characterised by informality and cash-based dealings) had directly affected the demand for ceramic products (Care Ratings Ltd. 2019: 16). Third, the ceramic industry is critically dependent on transport services (particularly, road) which was severely hit due to cash shortages that arose during the post-demonetisation period. However, as some opined during the survey, the entrepreneurs were slowly emerging out of that crisis with the passing of time. As a study observed, demonetisation 'disrupted' the demand situation across the country and normalcy in the ceramic business had been restored after almost six months (Sawdust 2018: 3).

The impact of demonetisation on the ceramic business has been deep and extensive as various reports indicate. Through an online survey of the larger units (10–30 acres area), the MCA held that 200 units had shut down by the last week of November 2016 due to shortage of both cash and raw material from Rajasthan; this had caused about 30 per cent of fall in business (Pathak 2016). Similarly, in a 2016 survey of a total of 470 units in the Morbi clusters conducted by the Morbi-Dhuva Glaze Tiles Association, it was held that while 60 per cent of the manufacturers had closed down production within a fortnight of the announcement of demonetisation, another 20 per cent were planning to follow suit soon. This was mainly due to their inability to pay wages in cash to their labour and their difficulty in transporting raw material and finished products. 'Production unit owners do not have cash to pay their labourers who are mainly from Uttar Pradesh and Bihar. Many of these workers do not have bank accounts. With caps on withdrawal, we are unable to draw required cash from the banks', the survey team was told (Damor 2016). The owners had asked many of their workers to stop coming to the units, and quite a few migrant workers had left for their home states in the absence of work. About 80,000 workers were affected by demonetisation. In the initial week, an average daily loss had been estimated at ₹150 million due to a drop in sales. That demonetisation had a definite unexpectedly adverse impact on the Morbi ceramic industry needs no underscoring.

GST and the Morbi Ceramic Industry

To attempt a realistic assessment of the impact of the goods and services tax (GST) on the ceramic clusters in Morbi is a difficult exercise as the new tax rates not just kept changing but also remained in most parts incomprehensible to the enterprises in the region. Previously, entrepreneurs paid a 5 per cent value added tax (VAT) and 12.5 per cent excise duty on ceramic products, although, given the high incidence of informality in the majority of the firms in the Morbi ceramic clusters, it would not have been unusual for them to have evaded VAT and excise duty to remain relevant in the market. However, with the enhanced provision of tax compliance under the new GST regime, local firms were certainly under pressure to allow their profit levels being compromised.

The effect of the GST has been deep and sharp on the Morbi firms as the GST Council had enlisted ceramics in the luxury category and, initially, imposed a tax as high as 28 per cent, which would push prices by 42 per cent for the final consumers. As argued by K. G. Kundariya of the MCA, the jump in prices of Morbi ceramics had an immediate and eventual effect in the drop in sales as Chinese products turned out to be less expensive than Morbi ceramic products due to cost competitiveness. In fact, during the first four months after the introduction of the GST on 1 July 2017, export shipments from Morbi had halved. The point was that the transport cost borne by the Morbi producers to send their products to different parts of the country turned out to be costlier than what the Chinese paid to ship their products to Chennai Port (Dhandeo 2017). In Thangadh, the ceramic units had insisted on reducing the GST to 5 per cent, as their products were typically low cost, especially the squat water closet pans that were in demand in villages all over India as part of the Swachh Bharat Abhiyan. With much resentment and protests, the relentless representations made to the GST Council by the MCA finally led to a reduction in the GST from 28 per cent to 18 per cent on 10 November 2017 (*Times of India* 2017). The entrepreneurs, however, continued to expect the rate to come down to 12 per cent.

Inter-firm Relationship and Collective Action

Intense competition between firms in an industrial cluster is not only inevitable but, from a business perspective, essential for the dynamism of the industry to be maintained. This is particularly the case when the constituent enterprises are small in size and try hard to capture as much of the market share as possible. Similarly, industrial clusters the world over are recognised as unique spaces for business, as firms often cooperate through joint action in non-competitive areas. Typically, cluster-level enterprise associations take up the task of articulating such challenges in appropriate fora. A substantive explanation of the sustained progress and increased competitiveness of the Morbi ceramic clusters lies in understanding the dynamics of inter-firm relations over the decades.

Key Issues in Competition

Even as, with fast-growing urbanisation in several Indian states and changes in sanitation behaviour across rural and urban areas, the demand for Morbi ceramics has been on the rise, local entrepreneurs are still wary of competition from firms within the clusters and also elsewhere. The most striking aspect of the responses is that there exists intense competition between firms within the clusters of Morbi. This could be interpreted as a positive feature of the Morbi clusters that acts as an intrinsic mechanism to raise the bar of competitiveness in the clusters – this would ultimately be every clustered firm's advantage as the reputation of Morbi ceramics would be held high. There are other ceramic clusters in Himmatnagar and Thangadh where both SMEs and large firms compete with Morbi firms. However, what assumes added significance is that as many as 19 respondents cited only one country, China, where medium and large firms are the real competitors to firms in the Morbi clusters.

In order to identify the factors that are considered critical in the otherwise dynamic Morbi ceramic clusters, the respondents were asked about their perception. With demand for ceramic products rising fast, it was not surprising to note that having the capacity to produce a larger volume tops the list. This is followed by access to skilled professionals and workers, which would be indispensable to maintaining a high standard of product quality. Sales promotion strategies have also assumed significance in broadening the consumer base. These factors are quite unlike those cited during the early 1990s when flooring tile manufacturers of Morbi competed by compromising on the quality of the input mix and adopting a range of unscrupulous business practices (Das 1998: 40–42). The other interesting aspect of these responses is that technological attributes are no longer considered principal issues in competition, as all enterprises are well aware of and prepared with building up technological capacity through investment in newer machines or by upgrading processes or introducing new designs, and so on.

Despite healthy inter-firm competition within the clusters, it is not unusual to come across instances of intense activities of an unscrupulous nature representing a sense of rivalry to out-compete a fellow entrepreneur. As noted by the respondents, providing incorrect or negative information on other firms' products or prices to customers or traders is one such major tactic in the rivalry. Hindering business activities of fellow producers and also trying to 'lure' skilled workers/technicians from others' units by offering higher remuneration or other incentives are all considered as reflecting rivalry between fellow entrepreneurs.

These are, however, not intractable issues and are often sorted out with the intervention of other members of the clusters.

Cooperation as a Business Strategy

Over the decades, entrepreneurs in the Morbi ceramic clusters have displayed a strong sense of cooperation and mutuality not always seen in many dynamic clusters in India. The MCA is a longstanding umbrella body of smaller associations around a certain type of products groups as vitrified tiles, wall tiles, floor tiles and sanitaryware. With the business growing nationally and internationally, the MCA has been beset with responsibilities of not only facilitating interactions between manufacturers with the concerned state authorities (regarding tax relief, fiscal concessions, access to land at reasonable rates, building transport infrastructure, and so on) but also constantly updating its members regarding the emerging regulations and expectations of trading partners. One specific issue that has engaged its attention in recent years relates to preventing fraudulent dealings involving its members, as it could sully the image of the entire industry. The formation of the initiative titled 'Fight against Fraud' is a collective commitment to maintaining ethical practices in business.

In terms of collective action addressing various challenges facing the industry, most respondents were positive about the initiatives taken in mutual interest. The respondents spoke about the constant endeavour of the entrepreneurs through several meetings – formal and informal – to identify sources of new machines, costs of replacement, the scope of acquiring second-hand foreign machines and also arrangement for repair and services of imported machines. Further, joint action, through the active support of the MCA, has been undertaken for the reduction of taxes, including GST, anti-dumping duties and other levies on utilities. Collective efforts at familiarising entrepreneurs with export procedures and identifying potential foreign importers have also been made on several occasions. Extending a helping hand to a fellow entrepreneur in times of financial difficulties has been noted by over one-third of the respondents; this is also to a large extent due to intra-community bonding existing in the clusters.

On being asked about the special role played by the local industry associations, it is clear that they have been at the centre of driving the clusters onto a high-road syndrome that has not only rendered them globally competitive but also helped iron out numerous rough edges in business matters. The associations have played a yeoman role in acting as a responsible conduit between the local state and the entrepreneurs. Several respondents pointed out the supportive role of associations in organising the distribution of large orders, including liaising with traders and exporters on their behalf. The industry collective has also facilitated group training of workers and has been helping individual entrepreneurs in sorting our legal hurdles.

Based on discussions with office bearers of the MCA and several individual entrepreneurs, it is obvious that there exists a strong community/social angle to the prevalence of an enviable cooperative ethos in the clusters, even though a select few of the entrepreneurs have been extraordinarily successful in expanding their business during the last decade or so. That almost all the members (may be with the exception of about four or five members) belonged to what could be labelled the Patel-Prajapati social group is cited as a vital community cohesive factor that prevents open conflicts between entrepreneurs. It is this, what Granovetter (1985) had described as social embeddedness of business, which needs to be recognised as a non-economic factor deeply influencing the success of a cluster in a small urban region.

Challenges Facing the Morbi Clusters

The *achieving* ceramic clusters of Morbi have been on a constant struggle to maintain competitiveness and grow into larger market spaces, in both the domestic and global spheres. Within the Indian market, the top position enjoyed by Morbi ceramics is asserted by the fact that over 90 per cent of such products used in the country are from these clusters. In the global market, there is a long way to go although quality-conscious manufacturers of Morbi have been pushing forward with new designs, sizes and cost savings. There are, however, several constraints faced by Morbi's ceramic manufacturers some of which have persisted over the years and some have been of relatively recent origin. Interestingly, the most-cited constraint (by 40 of the total 50 respondents) is about the dithering or irresolute approach of the state in fulfilling their expectations. The other constraints related to rising transportation costs due to oil price hike, which exerted pressure on the profitability of firms. This also implied that Chinese products could still be sold cheaper in the Indian market as the products from Morbi became costlier due to high transport charges. Absence of provision for loan funds has been a barrier for large investments, such as changing machines or shifting to new processes of firing, expanding production or sales capacity, or even purchasing additional land. Lack of infrastructure, delayed payments and difficulty in

Table 5.7   Expectations from the state

Expectations	Responses (%)
Provision of infrastructure (mainly, land, roads and water)	57 (33.3)
Subsidy and/or soft loans with fast processing (single window)	36 (9.4)
Electricity at a low price	23 (13.5)
Reduce gas price	18 (10.5)
Facilitate easy export	16 (9.4)
Lower all taxes	6 (3.5)
All	155 (100.0)

Source: Field survey.

Note: Multiple responses.

finding machines made in India are also cited as constraints to conducting a profitable business.

In Table 5.7, the expectations from the state have been described, and it is clear that the two main supports desired are related to physical infrastructure and the provision of easy loan finance. Reduction of prices of electricity and gas remains a major expectation of the entrepreneurs. Some even expected the state to facilitate exports. However, as shall be noted soon, the Government of Gujarat has, in fact, contributed substantially in developing infrastructure in the clusters and has indirectly helped export activity to grow.

Firm Strategies for Expanding Business and Enhancing Competitiveness

The respondents were asked about firm strategies to expand the business to have a larger presence in both domestic and global markets. Of the several strategies, improving product quality by adopting new technology dominated their thoughts, followed by efforts to expand production capacity, improved designs, and making provision for quality testing all targeted at accessing high-end markets. The concern for building up a sustainable stock of key raw materials, engaging skilled workers/technicians and even collaborating with foreign companies points to an outward-oriented local industry that is concerned with upgrading technology and setting a reputation for Morbi ceramics.

As part of aiming to be globally competitive, the respondents' attention was drawn to the specific challenges confronted due to China's known advantages in massive production capacity, low costs of manufacturing and facility to broad-base its reach, including making an important presence in the Indian market. Several of the local entrepreneurs sounded confident that the demand for Morbi ceramics would only rise in the coming years, as there exist collective efforts to improve product quality, reduce the cost of production through expanding scale and lower dependence on imported Chinese machinery.

Policy Support as Key

The Morbi trapezoid (the region between Morbi, Wankaner, Thangadh and Jetpar) is being developed as a high potential ceramic manufacturing zone, and the state has contributed immensely to this process (Maps 5.1 and 5.2). Discussions during the field survey and media reports indicate that the provincial state (Government of Gujarat) has been extremely supportive of the local industry in terms of providing a dedicated gas line to units, building

Map 5.1   The Morbi ceramic clusters trapezoid

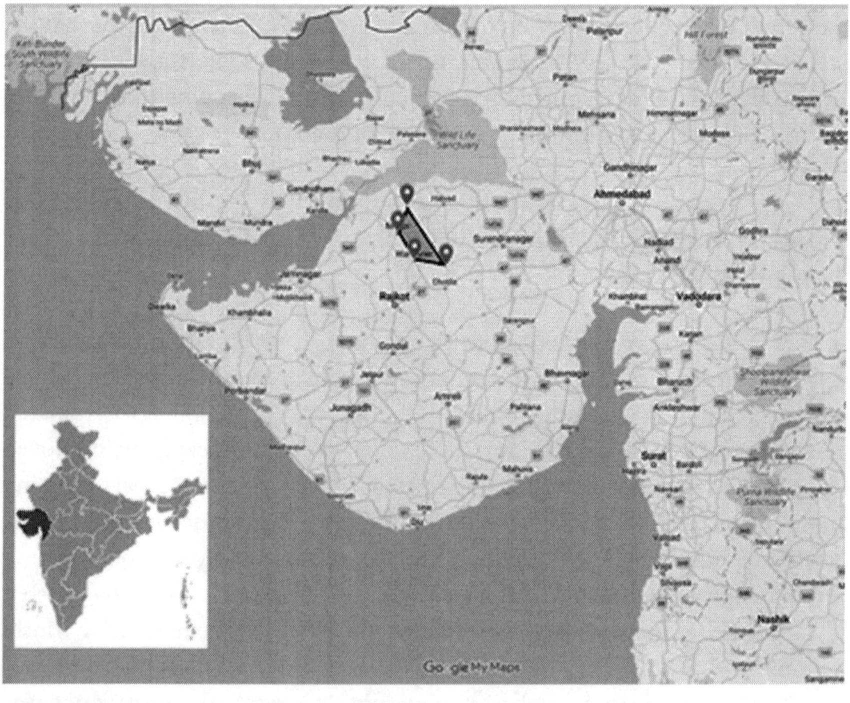

Source: Google Maps.

Note: Map not to scale and does not represent authentic international boundaries.

Map 5.2 The Kandla Port link roadway to Morbi ceramic clusters trapezoid

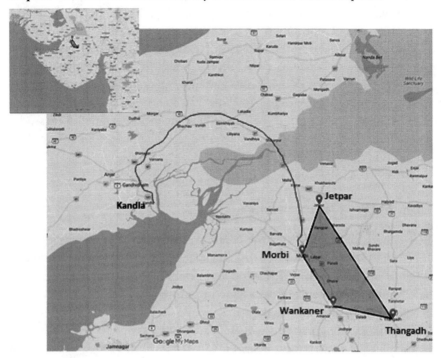

Source: Google Maps.

Note: Map not to scale and does not represent authentic international boundaries.

roads (including linking to the Kandla Port), providing uninterrupted power supply, and so on, and facilitating the holding of the huge Vibrant Ceramics Expo event periodically.

The state has contributed in a major way to the growth and upgradation of the industry and business infrastructure by providing (*a*) industrial gas line in the area in 2008, (*b*) uninterrupted power supply from the Gujarat Electricity Board, (*c*) well-developed transport network (national highway), especially the road linking Pipli and Jetpar since 2012 and (*d*) port facilities at Mundra and Kandla. The units also cater to the export market in Europe, Middle East, African Countries, Sri Lanka, Bangladesh and recently to Latin American countries. In recent years, Morbi has also become an important manufacturing outsourcing zone.

The favourable role of the state in supporting this industry can also be comprehended through the massive political patronage it enjoys for being a crucial (and influential) Patel belt in the Saurashtra region. The ruling party can ill-afford to side-line this bustling industry due to its potential as a major vote bank. Interestingly, during 1995–2017 for the Morbi Assembly Constituency and since 1996 for the respective Lok Sabha Constituency (Kachchh), candidates of the Bharatiya Janata Party (BJP) have consistently won. Moreover, the same party has been in power in the state since 1998.

Despite this industry's dynamism and huge market share in the domestic sphere, the global presence remains low (at about 6 per cent, while China's share is about 42 per cent). To be able to build up export competitiveness, the industry requires multi-pronged interventions, including raising the product and process standards and levels of skill.

Concluding Observations

The remarkable progress of the ceramic clusters in Morbi points to the effectiveness of collective (industry and state) strategies towards technology upgradation, product diversification and external orientation. These efforts have resulted in lowering of costs, creating jobs and accessing newer markets in both the domestic and global spheres. While the Morbi clusters, with a high level of automation, may be close to hitting what may be termed, following Hobday's conceptualisation (Greitemann et al. 2014; Hobday 2005), the *technological maturity* – below which they fail to compete with imports – macro policy benefits (such as undervalued exchange rate, cheap credit and other state support measures) would still keep the industry dynamic. Enlarging the potential of scale remains a key challenge if the Morbi clusters are to move ahead building on their hard-earned achievement, including in the global sphere; the role of *rescaling* the territory would be useful to bring in here.

The potential for jobs would depend on the growth accompanying the maturity of the cluster along with a substantive focus on re-skilling.

Notes

1. See http://www.morbiceramicindustry.com/.

References

ASSOCHAM (Associated Chambers of Commerce and Industry of India). 2013a. *Huge Imports from China Impacting Domestic Ceramics Industry: Study*. Surat: ASSOCHAM. Available at http://assocham.org/newsdetail.php?id=3977, accessed on 16 August 2017.

————. 2013b. *Indian Ceramic Industry: Challenges Ahead.* New Delhi: ASSOCHAM.

Care Ratings Ltd. 2019. 'Indian Ceramic Tile Industry: Structural Shift with Focus on Higher Value Added Products'. *Care Ratings*, 1 April. Available at http://www. careratings.com/upload/NewsFiles/SplAnalysis/Indian%20Ceramic%20Tile%20 Industry.pdf, accessed on 6 April 2019.

Damor, Kalpesh. 2016. 'Cash Crunch Forces 60% Morbi Ceramic Units to Close'. *Times of India*, 24 November. Available at https://timesofindia.indiatimes.com/city/ahmedabad/ Cash-crunch-forces-60-Morbi-ceramic-units-to-close/articleshow/55589288.cms, accessed on 6 March 2019.

Das, D. K., K. Sen and P. C. Das. 2015. 'Labour Intensity in Indian Manufacturing'. In *Labour, Employment and Economic Growth in India*, edited by K.V. Ramaswamy, 153–80. New Delhi: Cambridge University Press.

Das, Keshab. 2005. 'Industrial Clustering in India: Local Dynamics and the Global Debate'. In *Indian Industrial Clusters*, edited by Keshab Das, 1–19. Aldershot: Ashgate.

————. 2017. 'MSMEs in India: Challenges of Informality and Globalization'. In *Micro, Small and Medium Enterprises (MSMEs) in Emerging India*, edited by M. Chinara and H. S. Rout, 33–52. New Delhi: New Century Publications, 2017.

Das, Keshabananda. 1998. 'Collective Dynamism and Firm Strategy: Study of an Indian Industrial Cluster'. *Entrepreneurship and Regional Development* 10 (1): 33–49.

Dave, Mahendra. 1972. *Morbinu Ashmita* (History of Morbi) (In Gujarati). Morbi.

Dhandeo, Keyur. 2017. 'Morbi's Ceramic Tile Sector Affected by GST'. *DNA*, 31 October. Available at https://www.dnaindia.com/ahmedabad/report-morbi-s-ceramic-tile-sector-affected-by-gst-2556518, accessed on 6 March 2019.

Giri, A. K. and S. P. Singh. 2017. 'Post Reforms Dynamics in India's Labour Market'. *International Journal of Economics and Business Research* 13 (1): 1–21.

Government of Gujarat. 1965. *Gujarat State Gazetteers: Rajkot District*. Ahmedabad: Government Printing, Stationery and Publications.

Granovetter, Mark. 1985. 'Economic Action and Social Structure: The Problem of Embeddedness'. *American Journal of Sociology* 91 (3): 481–510.

Greitemann, Josef, Elias E. Christ, Anna C. Matzat and Gunther Reinhart. 2014. 'Strategic Evaluation of Technological Capabilities, Competencies and Core-Competencies of Manufacturing Companies'. *Procedia CIRP* 19: 57–62.

Hobday, Michael. 2005. 'Firm-level Innovation Models: Perspectives on Research in Developed and Developing Countries. *Technology Analysis & Strategic Management* 17 (2): 121–46.

Mehrotra, Santosh and J. Parida. 2019. 'Dial 'M' for Manufacturing'. *The Hindu*, 2 August. Available at https://www.thehindu.com/opinion/op-ed/dial-m-for-manufacturing/article28797380.ece?fbclid=IwAR0vPJV3yenVppkO2nXUMQRihty 3h7 mR8VgyM8MbRoRIJtKEIID4qT4vZOo, accessed on 14 August 2019.

Pathak, Maulik. 2016. 'Ceramic Industry Stares at 60% Slowdown as Diamond Capital Extends Diwali Vacation'. *Live Mint*, 5 December. Available at https://www.livemint. com/Companies/PYlfYDjHFMe7L7mnsdp9zH/Ceramic-industry-stares-at-60-slowdown-as-diamond-capital-e.html, accessed on 6 March 2019.

Rao, Harish. 2018. 'GCC May Impose Anti-dumping Duty on Indian Tiles'. *Sawdust*, 1 December. Available at https://www.sawdust.online/news/gcc-may-impose-anti-dumping-duty-on-indian-tiles/, accessed on 7 April 2019.

Sawdust. 2018. 'The Indian Ceramics Industry: A Report'. August. Available at https://www.sawdust.online/wp-content/uploads/2018/08/ceramics-industry-update-2018.pdf, accessed on 8 March 2019.

Srivastava, R. S. 2016. 'Myth and Reality of Labour Flexibility in India'. *The Indian Journal of Labour Economics* 59 (1): 1–38.

Times of India. 2017. 'GST Changes Save BJP the Blushes in Ceramic Hubs', 12 November. Available at http://timesofindia.indiatimes.com/articleshow/61611375.cms?utm_source=contentofinterest&utm_medium=text&utm_campaign=cppst, accessed on 27 February 2019.

Tooze, A. 2017. 'Notes on the Global Condition: India's Informal Capitalism under Pressure'. Available at https://www.adamtooze.com/2017/02/27/notes-global-condition-indias-informal-capitalism/, accessed on 28 February 2017.

CHAPTER 6

Sports Equipment Manufacturing in India

A Firm-level Inquiry into Growth and Employment Dynamism

VARINDER JAIN

Introduction

Globally, the size of sports equipment market, by 2025, is expected to be US\$89.22 billion. Though this growth will take place mainly in Europe and North America (USA and Canada), the Asian economies of China, India, Pakistan and Thailand will also be the major gainers (GVR 2018). It is considered that rapid technological advancements and continued innovations to keep pace with dynamic consumer preferences will work towards this end. Moreover, a variety of factors such as rising awareness about general health and fitness, easy purchases through e-commerce and m-commerce channels, building of sports infrastructure, better quality raw materials, growing commercialisation and media coverage of mega global sports events such as the Fédération Internationale de Football Association (FIFA) World Cup, Commonwealth Games, Olympic Games and Indian Premier League (IPL) matches may work as growth stimulants to this industry.

In such a situation, this study examines India's sports equipment manufacturing sector by focusing on the Jalandhar and Meerut clusters where this industry is mainly concentrated. In fact, this industry in India evolved during the pre-independence period when access to raw materials, cheap labour and craftsmanship of local people led to its emergence in Sialkot (now in Pakistan). India's partition in 1947 led to forced migration of Hindu entrepreneurs to Jalandhar where they strived to initiate their own micro enterprises (Chattha 2016). Soon after, the industry spread to Meerut and over time, there took place a major concentration of this industry at these two places. Nonetheless, various local conditions and favourable factors facilitated its evolution at other locations such as Jammu and Kashmir, Gurgaon, Delhi, Agra, Moradabad, Mumbai, Pune, Bangalore, Chennai, Tirupur, Kolkata, and so on (Nisar 2013: 84).

Two key questions continue to prevail: first, what sort of growth pattern is observed by this industry and what have been the growth and survival challenges and, second, what has been the plight of labour. Addressing these two questions, this study proceeds with examining the post-1990 state of this industry (the second section) which is followed by cluster specificities (the third section), firm-level operational dynamism (the fourth section), exporters' concerns and approaches (the fifth section), labour-related issues (the sixth section) and policy framework (the final section).

Post-1990 State of Sports Equipment Manufacturing in India

The sports equipment manufacturing industry in India is generally of small size. Nonetheless, a few large units also exist. In 1994–95, there were 89 factories in the organised sector, which grew up to 192 in 2014–15. However, fixed capital in these units grew at a compound annual growth rate (CAGR) of 12.82 per cent from ₹11.6 billion (in 1994–95) to ₹129.4 billion (in 2014–15) – this growth has been the highest during the 2000–01 to 2005–06 period. These units employed 13,288 persons in 2014–15, and output grew from ₹2.20 billion (in 1994–95) to ₹19.95 billion (in 2014–15). The overall growth of output has remained positive over the 1994–95 to 2014–15 period.

Average employment in these units rose from 39.88 workers (in 1994–95) to 69.21 workers (in 2014–15) along with a rise in capital intensity levels from ₹3.268 million (in 1994–95) to ₹10.067 million (in 2011–11) – it declined marginally to ₹9.738 million in 2014–15. This led to an improvement in labour productivity. Average output per worker improved from ₹0.619 million (in 1994–95) to ₹1.501 million (in 2014–15). In fact, these enterprises cater mainly to the export markets and, thus, their growth remains contingent on not only the availability of export orders but also their international competitiveness vis-à-vis their counterparts in other competing nations. Such vulnerability gets reflected in low capital productivity levels (Table 6.1). In fact, the limited growth of the organised sector units that hold the potential to cater to export markets should be a cause for concern as it affects the pace of direct and indirect employment generation in this sector.

Table 6.1   Selected indicators of the organised sports equipment industry in India

Year	F*	FC#	PE*	O#	AEmp	LP^	CP	CI^
1994–95	89	11.6	3,549	2.20	39.88	6.19	0.19	32.68
2000–01	136	13.3	5,919	3.42	43.52	5.77	0.26	22.47
2005–06	115	45.1	6,268	4.54	54.50	7.24	0.10	71.95
2010–11	168	102.9	10,221	13.54	60.84	13.24	0.13	100.67
2014–15	192	129.4	13,288	19.95	69.21	15.01	0.15	97.38
Period	*Compound annual growth rate (CAGR, %)*							
I	7.32	2.31	8.90	7.63	1.47	–1.17	5.20	–6.05
II	–3.30	27.99	1.15	5.83	4.60	4.62	–17.10	26.21
III	7.88	17.94	10.27	24.43	2.22	12.83	5.50	6.95
IV	3.39	5.90	6.78	10.17	3.27	3.18	4.04	–0.83
Overall	3.92	12.82	6.82	11.65	2.80	4.52	–1.03	5.61

Source: Based on Annual Survey of Industries, various years.

Notes: F – Factories, FC – Fixed capital, PE – Persons engaged, O – Output, AEmp – Average employment per factory, LP – Labour productivity, CP – Capital productivity, and CI – Capital intensity.

*, # and ^ imply the values are in No., ₹ billion and ₹ lakh (1 lakh = 100,000), respectively.

Period I (1994–95 to 2000–01), Period II (2000–01 to 2005–06), Period III (2005–06 to 2010–11), Period IV (2010–11 to 2014–15) and Overall Period (1994–95 to 2014–15).

However, most sports equipment manufacturing enterprises have evolved over time in the unorganised segment. The National Sample Survey Organisation's (NSSO) quinquennial rounds indicate that there were 5,374 unorganised enterprises in 1994–95 which grew to 11,954 by 2000–01. In 2005–06, this number went up to 20,958. From there, a limited increase in number was noted until 2010–11. Subsequently, in 2015–16, there has been a decline in their number to 12,853 – a level similar to 2000–01. In fact, various factors influenced such outcomes. Prime among them has been a key state intervention in 2007 that de-reserved sports goods.[1] Though this change in policy aimed at enhancing opportunities for increasing exports, upgrading technology and strengthening firms' competitiveness by raising economies of scale in an environment of liberalisation and globalisation, the experience has been the opposite as it exposed various micro and small enterprises to enhanced competition. With wide cost differences vis-à-vis Chinese counterparts, this debilitated their competitive position. Indian unorganised enterprises largely adopt labour-intensive methods involving limited use of machinery, which raises their cost of production above that of Chinese firms who, being of large size and capital-intensive in nature, enjoy economies of scale. Other factors such as shortage of skilled labour, inter-state differences in taxation structure,[2] non-implementation of certain policies,[3] firm's ignorance about government policies, raw material shortages and finance constraints remained to the disadvantage of these firms.

Jalandhar and Meerut Clusters: Hub of Sports Goods Manufacturing in India

Jalandhar is an important industrial city of Punjab. Being close to two other industrial cities, namely Ludhiana (70 kilometres) and Amritsar (60 kilometres), there has emerged other clusters of hand-tools and leather goods in Jalandhar district, spread across both rural and urban areas. Meerut is situated in western Uttar Pradesh at a distance of about 85 kilometres from the national capital of Delhi. There are also others clusters of scissors, glass and wooden beads, embroidery, artificial jewellery and electric transformers in Meerut. In fact, various similarities and contrasts characterise sports goods manufacturing in both these clusters.

Enterprises in both clusters were started by entrepreneurs of similar caste/community background. Khatris, Aroras and Ahluwlias formed entrepreneurial class, and Ad-dharmi, Meghs and Chamars formed a majority of working class. As most of them were engaged in sports goods manufacturing in Sialkot, after partition when Sialkot went to Pakistan, they migrated to Jalandhar and Meerut and started their own enterprises. Both had similar connections in export markets. In both clusters, manufacturers are also traders having their sales outlets in main markets. Most of the enterprises in both these clusters are micro and small in their scale of operation.

Nonetheless, the two clusters differ in size. In 2013–14, the Sixth Economic Census identified 2,684 enterprises in Jalandhar, whereas the number stood at 1,634 in Meerut. The enterprises in Jalandhar are mainly urban-centred (95 per cent), whereas in Meerut they are spread in both rural and urban areas – in 2013–14, the share of urban enterprises in Meerut was 53.9 per cent (Table 6.2). The clusters differ in export performance as well, with Jalandhar continuing to dominate. Cheap availability of skilled labour and proximity to the national capital remain favourable to Meerut. There is some disparity in

Table 6.2   Size of sports goods clusters in Jalandhar and Meerut

		Jalandhar		Meerut	
		2005–06	*2013–14*	*2005–06*	*2013–14*
Units (no.)	Rural	140 (8.2)	135 (5.0)	326 (32.83)	753 (46.1)
	Urban	1,559 (91.8)	2,549 (95.0)	667 (67.17)	881 (53.9)
	All	1,699 (100)	2,684 (100)	993 (100)	1,634 (100)
Social group of owner	Scheduled Caste (SC)	1,080 (63.5)	1,969 (73.4)	293 (29.5)	434 (26.6)
	Scheduled Tribe (ST)	51 (3.0)	19 (0.7)	9 (0.9)	47 (2.9)
	Other Backward Classes (OBC)	151 (8.9)	79 (2.9)	308 (31.0)	440 (26.9)
	Other	417 (24.5)	617 (23.0)	383 (38.6)	713 (43.6)
Workers	Adult males	5,557 (84.6)	6,778 (67.14)	3,465 (78.4)	6,091 (84.3)
	Adult females	940 (14.3)	3,318 (32.86)	722 (16.3)	1,134 (15.7)
	Children	70 (1.1)	–	232 (5.3)	–
	Total	6,567 (100)	10,096 (100)	4,419 (100)	7,225 (100)

Source: Fifth and Sixth Economic Census, Government of India.

product mix. Moreover, a relatively better state support, in the form of limited value-added tax (VAT) during the pre–goods and services tax (GST) regime, has facilitated the growth of the cluster in Meerut.

Owing to the disparity in cluster size, a relatively large proportion (68.57 per cent) of sample was selected from Jalandhar (Table 6.3).

Table 6.3   Sample size of the study

Enterprise type		Jalandhar	Meerut	Total
Micro	Home-based	70 (29.17)	30 (27.27)	100 (28.57)
	Non-home-based	100 (41.67)	50 (45.45)	150 (42.86)
	All	170 (70.83)	80 (72.73)	250 (71.43)
Small		50 (20.83)	20 (18.18)	70 (20.00)
Exporting units		20 (8.33)	10 (9.09)	30 (8.57)
Total		240 (100.0)	110 (100.0)	350 (100.0)

Source: Author.

The sample enterprises were comprised of micro, small and exporting units. The micro enterprises represented 71.43 per cent of our sample, and the shares of small and exporting units were 20 per cent and 8.57 per cent, respectively (Table 6.4). 42.86 per cent of the sample enterprises were located within household premises, and the share of such enterprises was relatively high in Meerut. Though these enterprises were mainly owned and run by males, female-run enterprises constituted about one-third of sample enterprises. The sample enterprises were mainly proprietary firms with a significant share of partnership firms.

The sample firms' ownership varied by social class. In Jalandhar, Scheduled Castes (SCs) owned a major share, whereas in Meerut most of these enterprises were owned by 'Others', followed by Other Backward Classes (OBCs), SCs and Scheduled Tribes (STs). Educationally, about 43 per cent of owners were either illiterate or could read and write but had no formal schooling. About 15 per cent were primary literate. Up to secondary literates represented 24.29 per cent, whereas 18 per cent were graduates or above – their share was higher in Meerut (25.45 per cent) than in Jalandhar (14.58 per cent).

Operational Dynamism of Sample Firms

It is widely recognised that the contribution of Jalandhar and Meerut sports goods clusters to the national output and export pool of sports equipment

Table 6.4   Selected characteristics of sample enterprises

		Jalandhar	Meerut	All
Firm type	Micro	170 (70.83)	80 (72.73)	250 (71.43)
	Small	50 (20.83)	20 (18.18)	70 (20.00)
	Exporting units	20 (8.33)	10 (9.09)	30 (8.57)
Location	Within house	100 (41.67)	50 (45.45)	150 (42.86)
	Outside house	140 (58.33)	60 (54.55)	200 (57.14)
Owned and	Male	160 (66.67)	76 (69.09)	236 (67.43)
run by	Female	80 (33.33)	34 (30.91)	114 (32.57)
Ownership	Proprietorship	138 (57.50)	64 (58.18)	202 (57.71)
type	Partnership	102 (42.50)	46 (41.82)	148 (42.29)
Working	Regular	168 (70.00)	66 (60.00)	234 (66.86)
nature	Irregular	72 (30.00)	44 (40.00)	116 (33.14)
N		240 (100.0)	110 (100.0)	350 (100.0)

Source: Based on primary survey.

is significant (Mukherjee et al. 2010). As per the Sports Goods Export Promotion Council (SGEPC), Jalandhar's contribution to India's sports good exports lies within the range of 56–64 per cent during the post-1990 period, whereas Meerut has contributed within the range of 25–35 per cent.[4] It is also observed that the industrial output in Jalandhar and Meerut has grown at the CAGR of 7.52 per cent and 10.83 per cent, respectively, during the post-1990 period. In such a situation, it is worth examining whether this growth is experienced uniformly across all types of enterprises or if there is any scale effect in growth performance. How do firms organise their production and in what kind of production relations the large and small firms cohabit? With changing external and internal business climate, how effectively could the firms adjust themselves? What kind of problems do they experience? How resilient are they to the changing business environment?

These issues are addressed in our primary survey. Regarding the growth aspect, we have made an inquiry by examining firms' sales turnover during the last five years. This indicator reveals that sample small firms could grow at an average annual growth rate of 5.12 per cent during the last five-year period – the firms in Meerut recorded a relatively high growth of 5.87 per cent compared to those in Jalandhar (4.37 per cent). This growth was negative for two continuous years (2016–17 and 2017–18), which was largely due to two major policy changes, namely demonetisation and the introduction of GST. Demonetisation led to a cash crunch in the market. The firms remained unable to pay workers and carry out production in a time-bound manner, which affected their orders. Similarly, the introduction of the GST caused confusion among factory owners about the government's tax policy. Subsequent revisions in GST rates and the existence of four tax-slabs added to the utter confusion of the sports industry owners – most of them, being not much educated, remained unaware of the procedures and intricacies of the GST regime.[5]

Figure 6.1a depicts variation in small firms' average growth in sales turnover by their plant size over the last five-year period. It is evident that having merely a large plant size does not ensure better growth of sales; rather, there are other key factors. Informal interviews upheld brand development, firms' capacity to network and develop relations with large firms and the ability to adjust product specifications as per changing market demands. Similarly, Figure 6.1b reports trend in average sales volumes of exporters in Jalandhar and Meerut. It indicates that average export volumes of exporters in Jalandhar have been higher than in Meerut. Though there has been a rising trend in exports, a decline is observed during 2016–17 and 2017–18.

Figure 6.1   (a) Small firms' average growth (%) in sales by plant size, 2013–18 periods (b) Exporting firms' sales (in ₹ crore) over the 2013–18 period

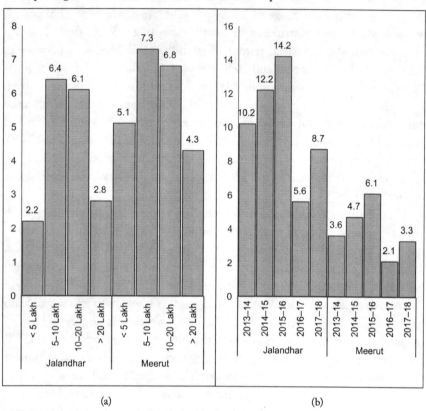

(a)   (b)

Source: Based on primary survey.

Notes: 1 lakh = 100,000; 1 crore = 10 million.

In fact, there also exist differences among firms in ways by which they organise their production. The micro enterprises manufacture their products themselves. They also work as subcontractors to large firms. The small firms get specific tasks done from outside firms that are mainly micro enterprises or home-based workers. Then they do the final assembling, packaging and branding. The large exporting firms, on the other hand, keep in-house the whole production systems, and they rarely contract-out their production tasks to outside home-based workers; rather, they prefer to get everything manufactured inside under controlled supervision. They, being known for their brands, are quality conscious.

Age and vintage of technology differentiate further. Micro enterprises operate largely with obsolete manually operated machines. Small firms besides manually operated machinery use mechanised tools and equipment. In exporting units, most of the machines are imported. Here, production is carried out automatically with minimal labour. Despite having machinery of global standards, the exporters raised concerns about the government's role in facilitating easy import of latest knowledge and technology. But, among small enterprises, more than 40 per cent firms are found to be operating with obsolete machinery. Some have domestically procured machinery, whereas some have innovatively modified it as per their requirements.

In fact, continuous worsening of business performance has been a major concern of micro and small enterprises in both Jalandhar and Meerut. Most enterprises in Jalandhar reported high severity of constraints such as erratic power supply, non-access to bank loans, no institutional support in product designing/finishing, low technical know-how and shortage of raw materials. Somewhat similar has been the situation in Meerut, but their degree of severity has remained relatively lower than those reported by firms in Jalandhar.

In an era of competition, micro and small enterprises strive hard to sustain in the market. But they can do so if they have developed resilience to shocks by gaining advantage in innovation, technology and various other aspects. In order to examine such resilience, we have conceptualised the 'resilience scale' as a yardstick for measuring firm-level capability to withstand any sort of market adversities. This scale assumes significance especially when the sports goods industry is experiencing tough times. In such a situation, this scale identifies those firms that are the most vulnerable. The resilience scale encompasses seven vital aspects, namely resource adequacy, technical edge, market knowledge, product uniqueness, commercial prudence, manpower planning and networking (Table 6.5).

In addition, the 'functional literacy scale' is defined that measures firm-level capability to adopt latest technology and knowledge for their business growth. It has four major components, namely computer/information and communication technology (ICT) knowledge, product designing capabilities, quality control and advertising skills (Table 6.6). The firms are inquired about these four dimensions and their responses to various queries under these broad dimensions are coded at the scale of five (one referring to nil and five indicating very high).

Table 6.5   Various constituents defining the resilience scale

	Broad dimension		Specific dimension
A	Resource adequacy	a	Sufficiency of working capital
		b	Ability to raise funds when needed
		c	Easy access to required quality raw material without monopoly price
B	Technical edge	a	Knowledge and adoption of latest production techniques
		b	Worker adoption & adaptability to new techniques
		c	Ability to add efficiency and effectiveness in production process
C	Market knowledge	a	Knowledge of market size, customers, their tastes and demands
		b	Competitors' threat to potential business growth
D	Product uniqueness	a	Product design as per customers' tastes and preferences
		b	Ability to innovate in product design
E	Commercial prudence	a	Ability to produce at low cost while maintaining quality standard
		b	Ability to foresee future demand and arrange production accordingly
F	Manpower planning	a	Adequate access to skilled/trained workforce
		b	Possibility of outsourcing production process to external small units
G	Networking	a	Ability to develop sound networks in input & output markets
		b	Ability to enhance market coverage beyond national boundaries

Source: Constructed by author.

Note: The responses to various queries under these broad dimensions are coded at the scale of five (one referring to nil and five indicating very high).

Table 6.6   Various constituents defining functional literacy scale

	Broad dimension		Specific dimension
A	Computer/ICT knowledge	a	Knowledge of internet usage
		b	Know-how to maintain account books in computer
B	Product designing capabilities	a	Innovative mind-set to add new and latest features to production
		b	Inquisitive thoughts on refining product appearance
C	Quality control	a	Know-how to produce competitive quality products
		b	Ability to judge weaknesses in own product and making refinements according to changing market demands
D	Advertising skills	a	Ability to highlight product features to gain competitive edge
		b	Ability to promote product usage in different markets
		c	Ability to introduce varied sales strategies to raise sales volume

Source: Constructed by author.

Note: In addition, we have also classified, as per this scale, the variables of (1) highest education attained and (2) possession of technical know-how related to sports goods manufacturing.

Figure 6.2 depicts disparity in firm-level resilience vis-à-vis the owner's functional literacy levels. The estimates are provided across firms with different plant sizes. It may be observed that the resilience levels for most firms across all plant sizes are very low. Nonetheless, they rise with an improvement in firms' functional literacy ranking. Such pattern is evident in both Jalandhar and Meerut, which reinforces the fact that if firms have to sustain themselves in this competitive world, they have to gain a competitive edge by improving not only their resource adequacy, technical and market knowledge, and so on, but also their command over computer/ICT knowledge, product designing capabilities, quality control and advertising skill. As 43 per cent of the owners are either illiterate or can only read and write, it is very difficult for this industry to gain a competitive edge in the global sphere.

A further inquiry into the deteriorating growth performance of the informal enterprises was made by exploring the trade route. In fact, traders are the prime channel through which the manufactured products reach the customers. They convince customers of the products' utility and cost-worthiness. They are the first to observe the changing tastes and demands of customers – an input of high significance for local manufacturers. Similarly, they also keep track of newly emerging designs and patterns of competing brands within the same

Figure 6.2   Firm-level variation in resilience scale

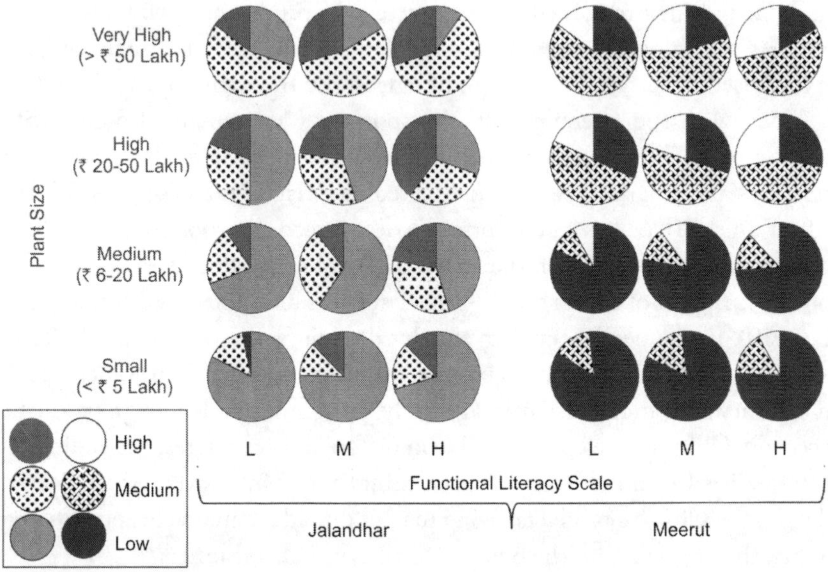

Source: Based on primary survey.

product line. Most of the sports equipment traders in Jalandhar and Meerut are also manufacturers. They have opened their retail outlets in market areas.[6] Informal interviews with these traders reveal that there has been an increased penetration of foreign brands. The local brands could survive only in a few product lines. In case of cricket bats, for example, the Indian brands such as SG, BDM, SS, GM and BAS Vampire dominate the market, and the entry of foreign brands such as Reebok has been limited. The Football market is dominated equally by Indian brands (such as Cosco, Nivia and Jonex) and foreign brands (such as Adidas, Nike and Victor). In lawn tennis racquets, the Indian brands (such as Pioneer, Jonex and Cosco) equally share market with foreign brands (such as Wilson, Yonex and Babalot). Similarly, in table tennis, the Indian brands such as STAG, Vixen and GKI are competing with foreign brands such as STIGA and Donic.

The traders revealed that customers' behaviour depict brand loyalty, and they are not much attracted to new brands as their loyalty emerges from product use. When convinced of the quality and durability, they hardly ever shift their choices. The branded products being superior in quality and durability gain customer attention. Customers bother little about the price. There has been an increased sale of foreign brands in recent years. The local industry products, which once formed a major share in the total sales volume, are witnessing a sharp fall. Two main factors led to such an outcome: first, the local industry remained non-competent in producing a wide variety of products matching consumer tastes and demand and, second, there has been an increased penetration of foreign brands in the Indian market.

Along with sports equipment, the sports market remains flooded with sports apparel. There are not many local brands supplying quality sportswear and shoes. The market remains dominated by foreign brands such as Adidas, Nike, Puma, FILA, Levis and Lotto. Traders agreed that sportswear and shoes account for a major share in their total sales volumes. They treat sportswear and shoes as part of sports goods – this issue was also noted by Mukherjee et al. (2010). It also became evident that local manufacturers lack the ability to produce a slightly differentiated product for different types of customers. Such an inability adds to the disadvantage of the local industry as foreign products, especially Chinese ones, are available in different price ranges, depending on their quality. Local industry products, being labour-intensive, remain dearer, whereas the Chinese products, being machine-made, remain cheaper. Owing to this, they fit well into the budgets of all types of consumers.

Targeting Export Markets: An Inquiry into Firm-level Initiatives

Having a modest origin from the ruins of partition, India's sports equipment industry could make its mark in global markets. Products manufactured in India became known for its quality and durability in Europe, North America, Latin America, Africa, Asia-Pacific and other locations. In terms of export volume, the trend indicates a rise across all locations, but the rise has been fast in Europe, Asia and North America (Figure 6.3).

These exports emerge mainly from Jalandhar and Meerut where production houses of major Indian brands such as NIVIA, SS, BAS Vampire, Stag, SG, BDM, GM, Jonex, Pioneer, Vixen and GKI are located. SGEPC attributes the export share of Jalandhar and Meerut in the ranges of 56–64 per cent and 25–35 per cent, respectively, during the post-1990 period, which indicates a significant contribution of both clusters to the national export pool. But by what strategies could Indian exporters maintain their stake in international markets? This aspect is explored through detailed discussions with exporters in both the clusters.[7]

Figure 6.3 Region-wise trend of India's export of sports equipment, US$ million

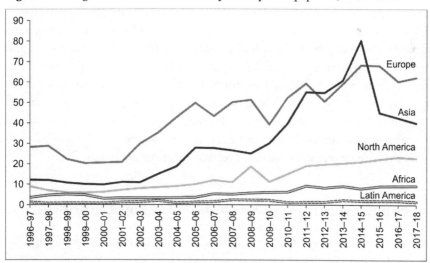

Source: Based on export data provided by Ministry of Commerce, Government of India.

Regarding channels through which they approached export markets, a common response was their self-effort and community links with already settled Punjabis in Europe and North America. Some acknowledged support gained through various schemes, but it was mainly their self-interest and initiatives that facilitated their access to global markets. Similarly, on the question of retaining a competitive edge, it was the care in product quality. Some owners did personal inspection of consignments to be delivered as they did not want to take any risk. They believed in maintaining the quality of their brands. Some said that they replaced defective articles without any question, which added to their goodwill and customers' faith in their brands. In fact, branding and quality certification have been the key strategies adopted by these firms to gain competitive edge. Regarding promotions, some sponsored international players, but it remained largely a missing aspect in their export promotion strategies. It is told that such strategy, being very costly, remains largely cornered by large companies situated in China and other competing countries such as Germany, Austria and USA.

On the question of developing links with large chain suppliers, there were not many who could develop supplier linkage with them. But some such as NIVIA Sports could once supply a large volume to Walmart. In fact, exporters urged the government to facilitate global advertisement of Indian brands. They wished that a sports industry delegation could also be part of the prime minister's delegation during his foreign trips. One major constraint hampering India's export growth has been the lack of world-class infrastructure in sports clusters, which are not attracting foreign brands. Informal discussions with exporters revealed that if the Indian state took interest in developing good infrastructure and adhering to labour standards, there were high possibilities for India to replace Pakistan in international sports equipment market for supplying inflatable balls. Similarly, India's democratic political system and security of property put it as a most desirable nation for investors to invest in but the lack of skilled labour and necessary infrastructure along with non-adherence to labour standards is adversely affecting the Indian firms.

Labour Engagement in Sports Goods Manufacturing

Sports goods manufacturing being labour-intensive and skill-oriented requires, a priori, certain skill acquisition by the worker. Given the scope for workers' engagement in tasks requiring varied skills, this sector has provided livelihood to many workers in Jalandhar and Meerut. The Sixth Economic Census indicates the employment of 10,096 workers in Jalandhar and 6,091 workers in Meerut during 2013–14. This figure was 6,567 and 4,419 for Jalandhar and Meerut, respectively, in the Fifth Economic Census (2005–06), which indicates that the CAGR of employment in Meerut has been 6.34 per cent in contrast to 5.52 per cent for Jalandhar during the 2005–06 to 2013–14 period. A relatively high level of employment growth in Meerut indicates a relatively better growth performance of this cluster during recent times.

In fact, a prime factor shaping the successful evolution of the sports goods cluster at Jalandhar during the post-independence period was the large availability of cheap migrant labour from Sialkot. Those who were not skilled were imparted the required skills in labour camps after independence at Jalandhar. Chattha (2011) notes that among those who migrated from Sialkot to Jalandhar, a large group belonged to SC groups such as Ad-dharmis, Meghs and Chamars who could diversify their traditional caste occupations and engage in manufacturing sports goods. The changing business climate after independence provided them the opportunity to emerge as entrepreneurs. These castes, especially Ad-dharmis and Chamars, controlled 70 per cent of the big units and about 80 per cent of medium and small units owned by these castes were producing surgical equipment in Jalandhar by the 1960s (Jodhka 2003). Bal and Judge (2010) also note their significant presence in sports goods and leather industries. The Sixth Economic Census, in 2013–14, records SCs' ownership of sports equipment enterprises at 73.4 per cent and 26.6 per cent in Jalandhar[8] and Meerut, respectively.

The workers in the sports goods industry are engaged in two ways: first, by working directly in manufacturing firms and, secondl, as home-based workers who are, most often, connected to manufacturing firm through a contractor. Our survey reveals that employment generation by firms depended on their scale of operation. Micro enterprises could not generate significant employment, and being a victim of uncertainty and irregularity, their survival, most often, remained at stake. Small and exporting units could generate employment. It is observed that these firms in Jalandhar could engage 225 workers directly with an average of 4.5 workers per enterprise – the same number stood at 122 workers (6.10 per enterprise) in Meerut. Similarly, exporting firms could engage a relatively large number of workers due to their high scale of operation. This apart, there have been many home-based workers who were attached to these enterprises but the availability of work to them has been irregular. Informal discussions revealed that, at present, these firms are unable to generate employment due to stagnant market demand but there were times when they used to engage many workers.

Through our survey, we could collect basic details of workers working within the enterprises. Our results indicate that male workers represent 83 per cent of workers working directly in small enterprises. In exporting firms, the share of female workers has been 30.53 per cent with a relatively large share (68 per cent) in Meerut. In terms of age, most workers in small enterprises belong to the 30–50 years age group, which is followed by the 18–30 years age group – the former group is relatively more in Jalandhar. Somewhat similar is the situation in exporting firms. In both small and exporting enterprises, a significant proportion of workers belong to the more-than-50-years age group. In small enterprises, about 15 per cent workers belong to the 15–18 years age group but in case of exporting units, the share of such workers is merely 2.67 per cent – 1.07 per cent in Jalandhar and 6.67 per cent in Meerut.

In Jalandhar, SC workers constitute a majority in both small enterprises and exporting firms. The highest proportion of workers belonged to OBCs, and the share of 'Others' and ST has been relatively lower. But in Meerut, OBCs constitute a majority of the workforce in small enterprises. In exporting firms here, a majority of the workers belong to STs. The share of SC workers is lower. In terms of education status, it is observed that a significant proportion of the workforce in small enterprises in both Jalandhar and Meerut is either illiterate or can only read and write – their share ranges between 42 and 47 per cent. But such is not the case with exporting firms where workers are relatively better educated.

Regarding working time, factories follow the standard working day of 8 hours (9 a.m. to 6 p.m.) with a one-hour lunch break. At times of bulk orders, these units ask workers for overtime – the overtime hourly wage payments remain within 0.5 to 1 per cent of their monthly pay.[9] For home-based piece-rate workers, there are no fixed working hours. They work as per market demand. The home-based work involves both male and female workers. The male workers generally perform tasks requiring hard labour, whereas female workers are preferred when tasks are relatively easy but tiring such as racket weaving, shuttle threading, ball stitching for kids, net weaving, and so on.

As this industry has provided employment opportunity to numerous home-based workers, we have made an inquiry into prevalent piece-based wages for these workers. We found gender disparity in piece-based wages, and this wage disparity is widely prevalent in the two sample clusters. The piece-based wages in Meerut, in general, are generally lower than those prevalent in Jalandhar. It is observed that a typical male worker in Jalandhar stitches football for ₹40, whereas the similar work can be done in Meerut in ₹28. Such is the comparative cost difference across various types of works. The piece-based wages prevalent in Jalandhar are 1.3 to 1.7 times higher than that prevalent in Meerut (Table 6.7).

Table 6.7 Prevalent piece-based wages (in ₹) for home-based workers

Industry type	Gender	Jalandhar (1)	Meerut (2)	1 times 2
Football stitching	Male	40	28	1.43
	Female	12	7	1.71
Rugby ball	Male	17	13	1.31
stitching	Female	8	5	1.60
Boxing kit/gloves	Male	80	50	1.60
stitching	Female	40	30	1.33
Net stitching	Male	50	35	1.43
	Female	50	30	1.67
Baseball stitching	Male	25	15	1.67
Badminton racket	Male	7	5	1.40
weaving	Female	3	3	1.00
Helmet basing	Male	30	20	1.50
Shuttle cocks	Male (feathering)	60/dozen	40/dozen	1.50
	Female (threading)	3/dozen	3/dozen	1.00

Source: Based on primary survey.

Informal discussions with football stitching male workers reveal that football stitching is a laborious activity. The males do heavy stitching. A male worker by sitting and stitching for 8 hours on a regular basis can stitch three to four footballs. With football stitching wages being limited to ₹40 per football, it provides a daily earning of about ₹120 to 160. In some instances, it remains even less than that gained by construction workers who earn ₹250 to 300 per day. The workers reported that factory owners pay them low wages and keep high margins with themselves. The same is the case with workers engaged in shuttle-making. Here, workers get about ₹5 to ₹7 per shuttle, which remains very low –shuttlecock manufacturing also faces competition from Japanese plastic shuttlecocks. Given such low piece-based wages, home-based workers compensate by working up to 12–13 hours a day, which affects adversely their health and well-being.

The study has also examined prevalent wage rates for factory workers. It has collected information from selected exporters on average wage payments across different levels of skill, as these wage rates may be considered as the benchmark wage rates for that product line in the industry. Industry-wise variation in these average wage rates is presented in Table 6.8. It becomes evident that the average wage payments remain conditioned by the type of work performed. The workers in Jalandhar earn, on an average, a relatively high monthly wage

Table 6.8 Average monthly wages paid in major exporting units in sample clusters

Industry type	Jalandhar			Meerut		
	Unskilled	Semi-skilled	Skilled	Unskilled	Semi-skilled	Skilled
Inflatable balls	4,000	5,500	8,000	3,000	4,500	6,000
Cricket bats, balls and accessories	6,500	8,500	14,000	5,500	8,000	11,000
Hockey sticks, balls and accessories	4,500	6,500	8,000	3,000	4,500	7,000
Badminton racquets, nets and accessories	3,000	6,000	7,500	2,000	3,500	4,500
Table tennis boards, balls, racquets, etc.	4,500	6,500	11,000	3,500	5,500	13,000
Indoor games	6,000	13,000	15,000	4,000	10,000	12,000
Athletics goods	5,500	7,500	10,000	3,500	5,500	8,000
Gym equipment	6,000	8,500	12,000	4,500	5,500	8,000

Source: Based on primary survey.

than those in Meerut in almost all types of enterprises considered here. The average monthly wage of unskilled workers in Jalandhar falls within ₹3,000 to ₹6,500 range, whereas the same has been between ₹2,000 and ₹5,500 in Meerut. Similar disparity across clusters is observed for semi-skilled and skilled workers. In industries manufacturing indoor games equipment, cricket bats, gym equipment, table tennis equipment, and so on, average monthly wages have remained higher than in those manufacturing inflatable balls, badminton racquets, and so on. With increasing competition within the sports goods industry, it has become difficult to pay even these wages.

The study has examined wageworkers' exposure to job insecurity and economic insecurity in small enterprises and exporting units. Job insecurity, in fact, represents the threat of job loss perceived by the workers. Similarly, economic insecurity hints at economic hardships experienced by workers due to income inadequacy and variability.[10] Table 6.9 indicates that the average incidence of job insecurity in Jalandhar is 2.35 and 2.10 in Meerut. Similarly, the average incidence of economic insecurity is 2.15 in Jalandhar and 1.95 in Meerut. Such incidence indicates the vulnerable state of the working masses and, thus, we may conclude that the sports goods manufacturing industry in Jalandhar and Meerut have not contributed much to generate quality employment, which should be a cause for concern.

Table 6.9   Average incidence of work-related insecurity among wageworkers

Indicator	Type	Job insecurity		Economic insecurity	
		Jalandhar	Meerut	Jalandhar	Meerut
Firm type	Small enterprises	2.85	2.42	2.56	2.12
	Exporting firms	1.76	1.53	1.43	1.25
Product type	Inflatable balls	2.75	2.62	2.30	2.12
	Cricket equipment	1.36	1.45	1.27	1.32
	Hockey equipment	1.75	1.66	1.45	1.37
	Badminton equipment	2.56	2.34	2.17	2.01
	Table/lawn tennis	2.48	2.43	2.15	2.08
	Skating equipment	2.32	2.25	2.14	2.12
	Indoor games	2.11	2.03	1.98	1.86
	Athletic goods	1.95	1.87	1.78	1.65
	Gym equipment	1.84	1.82	1.77	1.56
	Others	2.23	2.11	1.98	1.76
Gender	Male	2.11	1.85	2.22	2.08
	Female	2.45	2.18	1.98	1.85
Skill status	Skilled	1.83	1.75	1.55	1.50
	Semi-skilled	2.15	2.36	2.54	2.21
	Unskilled	2.69	2.27	2.62	2.32
Payment	Time-based	1.97	2.04	1.71	1.84
mode	Piece-based	2.73	2.56	3.01	3.15
All		2.35	2.10	2.15	1.95

Source: Based on primary survey.

State Policy Framework

In fact, sports equipment exporting firms in India experience various constraints related to input, financial, marketing and technological domains. Input constraints reflect skilled labour shortages and scarce fine-quality raw materials; financial constraints concern availability and cost of finance; marketing constraints reflect challenges in export marketing, packaging, branding and creativity; whereas technological constraints hint at issues related to technological access by these firms (Khara and Dogra 2009). Informal interviews revealed that except a few, the firms in general could not grow much. Given their limited resources and reach, market competition either wiped them out or they could operate only at a limited scale. State support to these enterprises has been negligible.

The state, in fact, introduced various schemes from time to time to promote this sector. Some prime schemes were 'Market Access Innovation Scheme', 'Market Development Assistance Scheme', 'Duty Free Import Scheme', 'Focus Product Scheme', 'Focus Market Scheme', 'Duty Drawback Scheme', 'Duty Entitlement Passbook Scheme' and 'Capital Subsidy Scheme'. But awareness among sample firms about these schemes has remained limited. Exporting firms, by and large, could benefit in both clusters, but a large proportion of non-exporting firms remained unaware, which indicates the limited reach and exporter-focused policy framework. However, more concerning is the fact that these schemes remained either uninitiated[11] or improperly implemented (Kalra 2012).

Given such apathetic Indian situation, let us examine the state support provided to this industry in Pakistan. In 1947, when partition ruined this industry in Sialkot, the state took active interest to revive this industry by considering it as a key generator of foreign exchange and employment (Chattha 2016). Soon after partition, the Punjab Department of Industries surveyed difficulties faced by the sports goods and surgical instruments industries in Sialkot. These difficulties were related to credit, industrial organisation and power infrastructure. The state set up the Small Scale and Cottage Industries Development Corporation in 1949. In 1950, Pakistan National Bank was opened along with other banks. The Government of Pakistan also persuaded the Bank of Egypt and the Bank of Turkey to open their branches in Sialkot. There have been numerous other efforts that collectively helped Sialkot's sports goods manufacturing industries to revive.

Recently, Pakistan has set up a common facility for manufacturing mechanised inflatable balls by establishing the Sports Industries Development Centre (SIDC) in Sialkot. SIDC ensures the provision of modern technology of football manufacturing as per standards approved by FIFA. It develops prototype balls for the Sialkot soccer ball industry, provides staff trainings and, thus, helps local manufacturers to switch over to the mechanised production system. It secures export orders for mechanised inflatable balls, develops quality vulcanisation and facilitates local development of modern machinery through reverse engineering along with the setting up of mechanised ball production lines in individual industrial units. It, by remaining open to all small and medium enterprises (SMEs), provides them access to world-class manufacturing technology. With an installed capacity of manufacturing 1 million balls per year on a single shift basis, SIDC has put Pakistan's sports goods industry on modern lines that has enabled exporters to meet global trends and challenges of football manufacturing. In fact, the introduction of mechanical stitching and the availability of fine-quality raw materials along with the enforcement of labour standards, factory-based working and other similar factors have attracted global brands (such as Adidas, Puma, Reebok, Umbro and NIKE) and leading international retailers (such as Walmart, Tesco and Carrefour) to source inflatable balls from non-branded manufacturers in Pakistan (Siegmann 2008; Nadvi, Thomsen and Khara 2011).

In China, the sports goods manufacturing industry recorded double-digit growth[12] in recent years. It attracted not only large investment but also the attention of the central government. In fact, when faced with enormous challenges of economic slowdown and restructuring amidst the US–China trade wars, the Chinese government found it difficult to sustain its double-digit growth. Keeping in view the fact that Chinese sports goods industry is still in its infancy and has scope to grow and create jobs, the central government made a strong top-down promotion plan with a series of high-profile policies. The most important has been the document, *Opinions on Accelerating the Development of Sports Industry and Promoting Sports Consumption*, which was released on 20 October 2014. This document is widely considered a milestone facilitating the take-off of the sports business in China in coming times. With this policy intervention, China's general administration of sports loosened. In 2015, it granted a subsidy of CN¥870 million (US$135 million) for 1,212 large sports venues to be opened for free or at low charge. In March 2015, another high-profile strategic plan, namely the *Overall Reform Plan to Boost the Development of Soccer in China*, was approved by China's central reform group. Earlier, in the old planned economy era, the China Football Association, a quasi-governmental sport governing body, was a major obstacle to the development of a free market-based sports industry and professional sports. But, with this reform, centralised sports governing systems got deregulated and the potential for growth of this industry released in China.

Given such supportive state role in competing nations, it becomes urgent for the Indian state to uplift this largely export-oriented sector. Similarly, being labour- and skill-intensive, it holds potential for generating employment. There is a need to work on aspects like infrastructural support, institutional support, human resource development, technology, raw material supplies, credit, business networking, brand promotion and marketing and taxation structure. We suggest some specific interventions under each aspect in Table 6.10. Rather than relying merely on state support, micro and small enterprises should also find possible solutions to their problems. These units being small

Table 6.10   Specific interventions aimed at promotion of India's sports equipment industry

Aspect	*Specific intervention*
Infrastructural support	Introduction of common production facility in various product lines
	Provision of adequate infrastructure in sports complexes
	Quality testing and support systems for micro enterprises
Institutional support	Supportive role of government departments to promote industrial growth
	Restructuring SGEPC along product lines and engaging all firms as active stakeholders in the matters of association
	Setting up of information centre to enable small firms gain latest knowledge on growing global trends in sports equipment sector
Human resource development	Opening Skill Up-gradation Centres and setting up specialised training institutes with public-private cooperation
	Higher research fellowships for process and product innovation
Technology	Encouragement to local industry to develop machinery
	Gaining economies of scale with better organisation of production
Raw materials supply	Removal of inter-state restrictions on movement of raw materials
	Setting-up raw material cells to contain price volatility
	Provision of 24-hour reliable power supply to enterprises
Credit	Easy and cheap availability of credit to micro enterprises
Business networking	Encourage small firms to participate in trade fairs and exhibitions
	Increased interaction with research institutes/universities
Brand promotion & marketing	Brand promotion and product/quality standardisation
	Increased preferences to Indian brands in local tournaments
	Concessional advertisement in national DD Sports channel
	State-sponsored global marketing of Indian brands
Taxation structure	Moderately low GST rates
	GST exemption on inter-state sale of sports goods
	Tax exemption to exports for raising global competitiveness

Source: Based on field insights (compiled by author).

do not have the means to undertake research and development (R&D). Owing to their small size and scale of operation, they remain unexposed to challenges and opportunities emerging in global markets. Here comes the role of education and computer literacy, which may enable firms to market their products through e-commerce channels. Moreover, it will also help in developing their business networks and an improved business relationship with larger firms.

Notes

1. Vide notification S.O.355 (E), the state de-reserved sports items such as 761 (all types of sports nets), 762 (shuttle cocks), 763 (hockey sticks), 764 (protective equipment, for sports like pads, gloves, and so on, soft leather goods), 765 (dumb-bells and chest expanders), 766 (cricket and hockey balls) and 767 (football, volley ball and basketball covers).
2. The value added tax (VAT), for example, was implemented in Punjab, but firms in Uttar Pradesh (Meerut) remained exempted, which influenced profit margins.
3. The Punjab government, for example, once announced 1 per cent freight subsidy but it was never given.
4. Interview with SGEPC officials, New Delhi, 20 June 2018.
5. When everyone was worried about the GST in Jalandhar, there was only one firm, namely Toppers International, that reported a positive impact of the GST on its business. In fact, its owner is well educated and aware of the procedures, though for him too it took some time to learn and get used to.
6. Some such examples are Spartan, Syndicate Sports, STAG, Vintex and Pioneer.
7. A total of 30 medium and large exporters were surveyed in Jalandhar (20) and Meerut (10). Some well-known exporters interviewed by us were WASAN Exports, WINTEX Exports, Sporting Syndicate, Soccer International, Rattan Brothers Ltd., Hansraj Mahajan Worldwide, Ceela International, Goodwin Sports, Kay Gee Sports, Robinson Sports, B.D.Mahajan & Sons, Bhalla International (Vinex), Stag International, PepUp Sports, Nelco (India) Pvt. Ltd., Gujral Industries (GISCO), Maxwell Exporters, Koxton Sports Equipments Pvt. Ltd. and Savi International.
8. As per the Census of India, 2011, the population share of SCs in Jalandhar is 38.95 per cent.
9. A worker, for example, earning ₹6,000 per month gets an hourly overtime payment within the range of ₹30–60.
10. Jain (2008) provides a detailed conceptualisation of 'job insecurity' and 'economic insecurity'.
11. For example, the Capital Subsidy Scheme of the Punjab government.
12. It recorded a growth of 35.97 per cent in 2015.

References

Bal, G. and P.S. Judge. 2010. 'Innovations, Entrepreneurship and Development: A Study of the Scheduled Castes in Punjab'. *Journal of Entrepreneurship* 19 (1): 43–62.

Chattha, I. 2011. *Partition and Locality: Violence, Migration and Development in Gujranwala and Sialkot, 1947–1961.* Karachi: Oxford University Press.

———. 2016. 'Artisanal Towns: A Comparative Analysis of Industrial Growth in Sialkot and Jalandhar'. *Lahore Journal of Policy Studies* 6 (1): 27–46.

GVR. 2018. *Sports Equipment Market Analysis Report by Product (Ball Games, Ball Over Net Games, Fitness/Strength Equipment, Athletic Training Equipment), By Distribution Channel and Segment Forecasts, 2018–2025*. San Francisco: Grand View Research Inc.

Kalra, P. 2012. 'Growth, Problems and Prospects of Sports Goods Cluster at Jalandhar'. Unpublished Ph.D. thesis, Department of Commerce and Business Management, Guru Nanak Dev University, Amritsar.

Khara, N. and B. Dogra. 2009. 'Examination of Export Constraints Affecting the Export Performance of the Indian Sports Goods Industry'. *European Journal of International Management* 3 (3): 382–92.

Jain, Varinder. 2008. 'Relative Advantage of Skill and Wageworkers' Exposure to Insecurity: How Debilitating Is the Impact of Migration Status and Social Class?' *The Indian Journal of Labour Economics* 51 (4): 927–38.

Jodhka, S. S. 2003. 'The Scheduled Castes in Contemporary Punjab'. In *Punjab Society: Perspective and Challenges*, edited by M.S. Gill, 26–42. New Delhi: Concept Publishing.

Mukherjee, Arpita, Ramneet Goswami, Tanu M. Goyal and Divya Satija. 2010. 'Sport Retailing in India: Opportunities, Constraints and Way Forward'. Working Paper No. 250, ICRIER, New Delhi.

Nadvi, K., P. L. Thomsen, and N. Khara. 2011. 'Playing Against China: Global Value Chains and Labour Standards in the International Sports Goods Industry'. *Global Networks* 11 (3): 334–54.

Nisar, H. 2013. 'Economic Significance of Sports Industries in India: A Case of National Capital Territory of Delhi since 2000'. Unpublished Ph.D. thesis, Department of Economics, Aligarh Muslim University, Aligarh.

Siegmann, Karin Astrid. 2008. 'Soccer Ball Production for NIKE in Pakistan'. *Economic and Political Weekly* 43 (22): 57–64.

CHAPTER 7

Aligarh Lock Cluster

Unravelling the Major Impediments

TAREEF HUSAIN

Introduction

One of the bright-dark characteristics of the Indian economy has been the remarkable growth rates of output with a low level of employment elasticity; as a result, the Indian economy slipped into the course of jobless growth. For researchers and policymakers, this jobless growth has been the main motivation behind shifting the attention from large to small enterprises. The importance of small and medium enterprises (SMEs) is quite discernible in the policy documents because of their significant employment-generating potential (Das 2008). Not merely the employment-generating capacity but also the ability to produce custom-made goods to satisfy the ever-changing demands of the consumer makes this sector even more significant from the industrialisation perspective. Hence, SMEs are supposed to have the dual potential of absorbing significant workforce by using labour-intensive technologies and handling the ever-rising international competition through adaptive skills.

Along with adaptability and flexibilities, SMEs mainly draw benefits from the concentration of horizontally and vertically related firms at a particular location. This characteristic of SMEs was first explained by Marshall (1920) who denoted this as an industrial district. Later, various new terms were coined, such as innovative milieu, learning region and cluster, where significant literature focuses on the idea of the cluster. The existing literature on cluster emphasises that the growth and competitiveness of small firms in developed as well as developing countries have been sourced from cooperative learning and innovation. Porter (1990) analyses that the competitive advantage of a nation is derived from the local characteristics of its industrial cluster. Similarly, Schmitz and Nadvi (1999) study the industrial clusters located in developing countries and explain that firms draw their competitive capabilities mainly from the externalities arising out of the proximity of firms in a certain geography.

The success stories of clusters in European countries, particularly of Italy, and of developing countries such as India set up the examples that SMEs cater to the needs of not only the local market but also the international market. Many Indian clusters, such as the knitwear cluster of Tirupur, the ceramic cluster of Morbi, the leather cluster of Kanpur, the brass cluster of Moradabad and the garment cluster of the National Capital Region (NCR), and others, have emerged to be successful exporters in the international market over a period of time. However, certain Indian clusters, such as the iron foundries of Howrah (Roy 2008) and the surgical instrument cluster of Jalandhar (Singh 2002), along with many others, are witnessing downward pressure. The main reasons are the obsolete technology, declining demand, shrinking pool of skilled labour, lack of collective actions and problems in distribution (Knorringa 1999; Roy 2008; Das 2008).

This study focuses on one of such Indian industrial clusters, namely the Aligarh lock cluster. This century-old cluster contributes approximately 80 per cent of India's lock manufacturing (*Business Standard* 2013). It encompasses as many as 2,500 enterprises with an aggregate turnover of around ₹15 billion, and being a labour-intensive cluster, it employs up to 10,000 workers (District Industrial Centre 2018). However, the prevalence of unorganised households or micro-enterprises (around 90 per cent) is one of the major predicaments in its upgradation. Moreover, foreign locks pose a serious threat not only to the growth but also to the survival of these unorganised manufacturers who are engaged in the manufacturing of low-technology and low-quality locks.

This study is an attempt to examine the major impediments being encountered by the Aligarh lock cluster. The major questions are, have the Aligarh lock manufacturing firms undergone technological improvement or do they remain reliant on low-technology and labour-intensive production processes? Is the manufacturer–trader relation dynamic, given that the successful relation between manufacturers and traders depends upon the trust between them, where trust is itself subject to various social and cultural factors (Knorringa 1999)? Likewise, in this era of ever-rising international competition, firms in a cluster cannot only rely on the incidental external economies; they need to collectively overcome the threats posed by foreign firms. And in a cluster, collective effort largely depends upon the active involvement of institutions like business associations. This study also sheds light on these collective actions and the involvement of business associations in the Aligarh lock cluster.

In the next section, the international trade composition of locks is covered, while the subsequent section deals with the review of the literature. The fourth section chalks out the historical development and overview of the cluster. The fifth section deals with the educational level of the owners and employees. The sixth section provides the status of technological development and innovation, whereas the seventh section uncovers distributional aspects. The eighth section sheds light on the ineffectiveness of business associations, and the ninth section deals with the role of inter-firm cooperation. The final section concludes the study.

International Trade Composition of Locks in India

The international trade composition of locks in India exhibits a rising trade deficit, especially in the last 10 years. It has increased from $10 million to around $68 million between the periods of 2004–08 and 2014–18. Based on the types of locks, the largest trade deficit was found to be in parts of padlocks, combination locks, keys and furniture locks. On the other hand, automobile locks have been the only ones showing trade surplus during the period of 2014–18 (Figure 7.1). Moreover, the trade deficits have been found

Figure 7.1 Average net export (export–import) for 2004–08, 2009–13 and 2014–18 by types of locks in US$ million

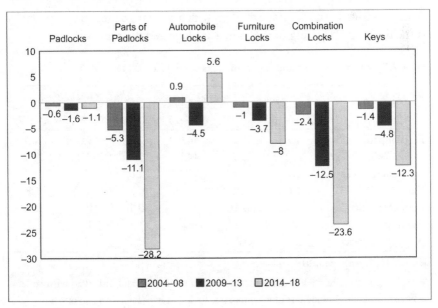

Source: UN Comtrade, 2019.

to be negligible with regard to padlocks, which are largely manufactured by the micro and /small manufacturers of Aligarh.

Given the statistics that around 70–80 per cent of Indian locks are being manufactured in Aligarh, this cluster seems to have a competitive advantage in the manufacturing of automobile locks and padlocks. The padlock product segment of Aligarh deals in the low-price market segment with the help of cheap labour. However, this padlock product segment is utterly lacking in the manufacturing of parts of padlocks, which are being imported significantly from Korea, Thailand, Japan and China. As far as the manufacturing of automobile locks in Aligarh is concerned, it deals mainly in the aftermarket for two-wheelers and three-wheelers. The better performance of the padlock and automobile lock product segments is associated with the availability of cheap labour having proficient skill in lever techniques (low-technology), which requires no usage of modern technology. However, the Aligarh lock cluster cannot thrive indefinitely based on its competitive advantage in the low-technology automobile lock and padlock product segments in the increasingly advanced technological nature of lock manufacturing. Automobile locks, despite the segment having a trade surplus, have also been found to be one of the largest imported items with imports o $30.6 million during 2014–18 (Table 7.1). This import is largely related to the high-technology locks. On the other hand, the marginal import and export of padlocks suggest that this segment is mainly catering to the domestic market, which seems to be shrinking gradually as the demand is shifting to the more sophisticated door locks.

Table 7.1   Average import and export of locks from 2004–08 to 2014–18

Products	Import in $ million			Export in $ million		
	2004–08	*2009–13*	*2014–18*	*2004–08*	*2009–13*	*2014–18*
Parts of padlocks	7.7	20.7	44.9	2.4	9.6	16.7
Combination locks[a]	10.1	29.7	44.7	7.6	17.1	21.1
Automobile locks	2.7	23.4	30.6	3.6	18.9	36.1
Keys	1.6	5.6	14	0.2	0.8	1.8
Furniture locks[b]	1.6	4.4	8.6	0.5	0.7	0.6
Padlocks[c]	2	3.2	6.2	1.4	1.6	5.1
All types of locks	25.7	87	149	15.7	48.7	81.4

Source: UN Comtrade, 2019.

Notes: a. Combination locks are those locks which are locked and unlocked with code.
b. Furniture locks include door locks, mortice locks, drawer locks, and so on.
c. Padlocks are the traditional detachable locks.

Furniture locks are also manufactured by a significant number of enterprises in Aligarh. These enterprises have somehow managed to perform well through reverse engineering and cater mainly to the domestic market. The export of these locks has been negligible, whereas import has increased from $1.6 to 8.6 million during the last 10 years because these locks are not at par with foreign locks, especially the Chinese ones, in terms of number of combinations[1] and quality. The main reason is the difference in machinery being used, for example, foreign locks are manufactured using the computer numerical control (CNC) machine while the Aligarh manufacturers are still using the old drill machine. As far as the combination locks are concerned, they have reported a huge trade deficit, as their import has been found to be much higher than the export. Moreover, only medium and large enterprises have been found to be engaged in the manufacturing of combination locks because of their ability to afford advanced technology.

Review of Literature

The competitive advantage of nations is necessarily rooted in the local economic structure, institutions, history and culture. Firms enjoy competitive advantage generated through vastly localised activities. Porter (1990) has proposed the certain home-based conditions, such as availability of demand, presence of vertically and horizontally related firms and a healthy rivalry among them, as the significant factors of competitive advantage for a nation. Firms in a cluster can innovate more because of the homogenous environment in terms of knowledge, proximity to the companies producing the same products, specialised workforce, easy access to resources, lower transportation cost and strong supply chains (Baptista and Swann 1998; Carlino 2001).

The question of whether small firms are more innovative than large firms remains as one of the main issues, and the available literature on developing countries supports the argument that large firms are more innovative than small firms. The surgical instrument cluster of Sialkot (Nadvi 1996) and the shoe cluster of Mexico (Rabellotti 1999) reveal that large firms are found to be more innovative than small firms. However, Knorringa's (1999) study suggests that industrial clusters in developing countries cannot be compared with those in developed countries in terms of innovative activities because the social boundary conditions of developing countries are less interactive than those in developed countries, for example, that of the Italian cluster. In developing countries, industrial clusters are more of a hub and spoke trajectory type, that is, the predominance of a few large firms instead of contributions from all firms through strong networking.

Along with visionary entrepreneurs (Schmitz 1999), demand–pull factors (Schmookler 1966) and technological capabilities (Lall 1992) are the important factors that tend to stimulate technological development. The literature on technological capabilities attempts to provide the justification regarding why despite facing similar demand pressure, technological change may vary among different firms as well as clusters. Technological capabilities include the technical skills and knowledge to absorb and use the available technology efficiently. These technological capabilities are lodged in people, organisational planning and technical routines (Bell and Albu 1999). The presence of these technological capabilities is responsible for firm-level technological activities; however, at the cluster level, the technological capabilities are determined by the presence of the capital goods sector (Pavitt 1984) and the availability of physical and technological infrastructure (Holmstrom 1998).

A field-based study undertaken by Sharma, Sharma and Naqvi (2005) on the Aligarh lock industry explain that technological development, as well as capabilities, has been found to be limited to a few large enterprises; as a result, the whole cluster underwent a drastic decline in terms of output. Moreover, inadequate power supply, rising prices of raw materials and rising import have also been the major causes behind the unsatisfactory performance of the industry (*Business Standard* 2013). The import of Chinese locks started rising a decade ago and, as a result, small manufacturers were affected badly while the comparatively large manufacturers responded to the international competition by improving their technology (*Indian Express* 2016). The Aligarh lock industry being one of the low capital-efficient industries mainly relies on labour, where child labour participate in a significant amount of manual work (Sekar and Mohammad 2001). Khan (2016) in a study on the major problems of the Aligarh lock manufacturers points out the lack of infrastructure, technological development and availability of labour as the primary problems afflicting the industry.

The trader–producer relation is an important source of growth opportunities for small enterprises, especially those located in a cluster. The assessment of manufacturer–trader relationship depends upon aspects such as the degree of cooperation between the two actors (Knorringa 1999) and the level of trust between them, which determines the cooperative relationship (Sabel 1992). In a diverse country like India, it is useful to differentiate between earned trust and ascribed trust, where the former is based on the business experience with each other and the latter is determined by the social and family background.

Historical Development and Overview of the Cluster

This century-old industry was established in Aligarh in the nineteenth century when the Governmental Postal Workshop was established; as a result, many artisans and entrepreneurs were attracted to the industry (Sekar and Mohammad 2001). Later on, many entrepreneurs established their firms under the broader classification as a cottage industry. Similarly, the government also helped in developing the industry by establishing the Government Metal Working School in the early 1930s. This industry witnessed a significant growth until the 1940s when it went through a very difficult time because of the global recession and the economic instability of nations involved in the Second World War. Moreover, at the time of partition, the lock industry witnessed a sharp decline in terms of output as well as employment, as most of the skilled workers migrated to Pakistan. The lock industry strived strongly to maintain its position by adapting to the changing policy environment; for example, in 1954, the Government of Uttar Pradesh introduced a quality control measure, which was embraced by the industry. However, the economic reforms of the 1990s posed more threats than opportunities to the lock industry because of the prevalence of small enterprises, especially by opening up the economy to international competition.

The lock cluster of Aligarh hosts more than 2,500 registered and unregistered lock manufacturing enterprises, which are mainly low-technology, labour-intensive and households/micro-enterprises that contribute to around three-fourths of the total lock production in India (*Business Standard* 2013). Out of 2,500 lock manufacturers in Aligarh, only 298 are organised/registered units with a capital investment of ₹254.1 million and employing up to 2,610 workers during 2015–16 (Table 7.2). The average employment in these

Table 7.2 Number of enterprises, employment and capital investment in the Aligarh lock industry

Years	Number of units	Employment	Employment per unit	Capital investment (₹ Millions)	Capital investment per unit (₹ Millions)
2014–15	242	1,918	7.9	324.9	1.3
2015–16	298	2,610	8.8	254.1	0.8

Source: District Industrial Centre (2018).

Note: These are the numbers of those units that are registered with the District Industrial Centre.

manufacturing units varies from 7.9 to 8.8 and the average capital investment from ₹1.3 to 0.8 million.

The major characteristics of this cluster are: the dependency of small enterprises on household units through subcontracting or outsourcing; the existence of disguised unemployment; and high prevalence of casual work. The existence of a large chunk of household/micro and small units in the industry could be attributed to the reservation policy adopted by the Government of India under which padlock manufacturing was reserved for small manufacturers until 2015.

Table 7.3 summarises the trends in employment and sale by the size of firms over the last five years, which shows almost all the household/micro units have witnessed declining trends during last five years in terms of sale as well as employment. Contrary to the household/micro-units, medium and large enterprises have reported rising performance in terms of sale and employment, the reason being diversification of products. Larger firms are manufacturing almost all kinds of locks and shifting their production from low-demanded padlocks to the high-demanded mortice locks.

Subcontracting has been the backbone of the Aligarh lock cluster. Lock manufacturing has attracted a large number of trading firms who supply locks under their own brands. The brand holders in Aligarh can be classified into four different categories. The first category brand holders are those who purchase the raw material in bulk and perform all operations on their factory premises. These units have the latest technology and a wide range of products. The second kind of brand holders are those who purchase the raw material in bulk and perform some processes in their own actories, provide the remaining

Table 7.3   Trends in employment and sale during the last five years by firm size

Firm size	Number of firms	Absolute number of workers	Workers per unit	Trends in employment			Trends in sale		
				+	=	−	+	=	−
1–10	23	106	5	1	2	20	1	3	19
11–50	23	456	20	6	5	12	8	5	10
51–100	10	624	62	4	6	0	7	1	2
More than 100	4	1570	393	4	0	0	4	0	0
All	60	2756		15	13	32	20	9	31

Source: Primary survey, 2018.

Note: + means increased, = means constant and − means declined over the last five years.

parts for manufacturing to subcontractors and finally assemble and package the products in their own factories. The third kind of brand holders also purchase the raw material in bulk and own godowns and factories – these kinds of brand holders get the locks manufactured by the artisans either by providing the designs to artisans or accepting the locks manufactured by them; moreover, these kinds of units also provide the raw material to the artisans or subcontractors without the involvement of any middlemen. The fourth category of brand holders purchase all parts from the artisans and assemble the locks in their factories and finally distribute them all over the country.

Education of Owners and Employees

The educational level of owners is summarised in Table 7.4. The descriptive statistics reveals that there is widespread illiteracy among households/micro-enterprises. In the existing literature, such as Bates (1990) and Basu (1998), the educational attainments of entrepreneurs are directly associated with the firms' growth. Out of a total 60 firms surveyed in this study, only 14 have been found to have owners with higher educational attainments. The owner of Nida Locks is the only entrepreneur in the sample firms who has a degree in mechanical engineering, and this firm is one of the most dynamic and growing firms in the cluster. On the other hand, more than 50 per cent of the owners among the surveyed firms are either illiterate or have a very low level of education, that is, upper primary. These firms are witnessing negative growth rates over a period of time and operating in the padlock product segment. However, in a few of these firms lately, the younger generation has joined the business, and most of them are undergraduates or postgraduates in management. Their approach towards business is based on diversification and upgradation of

Table 7.4   Education of firm owners by their size

Firm size	Illiterate	Up to upper primary	Up to higher secondary	Graduation	Masters
1–10	7 (30.4)	7 (30.4)	8 (34.3)	1 (4.3)	0 (0.0)
11–50	7 (30.4)	8 (34.4)	4 (17.4)	3 (13.0)	1 (4.3)
51–100	1 (10.0)	1 (10.0)	2 (20.0)	3 (30.0)	3 (30.0)
More than 100	1 (20.0)	0 (0.0)	0 (0.0)	2 (40.0)	2 (40.0)
All	16 (26.7)	16 (26.7)	14 (23.3)	9 (15.0)	5 (8.3)

Source: Primary survey, 2018.

products, and they believe that innovation is the most important component for firms' growth and survival.

Moreover, there is no provision for formal training of lock manufacturing. In the Aligarh lock cluster, labour acquires the necessary skills through informal on-the-job training at the early age of 14–18. However, in the recent past, this process has slowed down as the new generation has been found to be not interested in joining the lock manufacturing business mainly because of the low wages, that is, ₹500–₹1,500 per week. On the other hand, the chief technicians are paid around ₹8,000–₹10,000 per month, who are usually employed by the comparatively larger (small and medium) firms; otherwise, in most of the factories, owners themselves perform the functions of the main technician. The chief technician in a firm is usually the most experienced worker who does not have any kind of formal qualification and training.

In the Aligarh lock industry, none of the workers or employees has ever attended any kind of training programmes. This is astounding because in Aligarh there is a training centre that provides training to various undergraduates or higher secondary students through part-time or full-time diploma in mechanical engineering. The head of the training centre responded that earlier they used to provide training related to lock manufacturing to the students, but due to very little job prospects, they have discontinued the programme. However, most of the owners in Aligarh have the advantage of possessing tacit knowledge of the industry, as out of the 60 surveyed firms, the owners of 45 firms had worked earlier in some other factories as workers.

Technological Development and Innovation

The proposition that enterprises located in developing countries follow the low-technology path can be substantiated in case of the Aligarh lock cluster as well. Out of the 60 respondents, as many as 52 of them have reported the negligible presence of the latest technology. Lock manufacturing involves numerous operations, a majority of which are being performed manually. The mechanical work mainly involves cutting, pressing, dye-making, and so on. Over the years, process innovation or machine-based technological advancement has been far from the satisfactory level. Except for a few medium and large firms, none of them has purchased any kind of machinery. This phenomenon supports the hypothesis that most of the SME clusters involved in the manufacturing of traditional goods undergo very little change in the process-related technologies.

Only the largest firms, such as Link Lock and Lock Master, have purchased machinery from foreign countries, especially from Taiwan. The technological advancement in these firms has certainly boosted their production capabilities and helped them to compete with foreign locks in terms of quality and design. Over the last 10 years, CAD (computer-aided design) in designing the dies of locks and electroplating is the only process-related technological advancement witnessed by the cluster. The Aligarh lock cluster has experienced slow but significant diffusion of CAD facilities. Given its significance, the government has set up a few CNC machines at the National Small Industries Corporation Ltd. (NSIC), Aligarh, to help the local manufacturers. However, the local manufacturers seem to be not utilising this facility because the NSIC unnecessarily consumes too much time. It is not surprising that like process innovation, product innovation is also taking place only in large firms. These large firms have not only been manufacturing all kinds of locks but also been building hardware such as door fittings and window fittings. Over the last few years, the large firms have started manufacturing products such as tubular latch, door bolt, self-lock tower bolts, mortice handles, and so on.

As far as imitative innovation is concerned, the manufacturers at Aligarh are comfortable in re-engineering the locks as long as those are from Aligarh but they are unable to imitate foreign locks, especially those from China. The differences arise in terms of design and weight. For example, the 50 millimetre padlock[2] manufactured in Aligarh is almost two–three times heavier than Chinese locks, said one of the respondents. On the other hand, the mortice lock (door lock) is the only product segment that has witnessed a significant diffusion of imitative innovation. These manufacturers have somehow managed to upgrade their products despite using old machinery[3] and have reported significant growth rates. However, the manufacturers of mortice locks hold less than 10 per cent share in the total number of lock manufacturing firms in Aligarh. So, despite some technological and innovative activities being undertaken by a few enterprises, the Aligarh lock cluster certainly falls under the category of low-technology and less-innovative clusters. The requirement for specific skills such as engineers and technicians is more important when there are process innovations. On the other hand, non-process innovations such as organisational and market innovations require employees who are well experienced in management and marketing activities. But the lock manufacturing firms of Aligarh have been found to be unable to recruit highly skilled employees or workers because of financial constraints and inadequate infrastructure. The inadequate infrastructure includes training-related facilities either internally or in government-run institutions. The NSIC is supposed to provide research-related facilities but it was found to be non-functional with respect to lock manufacturing. There is an acute shortage of research-related infrastructure in Aligarh, including research institutions and testing laboratories.

Predicaments in Distribution

In a labour-intensive cluster like Aligarh, a large chunk of manufacturers belong to the informal sectors, which are assumed to be proficient in manufacturing only. The distribution is usually handled by traders situated in the cluster where these complementarities require a sound and professional relation between the manufacturers and traders. However, in different clusters, the relation between these two actors varies from the exploitative (where most of the surplus is extracted by the traders) to the complementary (where the small manufacturers also witness sound growth opportunities). To understand the distributional aspects of various firms in a cluster, it is useful to incorporate the market channel approach suggested by Knorringa (1999), where growth opportunities are different for the firms catering to different markets. In Aligarh, the firms catering to the low segment of the domestic market are the most vulnerable, as they are selling their products at a very low profit margin. These are the household, micro and small firms manufacturing padlocks,[4] which are around 80 per cent of the total firms in Aligarh. On the other hand, the medium and large enterprises catering to the upper market segment are operating at higher profit margins. As far as export is concerned, locks are being exported indirectly to the Gulf, African and some Asian countries.

In the market channel approach, the producer–trader relation is of utmost importance, which depends upon the trust between the actors. However, in different clusters, trust between the manufacturers and traders is based on either earned trust (trust based on experience with each other) or ascribed trust (trust based on social characteristics such as family background or ethnicity) (Knorringa 1999). The social[5] characteristics of manufacturers and traders are different in the Aligarh lock cluster, which was, however, found to be marginally affecting the relation between them. A few manufacturers have reported that sometimes the differences in social identities affect the relation.

The main marketing options for the lock manufacturers of Aligarh are either through local traders or through traders outside Aligarh, whereas a few large firms have been selling directly through different outlets located in various parts of the country under their own trademarks. A large chunk of micro and small manufacturers are working on orders received from local traders. These are mainly households or small firms receiving the orders for inexpensive locks from local traders. In this market channel, the relation between manufacturers and traders remains antagonistic and does not last for a long period of time, such that most of the manufacturers have changed their distributors during the last five years. The reason cited by manufacturers is the price difference arising from traders offering lower purchase prices than what manufacturers claim for the product. A significant number of manufacturers have reported unremunerative pricing of their products as one of the major problems in distribution. The micro and small manufacturers do not have enough bargaining power as the local traders are their only source of marketing. According to one of the traders, there is an outsized number of lock manufacturers in Aligarh, and whosoever is ready to manufacture the locks at the lowest price gets the order.

Ineffectiveness of Business Associations

The presence of business associations may tend to enhance the collective efficiency of firms in a cluster by providing various kinds of business promoting services. The main roles of the business associations are to regulate the competition among local firms and promote cooperation, thus bringing down the information cost regarding new standards and technologies, upgradation of products and workforce training. These local business associations in clusters in developed countries such as Italy have been successful in providing business, financial, managerial and technical services to the local firms (Best 1990).

In the Aligarh lock cluster, there have been a few associations working for the betterment of the industry. The All India Lock Manufacturers Association (AILMA) was one of the oldest associations in Aligarh, formed in the 1980s. The main objectives of the association were to provide necessary market- and technology-related information to the manufacturers and to develop necessary infrastructure along with lobbying the government on contemporary policy issues. However, this association has virtually ceased to exist in recent times because of its inability to perform on the said objectives. The head of the association reported that the non-participation of the small firms and the government's lack of interest in fulfilling the basic requirements of the lock industry (as put forth by the association) were the main reasons for the association's collapse. For example, from the very beginning, the association had been demanding the availability of electricity for 24 hours, but the supply of electricity for only 15–16 hours and power cuts during working hours continue to be the biggest obstacle for the industry's growth. Power cut in Aligarh directly increases the per hour cost of electricity by approximately ₹100 to ₹175 if generators are used. Moreover, the formation of other manufacturers' associations in recent times caused a lack of unanimous voice of the industry. Apart from the AILMA, the other business associations in Aligarh are the Aligarh Small Scale Lock Manufacturers Association (ASSLMA), the Aligarh Udhyog Vyapar Pratinidhi Mandal (AUVPM) and the Aligarh Lock Manufacturers and Traders Association (ALMTA). According to the ASSLMA secretary, due to the high competition among small manufacturers, they tried to set up minimum prices for various types of locks so that the profit margins of the small manufacturers could be increased from the currently bare minimum. But due to non-member as well as a few member firms continuing to manufacture locks at lower than the minimum prices, they could not succeed in their objective of raising the profit margin.

Membership density[6] is one of the important factors responsible for the effective functioning of business associations. In a cluster such as Aligarh, associations can have a monopoly in production if they are very dense, and may turn out to be very effective in promoting collective actions against foreign competition and inefficiencies in the local administration. However, in the present study, out of 60 firms, only 6 have been found to be members of any business association. A few of the respondents reported that they used to be members of some associations earlier, but due to the associations' ineffectiveness, they had withdrawn their membership. Moreover, the members have also been found to be unsatisfied with the associations as meetings were not held frequently, and no one followed the decisions made in the meetings. The density of membership depends upon the benefits offered by the associations. If the association is providing various benefits such as warehousing, marketing, testing, designing, upgrading, and so on, the membership of the association becomes valuable and exit is costly. In the case of business associations in Aligarh, none of the associations has been found to be providing any such kind of facilities to the members; as a result, the participation of entrepreneurs in the association activities is negligible. Likewise, the presence of rival associations may also impact associations' effectiveness. In Aligarh, there seems to be a conflict of interest between the small and larger units regarding setting of prices, technology advancement, product and quality upgradation, and so on, where large firms continue to put pressure on small firms to upgrade the technology but the small firms are not confident about their performance after the technological upgradation.

Role of Inter-firm Cooperation

The horizontal cooperation among enterprises has been acknowledged as one of the important elements in promoting the cluster's growth. Most of the clusters in developed as well as developing countries have grown tremendously or were able to respond positively to the growing international competition through increased inter-firm cooperation. According to Marshall (1920), the firms located in industrial districts get benefits from incidental external economies. The basic economic theories also explain that the external economies are involuntary. These incidental external economies are the primary factor responsible for the competitive advantage of the firms located in the cluster. However, these external economies are the necessary but not the sufficient condition for the performance of a cluster. Schmitz (1999) identified that consciously taken collective actions are the sufficient conditions for the growth of a cluster, along with the incidental external economies. Interestingly, in the Aligarh lock cluster, only incidental external economies seem to be in operation, while deliberative collective actions have been found to be almost missing.

In Aligarh, the lack of inter-firm cooperation can be attributed to the specific understanding of competition on the part of micro and small firms, who consider only local manufacturers as their competitors, not the foreign manufacturers. Inter-firm cooperation has also been measured through a stable relation with suppliers and local producers. The question asked was whether they frequently changed their suppliers and subcontractors. The relation with raw material provider/supplier seems to be more stable across all sizes of units, where most of the firms are obtaining raw materials from the same suppliers for the last 10–15 years. Likewise, the relation with subcontractors has also turned out to be strong, as most of the firms are working with the same contractors for the last 10–15 years.

The horizontal bilateral relationship has also been measured through whether the firms cooperated with other firms in matters such as 'exchanging the information about new products, processes and market', 'negotiation with respect to payment and delivery of locks', 'combined labour training', 'combined quality control' and 'combined product development'. This type of bilateral relationship among different manufacturers in Aligarh has been found to be negligible. Out of the 60 firms, none of them has reported having any kind of relationship with other local manufacturers. This is one of the serious drawbacks of the Aligarh lock cluster, where the relation between horizontal firms is based on severe competition rather than cooperation. The main reason for the lack of horizontal cooperation among firms could be attributed to the inactive associations in the cluster. The bilateral relation among the local producers is greatly shaped by the active involvement of associations. For example, in the Tirupur knitwear cluster, there are as many as 22 associations actively coordinating various activities of producers and traders and bringing them on the same platform, and they participate in various negotiating activities, such as organising training for workers, handling disputes among various actors, facilitating joint designing and development of technologies (Roy 2009).

The literature on cluster suggests that social characteristics play an important role in facilitating combined action. Likewise, the existing firms support the new firms through financial and technical support if they are socially related to each other. Therefore, the trust among enterprises is mainly sourced from the family or social relations among the entrepreneurs. However, the Aligarh lock cluster has witnessed a complete lack of horizontal cooperation despite the same ascribed characteristics of most of the households and small manufacturers in Aligarh, as they belong to the same religion.

Conclusion and Policy Implications

Industrial clusters located in developing countries have appeared to get significant consideration because the firms in a concentrated region are more competitive than isolated firms. The reason is the working of incidental as well as deliberative external economies that tend to effectively overcome the threat, challenges and growth constrictions. Thus, clusters could turn out to be an effective solution to one of the major problems currently facing the Indian economy, that is, jobless growth, by absorbing a significant portion of the working population. The Aligarh lock cluster is one of the important labour-intensive clusters in India that could partake robustly in employment generation along with industrialisation if it remains competitive in the face of growing international competition. Hence, it is useful to understand the major challenges the Aligarh lock cluster is currently facing to recommend the relevant policy intervention on the part of the government.

Firms' performance in the lock cluster varies based on their size and types of products manufactured. The medium- and large-sized firms have been able to achieve critical growth rates, whereas the household/micro and small firms have continuously struggled to sustain themselves in the market. Likewise, the manufacturers of mortice locks have performed well, while the padlock manufacturers witnessed declining trends over the last few years. Differences in the firms' performance lie in product diversification, technological progress and innovation, better quality and designing, and the intensity of internal as well as external competition. Moreover, the formal education of owners could also be related to the firms' performance, as a large chunk of the owners of household/micro and small enterprises have been found to be either illiterate or educated up to only primary/upper primary and therefore unable to maintain simple sale and purchase accounts.

The extent of technological progress and innovation in the Aligarh lock cluster is taking place at a very slow pace, which is limited to a few medium and large enterprises. The primary form of innovation in the Aligarh lock cluster is product innovation, where not only the large but also a few small firms are active. However, these innovations are minor and imitative. The cluster has witnessed an almost negligible change in process-related technologies. The slow pace of technological change and innovation in Aligarh might be the major factor responsible for the unsatisfactory performance of a significant number of firms in the cluster.

This study reveals that rising international competition and global policy orientation towards liberalisation and globalisation do not necessarily promote technological advancement in industrial clusters like Aligarh. The indication is that there is an utter lack of a technological support programme in the Aligarh lock cluster, and the available technological support provided by the NSIC is almost inaccessible to the majority of the units. There is a need for a research and development (R&D) centre or a common facility centre in Aligarh to undertake innovative and technologically advanced activities and disseminate them particularly to the micro and small enterprises, as the majority of the units belong to these categories. The unbearable sunk cost has turned out to be one of the major barriers to undertaking technological advancement and innovation by the majority of the units. If this sunk cost is met by the agencies or an R&D centre, technological advancement and innovation might get a push and these activities could get promoted at the cluster level. The formation of a common facility centre where all the micro and small enterprises could avail the services of pin cylinder technology could turn out to be a major breakthrough in the development of the cluster.

Firms in the Aligarh lock cluster have also shown different performances based on their distribution channels. The medium and large enterprises having a healthy relationship with distributors are capable of responding quickly and positively to the orders received from traders situated in or outside Aligarh. The relation between these manufacturers and traders has been found to be based on mutual growth where they complement each other. On the other hand, though the local traders have helped the household/ micro and small enterprises through distributing their products, the relation between the two has turned out to be not as strong as in case of medium and large enterprises. The relation between traders and household/micro and small manufacturers has been found to be antagonistic and do not last for a long period of time.

Despite facing stiff competition from Chinese locks, the cluster's associations have remained passive in terms of undertaking activities to strengthen local cooperation and provide various services to the firms. This requires an acute intervention on the part of the local and central governments to ensure that the local business associations played their roles in the development of the cluster. First, the government should implement policies that promote the active functioning of business associations. Second, there is a need for active coordination among the business associations and governments. The government should also ensure that the associations delivered the various complementary services to the member firms. The active functioning of business associations will also facilitate joint action among various manufacturers, which seems to be missing in the Aligarh lock cluster.

There is a need for a local cluster development agency that provides continuous assistance to the local firms. This agency should look into the various problems being faced by the firms. First, uninterrupted power supply is the urgent need of the lock cluster, which will help in achieving continuous manufacturing, technological upgradation and reduction in the cost of production. Second, the agency should focus on developing the technological and innovative environment. It needs to ensure active coordination and cooperation among different actors at the vertical as well as horizontal levels.

Notes

1. The number of combinations refers to how many locks can have a unique key; for example, if a lock has 100,000 combinations, it means 100,000 locks have unique keys.

2. The Chinese padlocks are based on pin cylindrical technology, whereas the padlocks manufactured in Aligarh are based on lever technology, which has fewer combinations compared to the Chinese locks.
3. Drill machine is the oldest technology for designing locks.
4. The cost of these locks varies from around ₹15 to ₹30.
5. Social categorisation is based on religion, where most of the manufacturers are Muslim and traders are Hindu.
6. Membership density is measured by the proportion of output produced by the members (Doner and Schneider 2000).

References

Baptista, R. and P. Swann. 1998. 'Do Firms in Clusters Innovate More'. *Research Policy* 27 (5): 525–40.
Basu, A. 1998. 'An Exploration of Entrepreneurial Activity among Asian Small Businesses in Britain'. *Small Business Economics* 10 (4): 313–19.
Bates, T. 1990. 'Entrepreneur Human Capital Inputs and Small Business Longevity'. *The Review of Economic and Statistics* 72 (4): 551–59.
Bell, M., and M. Albu. 1999. 'Knowledge Systems and Technological Dynamism in Industrial Clusters in Developing Countries'. *World Development* 21 (9): 1715–34.
Best, M. 1990. *The New Competition: Institutions of Industrial Restructuring*. Cambridge: Polity Press.
Business Standard. 2013. 'China Locks Out Aligarh Units'. 5 February. Available at http://www.business-standard.com/article/sme/china-locks-out-aligarh-units-107011901091_1.html, accessed on 15 May 2018.
Carlino, G. A. 2001. 'Knowledge Spillovers: Cities' Role in the New Economy'. Working Paper No. 01-14, Federal Reserve Bank of Philadelphia, Philadelphia.
Das, K. 2008. 'Micro Small and Medium Enterprises in India: Unfair Fare'. Working Paper No. 181, GIDR, Gujarat.
District Industrial Centre. 2018. *Brief Industrial Profile of District Aligarh*. Aligarh: District Industrial Centre. Available at http://dcmsme.gov.in/old/dips/Aligarh.pdf, accessed on 19 February 2018.
Doner, R. F. and B. R. Schneider. 2000. 'Business Associations and Economic Development'. *Business and Politics* 2 (3): 261–88.
Holmstrom, M. 1998. 'Bangalore as an Industrial District: Flexible Specialization in a Labour Surplus Economy?' In *Decentralized Production in India, Industrial Districts, Flexible Specialization and Employment*, edited by C. Philippe and H. Mark, 169–229. New Delhi: Sage Publications.
Indian Express. 2016. 'Aligarh Lock Industry Gasping for Breath Note Ban Adds to Woes'. 28 November. Available at https://indianexpress.com/article/india/india-news-india/aligarh-lock-industry-gasping-for-breath-note-ban-adds-to-woes-4399184, accessed on 15 May 2018.

Khan, N. 2016. 'Problems of Entrepreneurs in Lock Industry of Aligarh: A Case Study'. *International Journal of Innovation and Rural development* 1 (1): 8–18.

Knorringa, P. 1999. 'Agra: An Old Cluster Facing New Competition'. *World Development* 27 (9): 1587–604.

Lall, S. 1992. 'Technological Capabilities and Industrialization'. *World Development* 20 (2): 165–86.

Marshall, A. 1920. *Principles of Economics*, 8th ed. London: Macmillan.

Nadvi, K. 1996. 'Small Firm Industrial Districts in Pakistan'. Ph.D. Thesis, University of Sussex.

Pavitt, K. 1984. 'Sectoral Patterns of Technical Change: Towards a Taxonomy and a Theory'. *Research Policy* 13 (6): 343–73.

Porter, M. E. 1990. *The Competitive Advantage of Nations*. New York: Free Press.

Rabellotti, R. 1999. 'Recovery of a Mexican Cluster: Devaluation Bonanza or Collective Efficiency'. *World Development* 27 (9): 1571–85.

Roy, S. 2008. 'Iron Foundries in Duress Identifying Impediments in Organisations and Institutions'. Working Paper No. 2008/01, Institute for Studies in Industrial Development, New Delhi.

———. 2009. 'Garment Industry of India: Lessons from Two Clusters'. Working paper No. 2009/01, Institute for Studies in Industrial Development, New Delhi.

Sabel, C. F. 1993. 'Studied Trust: Building New Forms of Cooperation in a Volatile Economy'. *Human Relations* 46 (9): 215–50.

Schmitz, H. 1999. 'Collective Efficiency and Increasing Returns'. *Cambridge Journal of Economics* 23 (4): 465–83.

Schmitz, H. and K. Nadvi. 1999. 'Clustering and Industrialization: Introduction'. *World Development* 27 (9): 29–41.

Schmookler, J. 1966. *Invention and Economic Growth*. Cambridge, MA: Harvard University Press.

Sekar, H. R. and N. Mohammad. 2001. 'Child Labour in Home-based Lock Industries of Aligarh'. Working Paper No. 18/2001, V.V. Giri National Labour Institute, Noida.

Sharma, M., H. Sharma and T. F. Naqvi. 2005. 'Survival of Aligarh Lock Manufacturing Industry'. *Economic and Political Weekly* 40 (39): 4257–63.

Singh, M. 2002. 'Surgical Instruments Industry at Jalandhar: A Case Study'. *Economic and Political Weekly* 37 (31): 3298–304.

CHAPTER 8

Continued Misery or a Change in Fortune?

The Case of the Howrah Foundry Industry

JUDHAJIT CHAKRABORTY[*]

Introduction

The contemporary literature on industrial development and the manufacturing sector in India acknowledges that both manufacturing sector output and employment have witnessed stagnation in the recent past. We make this observation mainly in terms of manufacturing employment with the backdrop that manufacturing output has also not increased significantly during the period under study (Table 8A.1). At the all-India level, we find that the percentage of manufacturing workers in total employment declined from 11.6 per cent in 2001 to 10.1 per cent in 2011. In 1991, this share was 9.5 per cent; so over two decades, there was hardly any change in the share of manufacturing in total employment (Table 8A.2).

At the state level, most of the major states showed a decline in the share of manufacturing in total employment. For some of the major states, the share even went below the level in 1991. For West Bengal, the share of manufacturing workers as a percentage of total workers declined from 18 per cent in 2001 to 15.3 per cent in 2011, marginally below the 1991 level of 15.9 per cent (Table 8A.2). Alongside employment, West Bengal's ranking in terms of real per capita total manufacturing net state domestic product (NSDP) also consistently declined between 1990–91 and 2011–12 (Nagaraj 2016). In 1990–91, West Bengal ranked sixth amongst the 17 major states considered,

---

[*] Thanks to all the other participants of this project for their valuable comments during the Mumbai workshop. I also thank R. Nagaraj (IGIDR) for his valuable comments and guidance.

and in 2011–12, it ranked 12th in terms of real per capita total manufacturing NSDP. The state ranked fourth in the year 1970–71. Therefore, there is enough evidence of industrial stagnation for the state of West Bengal in terms of both manufacturing employment and output.

In this chapter, we try to study an industrial cluster in the state and illustrate the macro stagnation by searching for similar evidence at the micro level and analyse a few reasons behind the stagnation of the chosen industrial cluster. We choose West Bengal as it was one of the leading states in the manufacturing sector but has over time failed to sustain its position. Within West Bengal, we choose Howrah district. With nearly 40 per cent of its workers in manufacturing, Howrah has remained one of the top industrialised districts in the state and in the country for more than two decades. Howrah does not show any sign of expansion; in fact, there is evidence of stagnation in the district in terms of its share of manufacturing in total employment. We choose the foundry or the cast iron industrial cluster in Howrah for the micro-study. The cast iron industry is a relatively labour-intensive industry and comes under the Basic Metals and Fabricated Metal Products industry group. The share of manufacturing workers as a percentage of total manufacturing workers in this industry group marginally increased to 9.6 per cent in 2011, from 8.8 per cent in 1991. This industry group, along with the machinery and transport equipment industry, had played a major role in the fast industrialisation of the East Asian economies such as South Korea and Taiwan. Therefore, it is of strategic importance for us to separately study divisions such as the cast iron industry under the Basic Metals and Fabricated Metal Products group.

Alongside the evidence of industrial stagnation, it is also observed that the distribution of manufacturing employment is highly unequal across states and districts,[1] and this distribution has hardly changed over two decades (Tables 8A.3–8A.6). To understand how this macro observation gets reflected at the micro level and within an industrial cluster which itself is large, one needs to study the units across the lanes and by-lanes of the industrial cluster. Is the distribution of manufacturing output and employment even more skewed and unequal within a district or industrial cluster? Therefore, we present this micro-study through a field survey of the foundry industry in Howrah (Map 8.1).

The foundry cluster in Howrah, West Bengal, was one of the four major hubs along with Agra in Uttar Pradesh, Coimbatore in Tamil Nadu, and Rajkot in Gujarat. The foundry cluster in Howrah once mainly served the railway industry. It even exported manhole covers to Paris (Rajeev 2003). However,

Map 8.1 Howrah cluster map

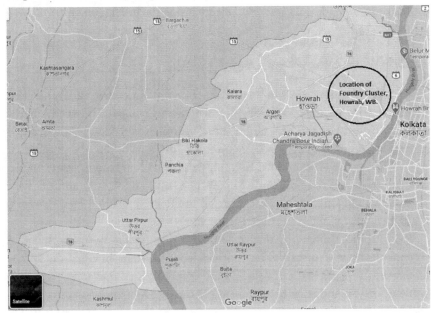

Source: Google Maps.

with a major fall in demand from the railways and a lack of alternative sources of demand, the foundry industry in Howrah was hit badly. Currently, the cluster is in a state of stagnation, while the foundry clusters in other parts of the country have expanded and are continuing to perform relatively better than the Howrah cluster. Therefore, in this chapter, we present an enterprise-level micro-study on the Howrah foundry cluster. We try to understand and document the changes in the labour, input and output markets, production organisation and the various institutional and technological challenges within the cluster. We also study the general perception around the upcoming foundry park, where the foundry industry in Howrah plans to shift. To put forward an exhaustive story, we interviewed a sample of owners and partners of the foundry units; we also interviewed few contractors, leaders of the key foundry associations and the government officials at the District Industrial Centre, Howrah.

The rest of the chapter is divided into literature review, data and methodology, observations from the field where we discuss the (*a*) micro insights to macro trends, (*b*) labour, input and output market, (*c*) production organisation, (*d*) institutional and technological challenges and (*e*) perceptions on the foundry park, followed by the conclusion of the chapter.

Literature Review

There are two main papers in the literature on the Howrah foundry industry. The first paper to our knowledge, which was a comparative study of the Howrah (West Bengal) and Coimbatore (Tamil Nadu) foundry industry, is of Rajeev (2003). Rajeev (2003) reports a significant difference in the kind of technology used for production in Howrah and Coimbatore. For example, the study observes that in Coimbatore 90 per cent of the small foundries have at least two induction furnaces compared to Howrah where the modern and high precision induction furnace is completely missing.

Rajeev (2003) mentions that a distinguishing feature is the presence of intermediaries in Howrah. The contract labour system emerged out of the labour-led lockouts in the 1970s. These contractors or intermediaries were workers in this industry before. The contractual system was preferable to the owners of the factory, as it gave them greater flexibility and control over operations, with the intermediaries now having complete control over the labour supply. However, with shrinkage in demand from the railways, a large section of the original entrepreneurs sold off their foundry units. According to the author, the new entrepreneurs had little experience of the backward linkages of demand of the foundry industry, and therefore it was a 'welcome situation' for them when the contractors or the intermediaries bought business orders and managed the labour. This led to the intermediaries (labour contractors) bringing in the business for the enterprise and managing the operations. On the other hand, the actual owners rented out the factory floor and other crucial inputs and equipment for production to the intermediaries. In this system, 'the intermediary is playing the role of an entrepreneur with the important deviation in that s/he has no control over investment (Coarse 1937). S/he is basically leasing capital and coordinating between different factors of production' (Rajeev 2003). The issue with this system is the 'non-entrepreneurial attitude' of the owner of the enterprise. The information gap arising out of this system has crucial long-run effects in terms of capital investment and overall quality of work, which further pushes the enterprise towards a low-level equilibrium.

On the contrary, in Coimbatore, the actual owner plays a pivotal role in fetching demand from the market themselves and in deciding on the production process, the backward and forward linkages. The role of the labour contractor is limited to the supply of labour to the units for daily operations. The direct link of the entrepreneurs with the market has helped them adapt to new technologies and changing market conditions. For example, the growth of the textile and pump machinery industry has given a considerable boost to the cast iron industry in Coimbatore. Many foundries were even started by the textile mill owners to vertically integrate the production process. Along with the absence of intermediaries, the availability of technical and advisory assistance from different associations and research organisations also helped the Coimbatore cluster immensely, something which was completely missing in the Howrah cluster.

The second paper, Roy (2013), studies the Howrah foundry cluster in the context of the new institutionalist theory. The theory assumes complete rationality of all economic agents and ignores the underlying social structures that are at the core of organisational and institutional changes (Roy 2013). Roy (2013) confirms with the findings of Rajeev (2003) concerning the role of the labour contractors. The labour contractors continue to do more than just supply labour to the enterprise, as they also bring business and manage other operations for the enterprise. On the other hand, the actual owners of the enterprise continue to simply rent out the factory floor and other essential inputs and capital equipment for production. This process is viewed as a 'mixture of both labour and industrial subcontracting' (Roy 2013).

Through observations from the field, Roy (2013) shows that the wages of the unskilled labourers are much lower than the minimum wages under the Minimum Wage Act. It is also shown that labour productivity in the Howrah foundries is almost three times compared to any average directory manufacturing establishment in West Bengal and 117 per cent higher than any establishment in India.[2] The same is the case for profitability in the foundry units in Howrah. With these observations, Roy (2013) shows that the sluggishness in the foundry industry in Howrah cannot be attributed to labour market inflexibility, nor the profitability of the firms. This is because with contractual labours, a flexible wage rate and a non-binding minimum wage regulation, the labour market in Howrah is quite flexible and the firms are profitable.

Further, studying the changes in backward and forward linkages around the foundry industry in Howrah, Roy (2013) observes that the market demand has considerably moved away from the cast iron products in favour of plastic pipes, steel items, and so on. Alongside this, there was a shock to the raw material prices with the decontrolling of prices and entry of a few private players in the supply of the essential pig iron, which was previously supplied by the government. The effect of this was a very volatile input market. For example, within a period of four months, the price of pig iron increased by 31.6 per cent (Roy 2013). These changes hit the small enterprises hard as they faced losses and difficulty in planning their production alongside a volatile input market. Finally, the decline of major ancillary industries such as textiles, jute mills and engineering industries within the state and the growth of automobiles, valves, pumps, and so on, away from the state led to a complete cut-down in derived demand for the foundry units in Howrah. However, having made these points, Roy (2013) argues that liberalisation and higher competition affected all industries, and this is not something unique to the foundry industry of Howrah alone.

Therefore, finding no major shortcomings in the labour process, market and policy-based factors, Roy (2013) turns to investigate the organisational and institutional aspects to explain the non-responsiveness of the industry to stagnation. Roy (2013) reiterates the underlying owner–trader–contractor relation in the foundry industry in Howrah and expands on the challenges associated with it, such as information gaps, 'impersonal management' and lack of 'systematic assessment of observations'. Further, in terms of institutional challenges, Roy (2013) mentions the lack of formal credit, lack of inter-sectoral linkages for research and innovations and no sign of cooperative efficiency within the cluster, which is in contrast to the stylised fact of 'bonding' over social capital between the enterprises of the industrial cluster.

Apart from these two main papers in the literature, Das (2013) reports a series of case studies studying production conditions in 18 foundry units. This study brings forward evidence on the awkward and static posture of work in all foundry units. In addition to this, the work environment for the labourers is highly risky as they are exposed to manual handling of heavy and dangerous materials. It is also documented that almost all the units in this study cater to the low end of the value chain. The highly volatile raw material prices, scarcity of labour with alternative opportunities, eroding domestic and international market and lack of collective action in the raw material market are identified as the major weaknesses of and threats to the Howrah cluster. Alternatively, the capability of the workers to produce high precision output using traditional technology, the past reputation of the cluster and the scope of exports due to the closure of foundry units in Western countries were seen as some strengths of and opportunities for this cluster.

In recent times, the foundry cluster in Howrah has not been studied, and therefore very little literature exists around it. In this chapter, we attempt to fill in this gap and document the changes (if any) in the Howrah foundry cluster. Therefore, our main objectives are as follows:

1. Do we find evidence of industrial stagnation and inequality in the distribution of manufacturing output and employment at the micro level?
2. Does the peculiar and inefficient owner–contractor relationship discussed in the literature still exist or has there been a major change?
3. What are the existing challenges in the input market? Has there been any major change in the product mix and hence is there any new forward linkage?
4. What is the general perception of the new foundry park among the entrepreneurs? Are they willing to move to this new park; how do the entrepreneurs look at this venture? Is there any fear of major closures in the transition to this new foundry park?

The above research questions will help add to the literature and will give a fresh perspective on state-led policies, especially on the new foundry park and the probable future of the cluster that was once a hub of cast iron in India.

Data and Methodology

We conducted fieldwork in the foundry cluster in Howrah between mid-April and mid-May of the accounting year 2018–19, with the above-mentioned research objectives. We studied 30 foundry units through a simple random sample; this is about 10 per cent of the total population of foundry units. We tried to cover small, medium and large units to have a sample that is closely representative of the population. We developed a questionnaire to collect information related to the history of the foundry unit; background of the owner; information related to labour, inputs and the output market; information related to credit and technology-related aspects; and a general perception about the overall state of the Howrah foundry industry, its future, the upcoming foundry park, and so on. However, during the survey, a lot of the owners were not very keen to share raw quantitative information, and for that reason, we also kept alternative open-ended questions (in a qualitative form). Therefore, we followed a mixed method (both quantitative and qualitative) to collect the relevant information that would suit our purpose. Apart from the owners or the partners of the foundry units, we also interviewed a few contractors, leaders of the key foundry associations and government officials at the District Industrial Centre, Howrah, to get a holistic view of the foundry cluster.

Observations from the Field

Micro Insights to Macro Trends

Through our fieldwork, we collected data on the output and employment of the foundry units studied. We asked the entrepreneurs their output and employment figures for the previous accounting year and the same five years earlier. This helped us to validate both the macro findings of industrial stagnation and the inequality in manufacturing output and employment as stated earlier.

We observe that in the last five years, both output and employment have reduced significantly across almost all the units studied. For only a few large foundry units, both output and employment have increased; this is mainly attributed to the growing exporting opportunities. There is strong evidence of industrial stagnation for the units solely catering to the local and domestic markets, both in terms of output and employment. Second, we also observe that, within the cluster, there is great inequality across the foundry units in terms of both output and employment. And most often these units are just a lane apart. In the survey, we interviewed an exporting foundry unit that produces about 6,600 to 7,200 tonne output per annum and employs around 300 direct and indirect workers. Moreover, in this unit, the furnace is used six days a week, and it makes an average weekly wage payment of nearly ₹250,000 to ₹300,000 – this information adequately signals the extent of production in this unit. This unit also has its own machining and finishing division and exports 80 per cent of its output and hence serves at the high end of the value chain. Another enterprise just on the adjacent lane is in a complete state of contrast. It produces 400–500 tonnes per annum and employs around 15–20 workers, most of whom are indirect labour. This unit only carries out job work and only supplies the rough or unfinished casting output in the local market and has consistently served in the low end of the value chain. These two examples show very different trajectories of industrial development within the same cluster and on two adjacent lanes. One can find many such contrasting examples across the entire foundry cluster in Howrah. Thus, the evidence of inequality in manufacturing output and employment at the macro level can be also observed and validated at the micro level within an industrial cluster spread within an average radius of 40–50 kilometres. Therefore, through the survey of the foundry cluster, we were able to make micro validation of the macro findings – industrial stagnation and inequality in the distribution of manufacturing output and employment.

Labour and Input–Output Market

Labour

All the units studied employ contractual labour and hold very few direct workers. Using contract labour is easy as it is flexible and does not require a fixed cost. The indirect workers in the foundry units studied are paid in different ways – per day, per week, per month and piece-rate (per kilogram) basis. The per-day wage ranges between ₹200 and 250 and the piece-rate wage ranges between ₹3 and 8 per kilogram. The piece-rate can be higher depending on the complexity of the cast iron output and other factors. Overall, labour is used predominantly on need basis and is therefore highly flexible.

The fieldwork revealed that the cumulative number of workers working in the units studied has fallen considerably in the last five years. All the foundry units studied complained about the shortage of labour and stated that the new generation workers are not willing to come to the foundry industry for work. This is mainly because the working conditions inside the foundry unit are extremely difficult and other employment opportunities are also easily available. Through our survey, we observed the labour within the foundry units working under extreme heat and taking very few safety measures. They also continue to have an 'awkward and static work posture', as observed by Das (2013) in his case studies. Foundry owners complain that alternative employment programmes such as the Mahatma Gandhi National Rural Employment Guarantee Act (MNREGA) and the permission to drive electric auto-rickshaws (which is called a *toto* in local language) within the Howrah municipality area have significantly eroded the availability of labour in the foundry cluster in Howrah. However, it is important to acknowledge that the labour shortage problem is not something unique to the Howrah cluster alone and is a consistent issue across the foundry industry. There is enough evidence of labour shortages in other major foundry clusters such as Coimbatore too. The Coimbatore cluster is heavily dependent on migrant workers from eastern states.

Input market

The essential raw materials for the cast iron industry is pig iron, scrap and coke. Earlier the government was the only supplier of pig iron in the market, but later it allowed the entry of private players and decontrolled the prices. Allowing the entry of private players in the market without a regulatory authority enabled these private enterprises to supply at high prices and hoard the supply to reap higher prices. The entry of private players in the pig iron market and the government's decontrolling of prices have only led to a volatile input market and distress among the small and medium foundry units. This has been discussed in the literature (Roy 2013) and comes out very clearly through our fieldwork. All the foundry units surveyed expressed concerns about the price volatility in the input market. For almost all the units studied, the frequent increase in pig iron prices has been a major problem, as they cannot plan production activity and quote prices accordingly, thus leading to a heavy drop in the margin and sometimes even losses. Among all the foundry units surveyed, only one unit responded that the frequent price rise of important inputs hardly affects their planning and production activities as they keep sufficient stock of raw materials covering a considerably larger period. With the time series data collected on prices through the fieldwork, it is observed that the pig iron prices increased by 11.5 per cent between December 2017 and April 2018. (On 22 December 2017 it was ₹29,600 per tonne, and this increased to ₹33,000 per tonne by 16 April 2018.) Along with this, allegations of hoarding were also quite widespread across the cluster. Therefore, this observation of rising input prices for the recent period, when seen in conjunction with the findings from earlier literature, shows that there is hardly any change in price volatility in the input market within this cluster in the last 10 to 15 years.

The fieldwork revealed that the pig iron suppliers are more interested in making steel-based pig iron rather than foundry-based pig iron, as the demand for steel-based pig iron is very large as compared to foundry-based pig iron. Also, the pig iron suppliers are facing a continued increase in iron ore prices, which is an essential raw material for pig iron production. Some of the senior entrepreneurs of the foundry cluster felt that there is a serious need to study the pig iron market itself and conduct research on iron ore availability and prices. However, it is important to note here that the increase in input prices is not something unique to the Howrah foundry cluster. During the same period as of the fieldwork in the Howrah cluster, there were reports of an increase in the prices of essential raw materials in the Coimbatore foundry cluster too.

Reports showed a 'decadal high' in pig iron prices at ₹36 per kilogram, while the prices of scrap and coke increased by 15 per cent and 30 per cent, respectively (Allirajan 2018). The foundry informatics centre also reported an increase in the pig iron prices led by low demand and a rise in iron ore prices during this period. Therefore, there is ample evidence to show that the input price increase is an industry-wide issue and nothing exclusive to the Howrah cluster.

Product mix

The majority of the units (mostly small and medium) predominantly produce hand pumps, agricultural equipment, jute mill parts, tea machinery parts, rice mill parts, cotton mill parts, sawmill parts and railway items. Only a few, the larger foundry units, produce exporting items such as different kinds of valves, pipe fittings, manhole cover, thermal power plant machinery, counterweights, industrial equipment, and so on.

The Howrah foundry cluster has failed to generate any major derived demand from the automobile industry as all major automobile industries are outside the state. Entrepreneurs from the Howrah cluster have failed to penetrate the markets of other states too. The automobile industry, on the other hand, generates a lot of demand and has been a major driving force behind the expansion of other foundry clusters in the country such as those in Pune, Coimbatore and Belgaum. Therefore, it seems that the Howrah foundry cluster has lost out on the opportunity to expand on the derived demand generated by the boom in the automobile industry. Additionally, there has hardly been any major change in the product mix of the Howrah foundry cluster if compared with the findings of Das (2013). For example, Das (2013) observes that only 1 out of the 18 foundry units studied produce automobile items, while we find only 2 units producing automobile items (one of which is the same as that of Das [2013]). This shows that there is a complete absence of any new forward linkage in the recent past, especially a linkage that can generate and account for a major share of the demand for the foundry industries in Howrah. Even leaving aside the growing automobile industry that is most predominant in other states, the foundry cluster in Howrah has no relations with the industries growing in the same state of West Bengal in which it is located. For example, although Howrah is one of the textile hubs of the country, it has never been a major forward linkage for the cast iron industry in Howrah. Among all the foundry units studied in the survey in Howrah, none of them manufacture textile machine components or parts. This is even consistent with the observations in Das (2013). However, in Coimbatore, the textile industry has been one of the major sources of demand for its foundry cluster, and there is evidence of strong linkages between the textile and foundry industries (Rajeev 2003).

Production Organisation

Through our field survey, it is observed that one of the most important and peculiar forms of production organisation within the foundry cluster in Howrah is where the owner of the foundry unit rents out his factory floor and other input and capital equipment essential for production. On the other hand, the labour contractors or intermediaries, along with supplying labour, also bring business or manufacturing orders for the enterprise. In our survey, we also observed that there are cases where the contractor and the labour are the same people. In this case, the labour with actual moulding skills brings an iron casting order and uses the floor and equipment of the factory. In this process, the contractor or the labour separately charges for the labour cost plus margins, and the owner of the enterprise who rented the floor for moulding and capital equipment charges the raw material cost plus margins from the reseller or the end-user. However, although this is the most prevalent form of production, it is not the only one. There are cases where the actual owner of the unit or the entrepreneur brings his/her own business either using social networks or years of fixed business relations or by tapping completely new markets (although this is very rare). In our survey, we found that about 37 per cent of the foundry units studied had a structure where the intermediaries played an important role in bringing business to the firm. In about 20 per cent of the units, both the types of structures were prevalent, that is, the intermediaries as well the entrepreneurs themselves brought business, and in 41 per cent of the units, the latter form of production organisation was predominant, that is, where the entrepreneurs bought a majority of the manufacturing orders. Within the set of firms where the entrepreneurs bring their own business more often, close to half of them are exporters. Therefore, it is important to note here that although we do see the prevalence of the intermediaries in the production organisation, which is also consistent with the observations of the earlier studies, there are units within the same cluster that not only bring their own business but also strategically try to enter other markets and reach the high end of the value chain.

The units where the intermediaries play a major role have peculiarly satisfied owners. The owners of these units are simply satisfied with renting out the floor for moulding and other important capital equipment for production – there is absolutely no urge to innovate and expand the production activities. Additionally, since in this type of production organisation the entrepreneurs are not directly connected to the market, they lack information about potential opportunities or are unable to reap the opportunities fully. We came across responses in which the entrepreneur did not have any knowledge about the exact forward linkage and only identified the contractor or the dealer who bought the order. The problem with this is that they are completely unaware of the value at which their manufactured products are getting sold to the end-user and hence unable to reap the full opportunity. This inadequate information also does not incentivise the unit to move higher up in the value chain. This has direct implications in the areas of innovation and technological improvement. For example, Subrahmanya, Balachandra and Mathiranjan (2004), while discussing two foundry units in Belgaum, mentions the case of Kapeel Foundry, which adopted reverse engineering to understand the details of high-tariff imported cast iron outputs. Further, it used this understanding to promote its own product design and then manufacture it in its own unit. This process helped the unit to expand its product base and enter new markets and hence eventually move higher up in the value chain. It is difficult to come across cases like this in Howrah, and a major reason for this is the 'impersonal management' (Roy 2013) of the entrepreneurs and the dominant role of the intermediaries.

However, as mentioned earlier, it is important to note here that the intermediary dominant production organisation is not the only type that exists in the foundry cluster in Howrah. As discussed earlier, we find that there are many units in which the entrepreneurs bring the business themselves. Therefore, although our survey confirms the wide prevalence of the type of production organisation (with the dominant role of intermediaries) discussed in the earlier literature, we also report the successful existence of other types of structures.

Institutional and Technological Challenges

Economic and social institutions and technological improvements play a major role in the development of an industrial cluster. Therefore, while surveying the foundry units in the Howrah cluster, we looked into the challenges associated with institutions and the prevailing technology within the cluster. Interviewing the entrepreneurs in the foundry cluster in Howrah, it was widely observed that formal credit is not easily available. For availing formal credit, the entrepreneurs face a lot of paperwork and the collateral requirement is also very high. For example, one of the entrepreneurs in need of credit had filed for a loan application with Andhra Bank in the year 2014, and it has been more than four years but his loan application has not been approved. The entrepreneur now prefers to move to a private sector bank. It was observed that most of the entrepreneurs do not have a formal loan, and almost all the entrepreneurs are active in the informal credit market through cash credits in both the input and output markets. The informal sources again become difficult to manage, especially when the entrepreneur must make an instant payment for the inputs (for example, pig iron suppliers such as Tata Metallics do not supply pig iron on credit) but gives the manufactured cast iron output on credit to retain the dealers or the end-users.

In Belgaum, some of the highly qualified foundry owners bought the State Bank of India's 'Project Uptech'[3] scheme in the Belgaum foundry cluster, and this helped them modernise their technology and automate the production process (Subrahmanya, Balachandra and Mathiranjan 2004). Success stories like these are completely absent for the Howrah foundry cluster. None of the units surveyed pursue dedicated credit facilities such as collateral-free loans for micro and small enterprises, and so on. The observations related to credit from the survey of the foundry cluster in Howrah has remained invariably the same as the earlier findings of Roy (2013).

One of the major shortcomings of the Howrah foundry units is the technology they use for production. None of the foundry units studied in the field survey used a modern induction furnace. In fact, out of the roughly 300 foundry units, there are only a handful that use an induction furnace. This is consistent with the earlier studies on Howrah (Rajeev 2003) and in complete contrast to the observations from Coimbatore. One of the major reasons behind this technological backwardness can be safely assumed to be the norms of the Pollution Control Board (PCB). The norms of the PCB restrict the foundry units in Howrah to make any sort of capital investments. The foundry industry is labelled as a red category (in terms of pollution levels) industry, and, as per pollution norms, a red category industry cannot expand alongside residential areas. These regulatory norms make it difficult for foundry units to make any capital investments and expand. Also, the areas in Howrah where the foundries are predominantly located do not have the required infrastructure such as high-tension electrical wires that are essential for running an induction furnace. Therefore, to introduce modern induction furnace in the foundry units in Howrah, apart from large capital requirements, there is a need to relax some of the major pollution regulatory norms and completely overhaul some of the old and primitive infrastructural capabilities.

Further, we could not find any evidence of inter-sectoral collaborations through the survey of the foundry units in Howrah. As already discussed earlier, the foundry industry in Howrah does not work closely with other growing ancillary industries. For example, the textile industry coexisting in Howrah and other parts of West Bengal alongside the foundry industry is one of the big textile hubs of the country and yet none of the foundry units studied produces textile machinery components. This lack of inter-sectoral collaboration is thus an outcome of complete absence of dedicated research and development (R&D) that can be facilitated under local institutions to best suit the market interests of both industries.

It is often believed in theory that there is high cooperative or collective efficiency across firms in an industrial cluster through the use of social capital and networks. With widespread acceptance, the theories of 'collective efficiency' and 'bonding' between enterprises are often put up as stylised facts of industrial clusters. However, while surveying the foundry units in Howrah, we find little evidence of cooperation among the foundry owners. Broadly, the foundry cluster in Howrah has owners from Marwari and Bengali communities, and these two groups do not seem to cooperate to any degree. In the survey, we did not come across a single unit with a Bengali owner who is involved in exporting. All the surveyed units that are engaged in exporting have owners from the Marwari community. Also, the information that a unit with a Marwari owner is exporting and has expanded substantially comes as a revelation to the Bengali entrepreneurs. For example, the president (a Bengali) of the Howrah Foundry Association (an association of more than 150 foundry units) is completely unaware that the vice president (a Marwari) of the same association is exporting to more than 20 countries for the past two years. Also, while surveying the foundry units, we felt that there is a great deal of secrecy around the large exporting units. Therefore, these observations show that the theories of collective efficiency and coordination using 'social capital' cease to exist in the foundry cluster of Howrah. Moreover, not only is there an information gap between the Marwari and Bengali communities of entrepreneurs, but the fact that some units within the cluster are exporting on a large scale took the officials of the District Industrial Centre in Howrah by surprise. Therefore, even the local industrial development bodies are not completely aware of the cluster variations.

Another important issue noted is the lack of transparency in data reporting by the government bodies. One of the leaders of the foundry association mentioned that the local and state industrial developmental bodies simply ask for the signature of the leaders of the association in blank sheets and fill the inflated output and employment numbers themselves.

Perceptions on the Foundry Park

As discussed earlier, the norms of the West Bengal Pollution Control Board (WBPCB) do not allow red category industries to operate and expand in residential areas. The foundry cluster in Howrah is a very old cluster, which is now completely trapped within residential areas. Thus, following the WBPCB norms, the Howrah foundry cluster in collaboration with the West Bengal Industrial Development Corporation (WBIDC) and the Indian Foundry Association has set up a new foundry park, away from the residential areas. The foundry park is in the Ranihati area of Howrah, which is about 50 kilometres away from the present foundry cluster. The newly dedicated foundry park promises to come up with common facility centres for R&D and the long overdue modern technology and equipment. It also plans to accommodate one of the major backward linkages by setting up a pig iron plant within the foundry park. The foundry park upon completion is expected to produce something between 300,000 and 500,000 tonnes of casting output and generate 10,000–20,000 direct and 30,000–40,000 indirect employment in the park. They have also set up a training institute for the workers of the foundry industry, which has a website, but the institute has not yet started. The work related to the foundry park started in April 2009 and was expected to complete its first phase by March 2014. However, as of May 2018, the foundry park was still not complete. Fieldwork revealed that the land allocation process is still ongoing, and the process is extremely slow.

It was observed that only a few units have been allotted land in the foundry park, but most of these units have not yet started the construction of their factories. Only one exporting unit was able to start construction activities on the allotted land, whereas others are finding it difficult to finance the factory construction. The rest of the units studied either have not opted for any land or have not been allotted land yet. These are mostly the small or low-end foundry units, who are finding it difficult to finance the land buying and registration process. On asking these entrepreneurs how they planned to finance the transition, which needs the factories to be rebuilt from scratch, they mentioned that the only way out was to sell the existing factory and land along with obtaining some subsidised credit or government aid. In this situation, it seems that these small unit entrepreneurs would be much better off selling the existing units to residential promoters and settling down with the lump sum amount, thus making these units highly vulnerable to complete closure. Responses like these have been common among the smaller units serving the low end of the value chain. Additionally, the units which have been allotted land in the foundry park also may sell the land if not properly incentivised with credit or market conditions.

Therefore, it is imperative for the government and other local industrial developmental bodies to carefully study these alternative situations. From our survey and interaction with different owners, it is observed that more than 50 per cent of the existing foundry units bear a medium to high risk of closure in this transition to the foundry park. The building of new units in the foundry park from scratch seems a difficult proposition for the small and medium units. Therefore, the concerned bodies for industrial development must lay down a plan to incentivise these entrepreneurs through cushioning credit schemes and better business opportunities for the units' sustainability in the short-to-medium run to mitigate the large cost of the setting up the new units. The Howrah foundry cluster should take lessons from the leather industry in Kolkata which had to move to a different location for similar pollution-related problems. According to the Indian Leather Products Association, in this transition process, around a hundred small units faced a high risk of closure as their operations did not match up to the cost of setting up a new unit in the dedicated leather complex.

Conclusion

The two broad objectives of this chapter were, first, to illustrate the macro findings at the micro level through a field-based study of an industrial cluster and, second, to study the cluster in terms of its labour market, backward and forward linkages, institutional and technological challenges, and the general perception of the foundry park among the entrepreneurs to identify the micro-level challenges of scaling up production and employment, and further discuss the future prospects of the cluster concerning its transition to the newly dedicated industrial estate. In the context of our first objective, we do find strong micro evidence of the macro trends, as cumulatively both manufacturing output and employment declined significantly for the units studied in the survey. Also, we observe highly contrasting performance across the foundry units, reflecting inequality in the distribution of manufacturing output and employment. A unit with a manufacturing output of around 7,000 tonnes per annum employing close to 300 direct and indirect workers has on its adjacent lane a unit that produces only 400 tonnes per annum of output employing 15–20 indirect workers. Examples like these make us believe that the distribution of manufacturing output and employment is even more skewed or unstable within the district.

In the context of our second objective, we observe that the foundry cluster in Howrah faces similar challenges like the other major foundry clusters in the country with respect to the labour market and the industry's backward and forward linkages. None of the challenges seem to be unique or specific just to the foundry cluster of Howrah. However, it seems that the foundry cluster in Howrah faces institutional and organisational challenges that are very typical and peculiar to the Howrah cluster alone. These organisational and institutional challenges, such as the wide prevalence of the intermediary dominant production organisation, a weak inter-sectoral linkage, virtually no sign of competitive efficiency, regulations inhibiting technological progress, and poor local governance, all augment the already existing stagnation of the foundry industry in Howrah. This observation of a non-market-led stagnation is similar to the findings in earlier literature; however, our survey reveals that market-based challenges such as the unavailability of easy credit and labour shortage are now impacting the Howrah cluster more than any other foundry cluster in the country. This is essential because the underlying decade-old challenges have augmented the existing stagnation to a stage where even minor fluctuations in the market can have an intense impact on the units. Therefore, we feel that alongside the organisational and institutional challenges, the market-based limitations are now having a deeper impact on the foundry cluster in Howrah.

In the context of the future transition of the natural foundry cluster in Howrah to a dedicated foundry industrial estate, as stated earlier, we feel that about 50 to 60 per cent of the small and medium units bear medium to high risk of closure, as they simply cannot finance the new units in the foundry park. If essential affordable credit and better business opportunities are not available, this transition will lead to the closure of many foundry units. As a workaround, we feel that there is an urgent need for the state to revise some of the regulatory norms concerning pollution and provide the essential infrastructure. It is imperative to allow the units to make necessary capital investments on the existing units (which is not permitted now because of regulations) for entering new markets and expanding their product base. Local governance will also have a major role to play in this process, along with a dedicated technology fund and a well-planned strategy.

Appendix 8A

Table 8A.1 Manufacturing employment and gross domestic product (GDP) in India

Year	Share of manufacturing in GDP (%)
1977–78	13.7
1983	14.7
1987–88	15
1993–94	14.6
1999–2000	15.1
2004–05	15.3
2009–10	16.2
2011–12	16.3
2012–13	15.8
2013–14	14.9

Source: Chaudhuri (2015).

Table 8A.2 State-wise share of manufacturing in total employment, 1991–2011

States/India	Share of manufacturing in total employment (main + marginal) (%)		
	1991 (%)	*2001 (%)*	*2011 (%)*
Andhra Pradesh	8.8	10.3	8.6
Bihar	3.9	7.5	5.5
Delhi U.T.	24.6	25.5	17.6
Gujarat	13.8	14.9	15.3
Haryana	9.9	12.5	11.0
Karnataka	10.2	11.5	11.7
Kerala	14.2	15.7	13.4
Madhya Pradesh	6.5	7.3	5.7
Maharashtra	12.4	12.4	11.3
Uttar Pradesh	7.4	11.3	9.2

Contd.

Table 8A.2 *contd.*

States/India	Share of manufacturing in total employment (main + marginal) (%)		
	1991 (%)	*2001 (%)*	*2011 (%)*
Orissa	6.5	8.8	8.3
Tamil Nadu	13.6	16.4	15.8
Rajasthan	6.4	8.2	7.1
Punjab	12.0	15.2	13.5
West Bengal	15.9	18.0	15.3
India	9.5	11.6	10.1

Source: Author's own calculations.

Table 8A.3   State-wise distribution of manufacturing workers (main), 1981–2011

States	1981 (%)	1991 (%)	2001 (%)	2011 (%)
Andhra Pradesh	9.1	8.8	8.1	7.4
Bihar	5.3	3.6	5.6	4.6
Gujarat	6.7	7.8	7.6	8.9
Haryana	1.9	1.7	2.2	2.1
Karnataka	6.6	6.5	6.3	7.2
Kerala	4.3	4.1	3.3	3.2
Madhya Pradesh	6.3	5.9	5.4	5.1
Maharashtra	13.5	14.3	11.8	12.9
Uttar Pradesh	11.6	11.2	12.8	11.9
Orissa	2.4	2.4	2.2	2.5
Tamil Nadu	11.5	11.2	10.7	11.8
Rajasthan	3.7	3.6	4.2	4.4
Punjab	2.6	2.6	3.1	3.0
West Bengal	10.2	11.5	10.9	10.0

Source: Author's own calculations.

Table 8A.4   State-wise ranking, by the share of manufacturing workers, 1981–2011

Rank	1981	1991	2001	2011
1	Maharashtra	Maharashtra	Uttar Pradesh	Maharashtra
2	Uttar Pradesh	West Bengal	Maharashtra	Uttar Pradesh
3	Tamil Nadu	Uttar Pradesh	West Bengal	Tamil Nadu

Contd.

Table 8A.4 *contd.*

Rank	1981	1991	2001	2011
4	West Bengal	Tamil Nadu	Tamil Nadu	West Bengal
5	Andhra Pradesh	Andhra Pradesh	Andhra Pradesh	Gujarat
6	Gujarat	Gujarat	Gujarat	Andhra Pradesh
7	Karnataka	Karnataka	Karnataka	Karnataka
8	Madhya Pradesh	Madhya Pradesh	Bihar	Madhya Pradesh
9	Bihar	Kerala	Madhya Pradesh	Bihar
10	Kerala	Rajasthan	Rajasthan	Rajasthan
11	Rajasthan	Bihar	Kerala	Kerala
12	Punjab	Punjab	Punjab	Punjab
13	Orissa	Orissa	Orissa	Orissa
14	Haryana	Haryana	Haryana	Haryana

Source: Author's own calculations.

Table 8A.5 Shares of the top three and bottom three states in net state domestic product in total manufacturing at constant prices among seventeen major states

Year	Top three states	Bottom three states
1970–71	47	2.2
1980–81	49.3	1.4
1990–91	44.3	1.4
2000–01	42.7	2
2005–06	41.9	2.5
2011–12	45.6	2.1

Source: Nagaraj (2016).

Table 8A.6 Share of the top and bottom 50 districts in total manufacturing employment, 1991–11

Year	Top 50 districts	Bottom 50 districts
1991	46.2	1.7
2001	41.4	2.2
2011	44.5	1.9

Source: Author's own calculations.

Notes

1. The share of the top states and districts accounted for the majority share of manufacturing employment and output, and this has hardly changed over a period of two decades. The share of the top 50 and bottom 50 districts has remained almost unchanged in the last two decades (refer to Tables 8A.3–8A.6).

2. An enterprise that employs at least one hired worker on a fairly regular basis is termed as an establishment. Paid or unpaid apprentices and paid household member or servant or resident worker in an enterprise are considered hired workers. They have been further been categorised into two parts: non-directory and directory (Ramaswamy 2014). A directory manufacturing establishment (DME) is an establishment that employs six or more workers. (Ramaswamy 2014).

3. Project Uptech is a scheme under the State Bank of India (SBI). Through this scheme, the SBI selects an industrial cluster with a 'growth potential, potential for quick technological upgradation and a supporting environment'. It then conducts a unit-level study and collects all the relevant information. Experts then study this information and recommend a 'business plan and suitable financial package for each unit'.

References

Allirajan, M. 2018. 'Foundry Industry Hit by High Raw Material Prices'. *Times of India*, 7 April 2018.

Chaudhuri, S. 2015. 'Import Liberalization and Premature Deindustrialization in India'. *Economic and Political Weekly* 50 (43): 60–69.

Das, S. 2013. *Need Assessment Study Report for Howrah Foundry Cluster (Under MSME Design Clinic Scheme, Supported by Ministry of MSME Government of India)*. Ahmedabad: National Institute of Design. Available at https://pdfslide.net/documents/need-assessment-study-report-for-howrah-foundry-cluster-under-.html, accessed on 14 January 2021.

Nagaraj, R. 2016. 'Regional Industrial Growth: Have the Economic Reforms Made a Difference?' In *International Trade and Industrial Development in India: Emerging Trends Patterns and Issues*, edited by C. Veeramani and R. Nagaraj, 103–19. New Delhi: Orient BlackSwan.

Rajeev, M. 2003. 'A Search for a Theory of Entrepreneurship: A Case Study of the Foundry Industry in Howrah and Coimbatore'. ISEC Working Paper 129, Institute for Social and Economic Change, Bangalore.

Ramaswamy, K. V. 2014. 'Small Enterprises in Indian Manufacturing and Inclusive Growth: Search for Compensatory Mechanisms'. IGIDR WP-2014-018. Available at http://www.igidr.ac.in/pdf/publication/WP-2014-018.pdf, accessed on 14 January 2021.

Roy, S. 2013. 'Foundries in Howrah: Impediments in Institutions and Organizations'. In *Small and Medium Enterprises in India: Infirmities and Asymmetries in Industrial Clusters*, ch. 5. London: Routledge Publications.

Subrahmanya, M. H. Bala, P. Balachandra, and M. Mathiranjan. 2004. 'Technological Innovations in Small-scale Industries: Case Studies of Two Foundries in Karnataka'. *South Asian Journal of Management* 11 (2): 111.

CHAPTER 9

Redevelop and Perish, or Survive and Grow?

The Case for Supporting Informal Leather Enterprises in Dharavi, Mumbai

KSHITI GALA

Introduction

There is a vast and growing literature focusing on the economies of scale and scope (Marshall 1920) that industrial units get by agglomerating themselves into 'industrial clusters' (Caniëls and Romijn 2003). Moving away from the micro-economic perspective of technological capacity at the firm level, these studies explore regional networks as contributing to technological capability and competitive advantage to industrial units (Pyke and Sengenberger 1992; Schmitz and Nadvi 1999). While thinking of small industrial clusters (SICs), it is often useful to consider them as networks of actors, grouped together in a geographical space, often competing with each other but also sharing technological know-how, facilities, skilled pool of labour and other resources (Varman and Chakrabarti 2011). For example, the clustering of knitwear units and their ancillary industries in Ludhiana played a critical role in its innovative transformation. However, the opening up of new market opportunities also explains the resilience of regional firms to the crises of 1990 and their recovery (Tewari 1999; Tewari and Pillai 2005). But mere survival does not mean that the cluster's technological capacity is close to competing at the international level, as the study of textile clusters in Panipat shows (Gulrajani 2006). The source of this dynamism lay in the strength of the organisational aspects of its production system, which did not guarantee its long-term survival. This study aims to focus on what policy support measures are required for industrial clusters in the informal sector to remain viable, innovate and acquire competitive advantage in international markets.

While in the literature, the advantage of industrial clusters and the policy support they require are often pitched in terms of the technological capacity and competitiveness of firms or the cluster in general, in the current context, industrial clusters have an important role in generating employment. There is a fair amount of evidence to show that the employment elasticity (rate of growth of employment with respect to the rate of growth of output) in India's manufacturing industry has declined in recent years. Keen observers of the economy have noted that 'unlike China's or South Korea's growth through manufactured exports that absorbed low-skilled-labour in vast numbers, India's growth episode was led by a high-skilled service sector that failed to adequately absorb unskilled labour from agriculture' (Kotwal and Sen 2019). In 1980–81, the share of manufacturing in the total workforce of the economy was about 11 per cent, which has remained nearly stagnant even after three decades (Nagaraj 2017). The rise in the share of industrial employment has been primarily due to the boom in construction sector employment. India's employment challenge is to generate job opportunities in the non-farm sector of about 17 million persons per year so that workers move out of agriculture (Mehrotra et al. 2014). The leather industry, being labour intensive, has a role to play in this transition. The point of departure of my study is to understand to what extent informal sector clusters can act as a vehicle of imparting this labour market dynamism, if appropriately supported in policy.

Study Area

General Description

The area I have chosen for study is Dharavi, Mumbai's most widespread and diverse informal settlement, which produces different commodities such as food products, leather goods, garments and pottery. According to the *New York Times* in 2011, 'Dharavi is a churning hive of workshops with an annual economic output estimated to be $600 million to more than $1 billion.' According to *The Economist* in 2005, 'In Dharavi, one of Asia's largest slums, covering 220 hectares (530 acres), some 1,00,000 people produce goods worth over $500m a year.' These numbers portray an optimistic picture but are difficult to verify. Such widely published but unverified news sources motivated me to give production activities in Dharavi a closer inquiry. I chose to focus on the leather goods cluster as it is a lifeline for a large number of households. It has the potential to create more jobs and lead to inclusive growth. Finished products such as bags, wallets, purses, jackets, belts, footwear and folders are manufactured and sold in Dharavi. While business appears to be thriving (with more than 300 leather goods sales shops on the Bandra–Sion link road), the cluster has not delivered on its full potential. My research focuses on:

1. Articulating the current state of the leather goods cluster in Dharavi
2. Mapping constraints that prevent it from becoming a world-class cluster selling high-quality, high-end leather products
3. Identifying policy support needed for it to overcome these constraints.[1]

Map 9.1   Map of Dharavi area

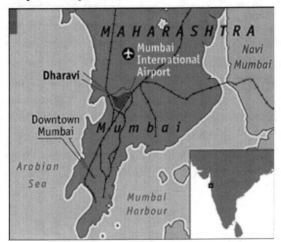

Source: *The Economist*, 19 December 2007.

Often described as a 'parallel economy', Dharavi is truly a backbone of the city of Mumbai. Also described as a 'self-created special economic zone for the poor' (Yardley 2011), it is a large conglomeration of densely populated informal settlements and an aspirational stepping stone for migrants. Spread over 3.5 square kilometres and located in the G North Ward of the Brihanmumbai Municipal Corporation (BMC) (Map 9.1), Dharavi, according to the 2011 Census of India, has a population of 599,039. However, its current population is estimated to be above 1 million. It has a dense network of units producing food products, soaps, plastics, leather and leather goods, garments, non-ferrous metal products such as buckles, door and window fittings, toys, rubber goods, recycling units and pottery.

Dharavi is comprised of hundreds of *gully*s or by-lanes, where thousands of people strive to make it in the city of dreams. It encompasses 85 *mohollas/localities/nagar*s, with each neighbourhood being unique in its ethnic and cultural identity, making it a microcosm of India's regional diversity. The population density in Dharavi ranges from 18,000 to 300,000 per square kilometre, making it one of the most densely populated areas in Mumbai. Households of 5–15 members each live in 100–300 square feet houses. Dharavi has poor water and sanitation services. While the informality of Dharavi and its lack of infrastructure are known, little is known about its economic role, particularly about its booming industrial sector that generates employment opportunities, especially for those living in Dharavi itself.

Informal employment is a key characteristic of the leather goods industry in Dharavi. Pias (2006b) documents the poor working conditions, wages and volatility in job security. The nature of employment is through subcontracting, which enables profitability and productivity for enterprise owners, depending on market needs. The primary mode of production is through subcontracting and then ex-post coordination among various informal units to achieve synchronisation. Employed workers may be informal sector workers working in informal or formal sector enterprises – both kinds of informalities are possible and a 'low road' to flexible specialisation is observed (Pyke and Sengenberger 1992).

Leather Goods Cluster in Dharavi

Leather is one of the oldest traditional manufacturing industries in India, with a long history ridden with caste-based discrimination (Roy 1994). It is one of India's least automated sectors and is strategically important for employment, growth and exports (Damodaran and Mansingh 2008). India has had a revealed comparative advantage in the manufacturing of leather products and continues to enjoy the same (Planning Commission 2011: 12). India has about 12.93 per cent of the world's production of hides, and it is the second largest manufacturer of footwear and leather garments. The sector can potentially create 250 jobs for every ₹10 million invested (Department of Industrial Policy and Promotion 2017). Additionally, female employment is highly concentrated in six industries, of which leather is one (Banerjee and Veeramani 2015: 11). It must be noted that micro and small units dominate the sector (characterised by high levels of subcontracting), and large units comprise only 5 per cent of the total manufacturing units (Planning Commission 2011: 15).

The presence of the leather industry in Dharavi dates back to the 1900s. To quote Roy (1994),

> Already in 1900, Bombay's neighbouring village Dharavi ... is entirely given up to the tanning industry. The tanneries were owned by the Bohra and Memon merchants, groups controlling Bombay's hide trade, though, interestingly, one tannery belonged to a Mochi. Shortly after the War, the city had 30 tanneries. The workforce consisted of Tamil-speaking caste tanners, who reportedly furnished better labour than the local tanners.

Historical and anthropological accounts (Sharma 2000; Engqvist and Lantz 2009) articulate that Dharavi has evolved since the 1930s, providing employment opportunities for migrants. Dharavi was a place where dead animals were cleaned to make rawhide. As the city grew, the 'dirty' process of tanning leather was shifted elsewhere, and raw material was procured from cities such as Agra, Chennai and Kolkata. Today, it has grown into a cluster that sells finished products to the domestic and global markets. Being a buyer-driven value chain, retailers and exporters purchase leather goods from Dharavi through bulk orders.

To arrive at the 'population' or the total number of leather goods manufacturing and commercial units in Dharavi, I searched various data sources such as journal articles, doctoral theses, government databases, civil society reports and newspaper features on Dharavi. The limitation in all data sources is that there is no definitive mention of exact numbers of registered enterprises, labour employment and exports. So, I sought information from the G North Ward of the BMC, the local governing body. After multiple appointments with the Senior Inspector – Licenses and Registrations, where I was constantly questioned on the reasons behind asking for information, I could finally access a list of all registered enterprises under the Shops and Establishments Act, 1948.

Since manufacturing enterprises in Dharavi are characterised by informality, I anticipated that the official list procured may not contain the exact number of enterprises that currently exist in Dharavi. When I set out on the field to do an on-ground check of the various enterprises, I found that many entries were incomplete and inaccurate. On enquiring with various shopkeepers, they revealed that despite trying to renew registrations, the lists were not always updated. BMC officials, on the other hand, blamed the entrepreneurs in

Dharavi for constantly hiding and not informing the ward office about shop closures and mergers.

Having chalked out the challenges in data availability that reinforce the need to study informal enterprises, I shall highlight the foundation on which these enterprises are built. The presence and vibrant growth of skilled and semi-skilled labour has been the backbone of leather goods enterprises in Dharavi. As a labour surplus country, India's key competitive advantage is the availability of abundant and cheap labour, and Dharavi is no exception. Artisans from different parts of India – Uttar Pradesh, Bihar, Tamil Nadu, Gujarat and other parts of Maharashtra – moved to Dharavi, with the aspirations of 'making it' in the city of dreams. Migrant artisans arrived with a diverse range of skill sets, often learned and mastered in their hometowns. Entrepreneurs and workers in the leather business in Dharavi are predominantly the *adi dravida*s (Dalits) from Tamil Nadu, Muslims from Uttar Pradesh and *chamar*s (Dalits) from Maharashtra (Sharma 2000). Primary interviews with entrepreneurs, workers and policymakers revealed that historical and traditional caste structures are reinforced in the leather industry, reflecting caste-based discrimination prevalent in Indian society.

The Strength of Skilled Human Capital

Since the leather business in Dharavi is not industrialised on a large scale, it is highly labour intensive. Skilled workers, who make relatively high-quality products in a short span of time, have driven the cluster's advancement. In my analysis, a key reason for the leather goods cluster's survival has been the availability of abundant skilled labour in Dharavi. Apart from stitching done on machines, the entire production process (for example, cutting, designing, stitching, finishing and packaging) requires human capital. There are variations in the skill set levels, and usually a new, untrained worker starts as an apprentice, slowly acquiring skills and increasing earnings over time. Highly skilled workers are those who can quickly emulate a design from its photograph. They are invaluable to their enterprises and hence the highest paid workers. Based on the speed of workers, they prefer to be paid either by the day or by the piece. For example, a worker making two bags a day might prefer getting paid ₹200 per bag as compared to a worker who can make one bag a day and gets a daily wage of ₹300. So, both time and piece-rate wages coexist (Figure 9.1).

Figure 9.1   Daily wage rate skilled workers doing product packaging and quality control

Source: Author.

Role of Caste, Community and Religious Networks

The role of community, religion, caste and kinship networks in the survival, profitability and resilience of these enterprises is strong. Leather-goods-related activities in Dharavi are closely linked to certain castes and religions, substantiating the continuation of occupations based on caste and religious identities. These networks are indispensable for resilience to market shocks, economic volatility and policy uncertainty. For instance, during the Covid-19 crisis, state support mechanisms had glaring limitations. While civil society organisations stepped in to provide humanitarian relief, migrant workers in small enterprises turned to community-, religion- and caste-based informal networks for economic survival.

Locational Advantage

Situated in the heart of the commercial capital of Mumbai, Dharavi is well connected to all parts of the city that were the traditional business hubs as well as the parts that have evolved as business hubs as the city grew. Dharavi's location in the heart of the commercial capital of Mumbai enables it to be well connected to the rest of the city. Leather business entrepreneurs have direct access to markets – local, national and international – because their businesses are located in the epicentre of Mumbai. At the local level, buying agents and corporate clients find it convenient to visit leather retail shops in person to finalise orders. For entrepreneurs, Dharavi's well-connected location aids in reducing transportation costs. At the national level, entrepreneurs find it easy to procure raw materials such as tanned leather from Kolkata, Tamil Nadu and Uttar Pradesh and send finished goods to these markets. At the international level, those looking to export have access to the international airport, which is 8 kilometres away. The location not only ensures access to markets but also facilitates forward and backward linkages for firms (for example, supplying raw materials, processing leather, embossing logos, providing imported fittings, packaging support – all available at a stone's throw within Dharavi). Leather is not the only business that is flourishing in Dharavi – it has a dense ecosystem of garment manufacturing and trading, food makers, recycling units and pottery artisans, to name a few. With the location comes a vibrant network of a skilled workforce, multiple manufacturing enterprises and shops that are deeply intertwined.[2]

Price Competition

Knorringa (1999) emphasises the price competition struggles for survival of traditional clusters such as the leather cluster in Agra. The combination of cut-throat prices amidst tacit location-based unity leads to competition enabled by cooperation in Dharavi. This distinctive feature contributes to the success of enterprises in Dharavi. Primary survey results reveal price-based competition among sellers. Of those interviewed, 45 per cent said they reduce prices or offer high discounts to become competitive.[3]

Constraints Faced by the Leather Goods Cluster

Design of Field Survey

Prior to conducting primary surveys and in-depth case studies, I made several visits to the leather goods manufacturing units in Dharavi during October–December 2017. This helped me get acquainted with the field area. During these visits, I interviewed employers (manufacturers and traders), domestic entrepreneurs and exporters, employees, trainers, policy makers and bureaucrats. From January–June 2018, I carried out primary field surveys of 200 enterprises to examine how domestic and exporting firms cope with competitive pressures. The entrepreneur is at the centre of the study, and the unit of study is an enterprise. Field-survey-based quantitative data has been supplemented with qualitative case studies and personal interviews. The years when the fieldwork was conducted, 2017 and 2018, were a turning point for the cluster, as enterprises were recovering from the impact of demonetisation, beef ban and implementation of the goods and services tax (GST).

Emergence of Organic Innovation

The evolution of leather goods manufacturing in Dharavi is a story of indigenous innovation. The word 'innovation' has a more fluid meaning here; it does not encompass conventional research and development conducted in design laboratories to make cutting-edge world-class products. It does not indicate redefining leather technology around the globe. Leather entrepreneurs in Dharavi did not have the time, financial and technological resources or educational qualifications to innovate as per global industry standards. But *adaptive strategies* in manufacturing goods and completing orders have enabled entrepreneurs to stay afloat and grow, despite market highs and lows.

Let me illustrate this through a historical example. In 1986, the Central Pollution Control Board (CPCB) issued directives to all Indian states and union territories to set effluent treatment standards for polluting industries, of which leather was one. Effectively, this meant that common effluent treatment plants were banned from being located in cities, and those located in rural areas were mandated to meet requirements under the Environment Protection Act, 1986. This judgment mandated grossly polluting industrial tanneries to move out because the effluent discharge adversely affected the air and water quality of the surrounding areas, as documented for Palar Valley in Tamil Nadu (Kennedy 2004).

Along with the CPCB's guidelines to protect the environment came large-scale economic ramifications, and all leather business in Dharavi were impacted overnight. For them, it was a negative externality, as tanneries could no longer operate in Dharavi. This was an inflection point when the entire network of manufacturing enterprises could have completely shut down but, instead, one sees a story of survival and resilience through innovation. During this time, Dharavi reinvented its *raison d'etre*, that is, the purpose of its existence. Earlier, raw leather and wet blue leather were tanned and processed in Dharavi. After the imposition of CPCB guidelines, Dharavi's leather business moved up the value chain and changed its product mix from raw materials to finished goods. As the leather cluster in Dharavi evolved, standing the test of time, so did the nature of products being manufactured, exemplifying innovative adaptive strategies deployed by entrepreneurs (Figure 9.2).

In terms of innovation in design, this is an organic process, done by imitating samples or by looking at pictures. Hence, there is no specific process for designing, but workers do try to stay updated on latest trends through information available to them.

> Designing is done mostly by customers who want a specific kind of design and give us a sample. The bigger players like Baggit and Wildcraft have their own designers and sometimes they share their designs with us. We don't have a specific designing process. We just pick up designs from the internet. (Interview with Sachin Shinde, entrepreneur, Maruti Leather, Dharavi, Mumbai, 3 February 2018)

In the leather goods cluster in Dharavi, on the one hand, there are small, labour-intensive enterprises, selling goods for the domestic market, and, on

Figure 9.2 Workers polishing and smoothening tanned leather procured from Kolkata that would previously be tanned in Dharavi

Source: Author.

the other hand, there are exporting firms, manufacturing high-quality goods for global brands. Exporting firms use less labour per unit of output, although their tasks remain highly labour intensive. Thus, an impetus on the design front to both domestic and exporting firms is desirable for creating more jobs and high-value products.

Prevalence of Weak Linkages between Small Enterprises and Large Exporters

Having interviewed both small enterprise owners and large exporters, I noticed a dichotomy between the two due to the paucity of effective linkages. On the one hand, there are labour-intensive enterprises, selling low-productivity, low-end goods. On the other hand, there are exporters, selling world-class products. Primary case studies of entrepreneurs who are exporters illustrate the factors that enabled them to compete, diversify, grow and create more value compared to smaller domestic enterprises.

Every entrepreneur does not have the capacity to export because he or she might not be able to reach the size, quality and environmental standards mandated globally. Hence, access to the domestic markets is very important. Having said that, weak linkages between small enterprises and large exporters do exist and need to be strengthened. Stronger linkages will play the dual role of helping small enterprises stay afloat and enabling large exporters to stay price competitive globally.

> In 1995, I got the first export order from Dubai for around ₹2 crores. Over the years, I have exported to Holland, Kenya, Russia, Africa and some Gulf countries. Currently, my annual turnover has reduced to ₹1.5 crores. Although the volume has almost remained the same, profit margins have gone down tremendously. I focus on exporting to Gulf countries. The export market is quite cut throat. China has lowered prices and customers are attracted to better design. It is a 'Use and Throw' generation where how the product looks matters more than its quality. (Interview with Rehmatulla Abdul, entrepreneur, High Design, Dharavi, Mumbai, 16 January 2018)

Low Investment Business with Reasonable Profit Margins

The number of small enterprises in the cluster have grown due to low initial investment needs and ease of entry. Of the entrepreneurs, 51 per cent said that investing up to ₹2 million was sufficient for starting the leather business. Additionally, in the absence of adverse policy measures (namely demonetisation, beef ban, gaps in GST implementation), the profit margin was up to 20 per cent for 65 per cent of the entrepreneurs, making it a viable business.

In order to build export competitiveness, small and informal manufacturing units need upgradation of product, process, standards and of skills. However, labour flexibility is a very important factor for surviving in a world of uncertain orders and short delivery times. While labour flexibility enables small enterprises to remain afloat in times of crisis, it acts as a double-edged sword, making labour dispensable and unemployed overnight.

Spatial Constraint

Space is the biggest constraint for manufacturing enterprises. Of the 200 units, 153 (76.5 per cent) operate in less than 500 square feet of space. Dharavi is highly congested (Figure 9.3). This is a challenge for scaling up – new machines cannot be installed and storage spaces cannot be expanded due to spatial constraints (Figure 9.4).

Figure 9.3 Spatial constraints are evident as three-fourths of the enterprises are crunched up in less than 500 square feet

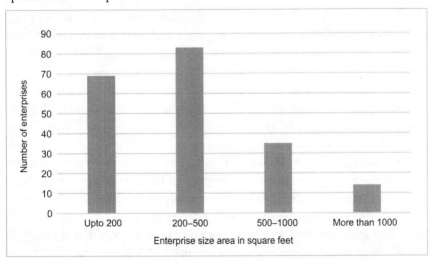

Source: Author.

Figure 9.4   The Indian Leather Art Co. is a space-constrained enterprise, like many others in Dharavi, with narrow steps and a rope for climbing to the manufacturing enterprise

Source: Author.

Prevalence of Exports through Multiple Intermediaries

The cluster caters primarily to the domestic market, and its clientele is private companies that place bulk orders for gifting purposes. The receipt of such orders is conditional upon the private sector's performance, and hence during an economic downfall, these orders slowly and steadily dwindle. There are indirect and direct exporters in Dharavi, and some exporters have moved manufacturing activities to Mumbai's suburbs. This is because scaling up requires outsourcing tasks and expanding the firm size, and Dharavi does indeed pose a structural constraint in terms of limited land availability. Small enterprises can be more profitable if they eliminate multiple intermediaries and are able to export directly. Anecdotes from the field survey revealed that domestic companies such as Bata and international companies such as Prada reduce costs by manufacturing their leather products in Dharavi. However, there are hardly any efforts seen on-ground to ensure international standards and dignified working conditions of those making their products.

Lack of Access to Formal Sources of Credit

Despite the leather goods industry having existed for a long time, it is surprising that 61 per cent of the entrepreneurs interviewed turn to personal finance or friends and family as a source of credit. Pranab Bardhan (1980) writes on interlocked markets and the paucity of formal credit in the rural economy and, clearly, access to formal sources of credit has not reached urban areas like Dharavi. An entrepreneur pointed out, 'I have never utilised any government schemes. Small players need financial support so that they can survive. Manufacturing businesses are pillars of productivity of any country and hence should be supported by the government' (interview with Rajendra Khade, Treasurer, Leather Goods Manufacturers' Association, Dharavi, Mumbai, 19 February 2018).

The unavailability of formal sources of credit gets exacerbated because of delayed payments from buyers. Of the entrepreneurs, 50 per cent said that they have to give companies up to 120 days of credit. So, on the one hand, the sources of formal credit are few and, on the other, selling on a credit basis (that is, a waiting time of four months to receive payments) to get business is the norm.

Potential for Machine Upgradation

At present, there is a low level of mechanisation, with 1–20 machines per enterprise. Brands of sewing machines used are Juki (from Japan) (Figure 9.5), Singer (from India) and Adler (from Germany). At present, entrepreneurs feel that imported machines can improve productivity and output quality. However, they are unable to use imported machines because of high costs of procurement. Additionally, low-price, low-quality products can be manually made without high-end machinery. An entrepreneur explains the need to upgrade machinery:

> In order to give more jobs to people, I need to increase my production capacity, for which I will need to increase my market area – either domestic or exports. In the domestic market, our biggest competitor is China. Unlike China, we do not have hi-tech machinery and as much support as is given by the Chinese government. Due to these reasons, our cost of production is increasing. In China, everyone specialises in only one task. Till we do not get hi-tech machinery, our cost of production will not reduce and production will not be faster. Those who want 20,000 bags give their order to China because we are not able to give such large quantities at China's cheap rates. So, with better machinery, we can increase production, have greater market size, deliver large orders and hence employ more people. (Interview with Rahul Gore, entrepreneur, Made by Dharavi, Dharavi, Mumbai, 15 March 2018)

Figure 9.5   A 15-year-old Juki machine, bought second hand, exemplifying the need to upgrade machinery

Source: Author.

Mixed Education Levels

More than formal degrees, there is a greater need for skill improvement and training (Figure 9.6).

Figure 9.6   Lack of training and vocational skills constrain Dharavi's leather entrepreneurs

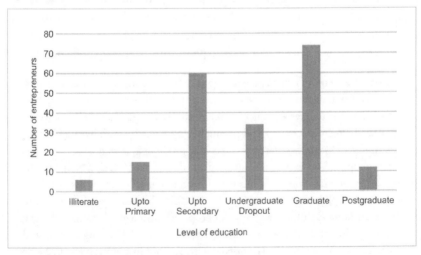

Source: Author.

Of the entrepreneurs, 83 per cent had never been trained in leather technology. And 92 per cent of their workers had never received any skill improvement training. Both entrepreneurs and workers are learning, on the job, without any training support. The skill sets they have are indigenous and experiential.

Marketing Intermediaries

There is intense competition, and strategies to cope with competition include reducing price and cutting down profit margins to get more orders. Current marketing channels include word-of-mouth sales, retail and wholesale buying agents. As of now, a bulk of the orders come from wholesalers, who impose large intermediary commissions, further reducing profit margins for entrepreneurs. Some untapped opportunities are marketing products online and participating in global export exhibitions, to eliminate intermediaries.

Figure 9.7 highlights the need to explore e-commerce and social media platforms for greater marketing outreach. Currently, conventional marketing methods like word of mouth, retail and wholesale are prevalent.

Figure 9.7 Conventional marketing methods prevail

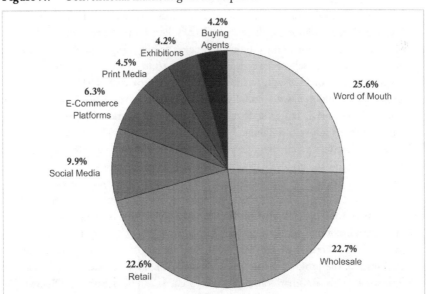

Source: Author.

Competition from Big Brands

The field survey revealed that the following brands outsource either a part of their manufacturing process or the entire process to Dharavi:

1. Domestically known brands – Bata, Provogue, Seagram, Esbeda, Woodland, Zara, Swaraj Fashions and Lifestyle
2. Sellers on e-commerce platforms like Flipkart and Amazon
3. International brands – Rasbeda, Burberry, Geigei, Asos, Steve Madden, Aldo, Mobil, Blakeley, Sanofi, Clarks and Debinims

Brand development is such an investment heavy endeavour that very few enterprises are attempting to create their own brands.

An exception is Made by Dharavi, started by two dynamic second-generation leather entrepreneurs. Made by Dharavi is built on a social enterprise model and specialises in handmade luxury leather products. Entrepreneurs Suresh Agawane and Rahul More's vision is to empower local leather workers by establishing their identity as artisans. They aim to appeal to the international elite who speak about 'conscious consumption' and make a mark in the ethical fashion business.

> By selling on Amazon and Flipkart, the profits are few and far in between. On Amazon, one can sell and advertise, so I am working towards building a brand so that I get better sales. So far, my Amazon experience has been that I can sell only if I have a large inventory, as there are lakhs of sellers for the same product. As a customer, you will open only the first 4–5 pages to buy a bag. Hence, not every one of the lakhs of sellers have visibility on Amazon. I had kept an inventory worth ₹10 lakh on Amazon but my daily sales weren't even ₹10,000. That is why, when I build my own brand, I will be able to sell not only on Amazon but also on other portals online so that I can diversify my market. The online and offline markets are very different. Amazon imposes courier charges and levies taxes, which reduce profits and increases the product cost compared to its quality. So, people tend to sell lower quality items at a cheaper price on e-commerce platforms. I know that the products I sell on Amazon are not the products I sell in retail stores (the latter is better quality). It is only the big brands that try to maintain some quality on Amazon. An additional issue on Amazon is that there are a lot of returns. For example, if I make a profit of ₹1,000, I still end up paying ₹250 as courier charges for 5 returned items. So, to sum it up, by selling on Amazon, the profits are barely any. And the Flipkart experience is similar. (Interview with Rehman Siddiqui, entrepreneur, Taiba Leathers, Dharavi, Mumbai, 20 April 2018)

Outsourcing, Subcontracting and Lack of Institutional Awareness

Forty-six per cent of the entrepreneurs regularly outsource work to smaller units and individual workers. Subcontracting is the only way they are able to survive and stay afloat, because hiring full-time workers is a liability. Thirty-five per cent of the entrepreneurs regularly undertake job work for big brands.

The field survey shows the dire need to create more awareness on institutions and their membership benefits (Table 9.1). Except for the Dharavi Leather Goods Manufacturers' Association (Figure 9.8), awareness of national-level

Table 9.1 Awareness and membership of industry organisations

Name of the organisation	Are you aware of this organisation? (%)			Are you a member/have you accessed any schemes from this organisation? (%)		
	Yes	*No*	*Maybe*	*Yes*	*No*	*Maybe*
Dharavi Leather Goods Manufacturers' Association	**51**	47	2	**16**	81	3
Central Leather Research Institute	**16**	81	3	**5**	90	5
Council for Leather Exports	**22**	74	4	**16**	81	3
Small Industries Development Bank of India	**16**	79	5	**5**	90	5
Footwear Design and Development Institute	**12**	84	4	**4**	92	4

Source: Author.

Figure 9.8 The Leather Goods Manufacturers' Association head office in Dharavi

Source: Author.

institutions was minimal. Less than 25 per cent of the entrepreneurs interviewed are aware of these institutions. Moreover, membership or association of any kind was less than 20 per cent. Thus, a serious evaluation and re-imagination of the relevance, value-add and entrepreneurial support provided by these institutions is needed.

Key Issues Highlighted by Entrepreneurs

For S. Dhavan and Sons, one of the larger exporters, timeliness of delivery and high quality of products matter, as Indian exporters struggle on these fronts. For Taiba Exports, a small exporter, a skilling centre for workers would be the most beneficial. For Made by Dharavi, a local upcoming brand, state support in creating a brand and selling in niche markets is of utmost importance.

The predominant sentiment among Dharavi's entrepreneurs is one of gloom. The leather market has had multiple consecutive setbacks. First, due to demonetisation – affecting cash flow. Second, due to the beef ban – a heavily politicised and divisive policy based on religion, affecting raw material availability. Third, due to GST – affecting profitability, with high GST rates imposed, delays in receiving refunds and practical difficulties in filing GST (Rashid 2015; Pinto 2017; Johari 2017).

For example, until 2016, 12 per cent as value-added tax (VAT) was levied on leather goods. In 2017, the initial GST rate on finished leather goods was 28 per cent. This led to a significant reduction in market size for entrepreneurs in Dharavi. Additionally, the GST on raw leather was 12 per cent. For example, a leather bag that would cost ₹1,000 earlier would now cost ₹1,280 after adding GST. This made it unaffordable to many customers. After multiple appeals from institutions and leaders within the leather industry, GST on finished goods was later reduced to 18 per cent.

Overall, the demand for leather-based products has been impacted and is extremely price sensitive (Figure 9.9). Leather goods are in the category of luxury goods that are not considered as mass consumption goods. Hence, buyers are mostly tourists and private corporations. The demand from tourists fluctuates drastically. As for corporate gifts, which were a huge trend earlier, especially in the pharmaceutical corporate industry, leather goods gifts have now gone out of fashion. Corporates prefer to gift food consumables and electronics during festive seasons. This has created a further shortage of domestic demand for the leather goods industry.

Figure 9.9 A buyer negotiates and bargains; as a result, the entrepreneur cuts prices, because every retail sale matters for his business to stay afloat

Source: Author.

Table 9.2 Entrepreneurs' view on the impact of international competition and national policy changes on their businesses

Has any of the following impacted your business adversely?	Yes (%)	No (%)	Cannot say (%)
Demonetisation	80	13	7
GST implementation	93	6	1
Beef ban	46	35	19
Competition from China	59	25	16

Source: Author.

Table 9.2 highlights that competition from China was a far lesser threat compared to unfavourable national level policy changes that were unilaterally implemented.

Mixed Signals to Entrepreneurs due to Policy Uncertainty on Redevelopment

The future of the cluster remains uncertain. Being located in the heart of Mumbai, there is an increasing pressure to redevelop Dharavi and relocate inhabitants. The Dharavi Redevelopment Plan does not recognise dual use of space, where the place of stay and the place of work are the same, thus substantially reducing costs. If redevelopment occurs by allocating residential buildings, leaving out the commercial aspects, then these manufacturing enterprises will be completely wiped out. One argument is that the real estate value of land is greater than the value of the output produced. Thus, the opportunity cost of the land is very high, making a case for the leather goods manufacturing to be relocated elsewhere. The future of Dharavi's leather cluster is closely tied to the state's ideas about land use planning. Informal settlements are an eye sore for city planners who imagine Mumbai as the next Shanghai, visualising the ideal city to be 'slum-free'. Thus, the future of the cluster is uncertain because any state support to the cluster would mean a step towards not only giving a boost to the leather industry located in Dharavi but also giving legitimacy to the rights of its dwellers. In the absence of state support for improving infrastructure, conducting vocational training, and acquiring new technologies, the cluster may not survive. Uprooting the cluster will lead to an irreversible loss of a repository of almost a century of rich knowledge, dense networks, able entrepreneurs and skilled artisans.

Policy Recommendations

The Head, Department of Leather Technology, Government Polytechnic, Mumbai, highlighted challenges such as obsolete machinery to train students and the leather sector not being an aspirational one to work in, due to the stigma associated with it.

> The machines we have are ones from the 1900s – from the time of the British Raj. Needless to say, students are not able to keep up with the latest technology in leather goods manufacturing as the machines are outdated. There is a dire need for better industry-oriented training and it cannot happen without having the latest technology.
>
> Another issue is that the Polytechnic's programmes are not publicised, rarely attracting good talent. In India where caste-based discrimination is prevalent, the stigma associated with working in the leather sector is still widespread. So, the youth don't want to make a career in the leather industry. Only students who do not get admissions anywhere else come to the polytechnic in the hope of finding a job, after course completion. (Interview, Head, Department of Leather Technology, Government Polytechnic, Mumbai, 22 June 2018)

The Regional Director, Council for Leather Exports, shared that the Indian leather industry is at the lower end of the pecking order in global value chains.

At international exhibitions and sales, India is merely looked at as an assembler of leather products. We are not perceived as an innovative country, creating new designs and cutting edge finished products. This is because our exporters lack creative thinking in design innovation. Our exporters do not invest in training human capital to create new products and designs.

Additionally, the exporters' directory and database is not updated regularly. There is incomplete and inaccurate information on the number of active exporters. Compared to rest of India, the western region needs an impetus in leather goods manufacturing. (Interview, CLE Western Region Head Office, Andheri, Mumbai, 24 April 2018)

Teething troubles on GST implementation were being recognised by officials:

GST implementation issues have affected exports and need to be resolved immediately. Systematic technological hurdles have led to delays in GST reimbursements and refunds. This is something we are working towards solving for. (Interview with the Assistant Commissioner GST, Mumbai, 30 May 2018)

Through my field survey, I found that connecting links and collaboration between entrepreneurs in Dharavi, government officials and policymakers were missing. For example, the Government Leather Polytechnic, the Council for Leather Exports and the Office of GST Commissioner were working in silos, rather than trying to find comprehensive solutions to what vocational training, export-promotion programmes and GST filing information sessions could help leather goods entrepreneurs in Dharavi. The complete disconnect between government policy and business practice was evident.

Policymakers must acknowledge that entrepreneurs and workers were making in Dharavi much before the 'Make in India' narrative and the Prime Minister's popular tropes of *aatmanirbharta* or self-reliance.

Based on their experiential business knowledge and acumen, entrepreneurs and not bureaucrats are better equipped to chalk out how small enterprises can grow.

My concluding reflections on policy implications of the chapter are summarised below:

1. The nature of production in Dharavi must be understood better. Particularly from the field survey and entrepreneur's in-depth interviews, it is evident that production is based on an intricate and locally dense network of relationships and commercial transactions among informal

enterprises in Dharavi. Exploration of any policy measure needs to be based on an understanding of this network.

2. Accurate estimates are needed of Dharavi's contribution to economic output and job creation in Mumbai. For this, the government will have to collect, organise and update data regularly, with a special focus on undocumented informal sector enterprises.

3. After taking cognizance of points 1 and 2, a relook and rethink of the Mumbai Development Plan 2034 and the Dharavi Redevelopment Plan is required. Dharavi's redevelopment needs to be re-evaluated keeping in mind the loss of inter-linkages between enterprises, learning networks and skilled labour.

   After undertaking the steps outlined in points 1, 2 and 3, in a situation where the state does not prove itself to be a threat to the survival of a vibrant industrial cluster, it may consider working towards the following points.

4. Substantial improvements in vocational and polytechnic institutes are required to provide relevant training. Industry-oriented vocational training will increase students' employability.

5. Enable and support leather businesses in Dharavi to obtain official cluster recognition (although, in practice, it is already a functional cluster). Allow registration under the micro, small and medium enterprises (MSME) cluster list. Cluster recognition will help firms get access to government schemes and benefits that currently exist, mainly on paper.

6. Provisions for affordable and timely credit through the much-publicised MUDRA scheme (Micro Units Development and Refinance Agency). Office bearers of the Leather Goods Manufacturers' Association (LIGMA) in Dharavi have been trying to access the MUDRA scheme for the last four years but have been unsuccessful. Formal sources of access to credit will enable entrepreneurs to take bank loans at low rates of interest. Instead of coming up with new schemes and policies, ensuring that existing ones such as MUDRA are implemented is important.

7. Technological upgradation and product design are essential for increasing the overall efficiency of enterprises in Dharavi and for helping them move up the global value chain. Better machinery through technological upgradation will help improve overall product quality and increase per output value. Designing facilities that are currently absent will help workers understand how high-value products for international markets are designed and made.

8. Eliminating intermediaries such as wholesale agents, negotiating fairer deals with e-commerce platforms such as Amazon and Flipkart and participating in international exhibitions will help entrepreneurs tap into newer markets.

9. Increasing the Council for Leather Exports's membership will give upcoming entrepreneurs a platform to tap into larger export markets. Domestically, it is important to grant licences regularly and keep accurately updating databases.

10. Last but not least, instead of homogenising the market, there is a need to focus on interlinkages between large exporters and small enterprises in Dharavi. Identifying lead exporting firms and supporting their growth will give more job work to small enterprises. This will strengthen the co-ordination and co-operation between large exporters and small enterprises. The result is greater collective efficiency and increasing returns (Schmitz 1999), making it a win–win for both.

Conclusion

In this chapter, I began with the question of declining labour intensity of India's manufacturing and the ways to enhance employment generation by supporting informal sector manufacturing enterprises. Taking the example of Dharavi, I have highlighted the historical context of manufacturing enterprises and the diverse states and religions its people come from. The case study of Dharavi's leather goods cluster shows how its entrepreneurs have leveraged skilled labour, locational advantages and indigenous innovation to not only survive shocks but also grow, both individually and collectively. For the last century, entrepreneurs in Dharavi have been doing things right. Their businesses have flourished, creating jobs for the marginalised urban poor, especially migrants. And hence their stories must be heard and documented, with the aspiration for a bottom up approach to policymaking. International media has been quick to celebrate the achievements of Dharavi's people (Saglio-Yatzimirsky 2013), but closer at home, plans are being made to uproot its industries and displace its people. It is important to recognise that affordable housing and job creation are precisely the two needs that Dharavi has fulfilled over the years, something that the state has failed at equitably achieving.

Bringing the production and employment mandate back into the government's development agenda (Amsden 1997; Andreoni and Chang 2016) is a pressing need and hence a need to re-look at labour-intensive enterprises like those located in the Dharavi cluster. Through the field research, I show that changes in national policies have often backfired for small enterprises. Instead of redeveloping Dharavi in a way that will displace and weaken its enterprises, the state needs to renew its lens and collect accurate data to fully understand Dharavi's economic contribution to Mumbai, Maharashtra and India. It ought to systematically improve vocational and training institutes, which have lost their relevance, and ensure that credit schemes are accessible. If the aspiration is to make India a global manufacturing hub, then we must enable small enterprises to survive, grow and move up the global value chain through sufficient state support.

Notes

1. It must be noted that as of May 2021, Dharavi has come into the spotlight during the Covid-19 crisis. This is because amidst a universal approach of work-from-home and self-isolation, there is lack of recognition that maintaining social distancing and washing hands is not possible in a densely populated area like Dharavi, with limited access to water and sanitation facilities.

   Moreover, the Covid-19 crisis has exposed large gaps in policymakers' lack of understanding of informal settlements, living conditions and small businesses functioning in informal settlements. It is clear that during a public health crisis, some sections of society need more support than others, and small, labour-intensive enterprises need state policy to survive during an economic and health crisis.

2. 'The biggest advantage of being located in Dharavi is that I get skilled workers easily. The shop rent in Dharavi is lower compared to the rest of Bombay. There are raw material shops and fittings wholesalers in Dharavi. Leather raw material for different products comes from different places: for shoes from Kanpur, for jackets from Chennai, for wallets from Kolkata. I have never had to visit any of these places to procure raw materials. For making one leather bag, you need the leather, chains, handles, foam, lining, pasting materials, etc. Everything is available in Dharavi. Even in the tiniest of rooms, 2–3 people can sit and work. I think there are about 1 lakh skilled leather workers in Dharavi' (interview with Suresh Agawane, entrepreneur, Made by Dharavi, Dharavi, Mumbai, 19 May 2018).

3. 'There is a lot of competition and I am a small player. Seventy per cent of customers want to purchase cheap, low-quality goods and only 30 per cent want good quality. I am trying to position myself in a medium-quality range. There are a lot of players trying to make low-quality products that are really cheap. So, I am trying to position myself as a medium-quality player with better designs so that I can keep some margin where there is high competition. Sellers are many and buyers becoming fewer. So, if you don't give a competitive price, the order will go to someone else' (interview with Rizwan Ahmed, entrepreneur, Sidrah Sales, Dharavi, Dharavi, Mumbai, 6 June 2018).

References

Amsden, Alice H. 1997. 'Bringing Production Back In: Understanding Government's Economic Role in Late Industrialization'. *World Development* 25 (4): 469–80.

Andreoni, Antonio and Ha-Joon Chang. 2016. 'Bringing Production and Employment Back into Development: Alice Amsden's Legacy for a New Developmentalist Agenda'. *Cambridge Journal of Regions, Economy and Society* 10 (1): 173–87.

Banerjee, Purna and C. Veeramani. 2015. 'Trade Liberalisation and Women's Employment Intensity: Analysis of India's Manufacturing Industries'. Working Paper, WP-2015-018, Indira Gandhi Institute of Development Research, Mumbai.

Bardhan, P. K. 1980. 'Interlocking Factor Markets and Agrarian Development: A Review of Issues.' *Oxford Economic Papers* 32: 82–98.

Caniëls, M. C., and H. A. Romijn. 2003. 'Agglomeration Advantages and Capability Building in Industrial Clusters: The Missing Link'. *Journal of Development Studies* 39 (3): 129–54.

Damodaran, Sumangala and Pallavi Mansingh. 2008. 'Leather Industry in India'. Working Paper, Center for Education and Communication, New Delhi.

Department of Industrial Policy and Promotion. 2017. *Leather Sector Achievements Report.* New Delhi: Department of Industrial Policy and Promotion, Ministry of Commerce and Industry.

Engqvist, J. H., and M. Lantz. 2009. *Dharavi: Documenting Informalities.* New Delhi: Academic Foundation.

Gulrajani, M. 2006. 'Technological Capabilities in Industrial Clusters: A Case Study of Textile Cluster in Northern India'. *Science, Technology and Society* 11 (1): 149–90.

IANS. 2017. 'Slaughterhouse Ban to Hit Leather Goods Industry, Impact Make in India.' *Business Standard,* 1 April.

Johari, Aarefa. 2017. 'Note Ban, Beef Ban and GST: Dharavi's Leather Industry Braces for a Triple Blow to Business'. *Scroll.in,* 3 July.

Kennedy, Lorraine. 2004. 'Local Assets and Liabilities for Economic Performance and Social Mobility in the Palar Valley Leather Industry'. In *Industrialisation and Socio-Cultural Change in the Tannery Belt of the Palar Valley,* edited by Lorraine Kennedy, 31–52. Pondicherry: French Institute of Pondicherry.

Kotwal, Ashok and Pranob Sen. 2019. 'What Should We Do about the Indian Economy? A Wide Angled Perspective'. The India Forum, October 2019.

Knorringa, Peter. 1999. 'Agra: An Old Cluster Facing the New Competition'. *World Development* 27 (9): 1587–604.

Marshall, A. 1920. *Principles of Economics,* 8th ed. London: Macmillan.

Mehrotra, S., J. Parida, S. Sinha and A. Gandhi. 2014. 'Explaining Employment Trends in the Indian Economy: 1993–94 to 2011–12'. *Economic and Political Weekly* 49 (32): 49–57.

Nagaraj, R. 2017. 'Economic Reforms and Manufacturing Sector Growth: Need for Reconfiguring the Industrialisation Model'. *Economic and Political Weekly* 52 (2): 61–68.

Pias, Jesim. 2006a. 'Some Features of Migration and Labour Mobility in the Leather Accessories Manufacture in India: A Study of the Informal Sector Industry in Dharavi, Mumbai'. Working paper no. 2006/06, Institute for Studies in Industrial Development, New Delhi.

———. 2006b. 'Wages and Earnings in Leather Accessories Manufacturing in India: An Analysis of the Industry in Mumbai'. *The Indian Journal of Labour Economics* 49 (4): 697–714.

Planning Commission. 2011. *Report of Working Group on Leather and Leather Products: Twelfth Five Year Plan Period (2012–17)*. New Delhi: Department of Industrial Policy and Promotion, Ministry of Commerce and Industry.

Pyke, F., and W. Sengenberger. 1992. *Industrial Districts and Local Economic Regeneration*. Geneva: International Institute for Labour Studies.

Pinto, Viveat Susan. 2016. 'Leather Goods Hub at Dharavi Struggles to Hide Cash Crunch Pain'. *Business Standard*, 16 December.

Rashid, Omar. 2015. 'Beef Ban Hits Dharavi Leather Traders Hard'. *The Hindu*, 14 June.

Roy, Tirthankar. 1994. 'Foreign Trade and the Artisans in Colonial India: A Study of Leather'. *The Indian Economic & Social History Review* 31 (4): 461–90.

Saglio-Yatzimirsky, M. 2013. *Dharavi: From Mega-Slum to Urban Paradigm*. New Delhi: Routledge India.

Schmitz, H. 1999. 'Collective Efficiency and Increasing Returns'. *Cambridge Journal of Economics* 23 (4): 465–83.

Schmitz, H., and K. Nadvi. 1999. 'Clustering and Industrialization: Introduction'. *World Development* 27 (9): 1503–14.

Sharma, K. 2000. *Rediscovering Dharavi: Stories from Asia's Largest Slum*. New Delhi: Penguin Books.

Tewari, M. 1999. 'Successful Adjustment in Indian Industry: The Case of Ludhiana's Woolen Knitwear Cluster'. *World Development* 27 (9): 1651–71.

Tewari, Meenu and Poonam Pillai. 2005. 'Global Standards and the Dynamics of Environmental Compliance in India's Leather Industry'. *Oxford Development Studies* 33 (2): 245–67.

The Economist. 2005. 'Inside the Slums: Light in the Darkness'. 29 January. Available at https://www.economist.com/asia/2005/01/27/inside-the-slums.

———. 2007. 'Urban Poverty in India: A Flourishing Slum'. 22 December. Available at https://www.economist.com/christmas-specials/2007/12/19/a-flourishing-slum.

Varman, R. and M. Chakrabarti. 2011. 'Notes from Small Industry Clusters: Making Sense of Knowledge and Barriers to Innovation.' *AI & Society* 26 (4): 393–415.

Yardley, Jim. 2011. 'In One Indian Slum, Misery, Work, Politics and Hope'. *New York Times*, 28 December.

CHAPTER 10

Growth Performance, Competitiveness and Employment in MSMEs

A Case Study of the Rajkot Engineering Cluster

DINESH AWASTHI AND AMITA SHAH

Introduction

The last three decades or so have often been labelled as the decades of 'jobless growth' in India. The employment content of growth has decelerated over the years. It has been stark in the organised manufacturing sector (Papola 2014). The share of the manufacturing sector in gross domestic product (GDP) still hovers around 16 per cent, up merely by 0.57 per cent during the last 10 years. The slow growth was ascribed to the stifling and over-regulated policy framework. The political dispensation in the 1990s realised these constraints and started dismantling some of the archaic rules and regulations, though at a snail's pace.

Realising that the growth of the manufacturing sector is vital to generate sustainable and decent employment, the Government of India envisaged the manufacturing sector to contribute 25 per cent, up from the current 16.57 per cent, to the GDP and create 100 million jobs by 2022, under its 'Make in India' campaign, announced on 25 September 2014. As per the campaign, both domestic and foreign entrepreneurs are encouraged to set up their manufacturing facilities in India, produce and trade globally, besides catering to the vast Indian market. Such investments, it is envisioned, will create incomes and jobs for millions of youth, besides augmenting exports and foreign exchange earnings.

Within the manufacturing sector, the track record of organised large-scale industries in creating employment, as stated earlier, has been somewhat disappointing. The performance of the micro, small and medium enterprises

(MSME) sector in this regard has been noteworthy (Gade 2018). MSMEs have continued to employ a larger number of semi-skilled and un-skilled workers, over the years, compared to the large-scale enterprises. Not only in India but elsewhere too, such as in the USA, small and medium enterprises (SMEs) have been generating more jobs than the large ones (Katua 2014; United Capital 2019). In India, a characteristic feature of the development of SMEs has been their emergence and growth in a clustered form (Awasthi 2004).

Industrial Clusters: A Road to Competitiveness

Both developed and developing countries have witnessed the congregated emergence of SMEs, widely known as 'industrial clusters'. From Marshal (1974 [1890]) to Porter (1990), industrial clusters have travelled a long way. Taking a cue from the Marshallian 'industrial districts', Porter (1998: 78) defines a cluster as

> geographic concentrations of interconnected companies and institutions in a particular field. Clusters encompass an array of linked industries and other entities ... [that] include, for example, suppliers of specialised inputs such as components, machinery, and services ... complementary products ... skills, technologies, or common inputs. Finally, many clusters include governmental and other institutions – such as universities, standards-setting agencies, think tanks, vocational training providers, and trade associations – that provide specialised training, education, information, research, and technical support.

These spatial concentrations give rise to various kinds of economic and non-economic inter-firm linkages (Shah 1994) due to their social embeddedness (Humphrey and Schmitz 1995). Such linkages have also been found to improve efficiency and global competitiveness of SMEs because of the economies of scale and scope (Nadvi and Schmitz 1994). Operational dynamics of clusters is characterised by a constant flow of innovations and knowledge, better access to market intelligence, flexible specialisation, social embeddedness and trust backed up by collective actions and various kinds of externalities resulting in lower transaction costs (Piore and Sabel 1984; Trigilia 1989) and also higher degree of competitiveness (Tendler 1987; Schmitz 1989). Industry associations, also known as business member organisations, also play an important role in promoting collective efficiency in clusters (Schmitz 1999).

It has further been observed that the firms operating in clusters have better resilience to policy changes than those operating in isolation (Krishna and Awasthi 1994). A few studies also indicate that SMEs working in clusters tend to perform better in terms of productivity than the stand-alone SMEs (Awasthi 2004; Branco and Lopes 2013). It has been often argued that micro and small enterprises suffer more because of their isolation rather than their size (Bagchi 1999). The clusters mitigate these limitations. It is expected of the cluster enterprises to grow faster, also leading to better employment opportunities. Moreover, a large proportion of SMEs has historically been operating in clusters in India. For example, as per the estimates based on the third census of small-scale industries, 80.73 per cent units employing 76.29 per cent workers, with 65.70 per cent investment and 62.69 per cent output, were found to be operating in 2,896 clusters in India (Awasthi 2005).[1]

Based on these discussions, we flag three facts: (*a*) the growth of the manufacturing sector is the key to generating sustainable and decent employment, (*b*) within the manufacturing sector, SMEs have historically generated and are likely to generate more employment and (*c*) most of the SMEs operate in clusters. Therefore, any policy focusing on industry for creating sustainable employment must focus on industrial clusters as well, besides other factors.

The Focus

The specific focus of this chapter is to explore the role of clusters in generating employment and inducing collective efficiency and competitiveness among MSMEs. For this, we studied the Rajkot engineering cluster, which is one of the largest engineering clusters in the country, as a case. The chapter attempts to address three sets of questions:

1. What has been the growth trajectory of the Rajkot engineering cluster in terms of overall productivity, growth, employment, technology and so on?
2. What are the operational dynamics of the cluster, focusing on subcontracting, competition, social embeddedness and role of networks?
3. What is the impact of recent policy pronouncements such as demonetisation and the goods and services tax (GST) on the cluster enterprises? What are the major operational and policy-related bottlenecks? And what are the policy imperatives?

The Locale and the Coverage

The Rajkot engineering cluster consists of a large number of engineering sub-sectors such as foundries, diesel engines, machine tools, auto parts and components, bearings, electric pumps, kitchenware, hardware, electrical and electronic items, and so on. Together, the number of engineering SMEs in Rajkot is about 10,000, which employ close to 200,000 workers, with a turnover of about ₹150 billion.[2]

The study covers a sample of 176 MSMEs consisting of about 20–30 enterprises from each of the select six engineering sub-sectors, namely foundries, diesel engine, bearings, auto parts and components, machine tools and electric pumps, covered in the study. They account for almost 80 per cent of the engineering firms in Rajkot. Besides, owners of 10 large enterprises, 1–2 from each segment, were also interviewed to get a macro perspective. Only those firms which had been in operation for at least five years were covered.

Profile of Sample Enterprises

The sample provides a reasonably large degree of diversity. Over 80 per cent of the sample enterprises are either proprietary or partnership firms. While 21 firms are between 5 and 10 years old, another 79 firms are between 10 and 25 years. In all, 152 units were registered under the Factories Act, 1948, and the remaining 24 were unregistered (Table 10.1). Of the total 176 sample enterprises, 42 (24 per cent) firms are micro, 115 (65 per cent) are small, and the remaining 19 (11 per cent) are medium-sized enterprises. In terms of investment in plant and machinery,[3] 42 firms had invested up to ₹2.5 million (micro enterprises) and 115 firms had investment between ₹2.5 million and ₹50 million. In all, 19 firms are in the category of medium enterprises with investment above ₹50 million. With regard to total employment, 24 (13.7 per cent) firms employ up to 9 workers. Only 5 firms employ more than 100 workers. The major concentration is around the employment classes of 10–25 workers and 25–50 workers. In terms of sales, 33 firms (all these 18.8 per cent are micro enterprises) had sales below ₹5 million in the year 2017–18. Sales of another 84 firms were between ₹5 million and ₹20 million, whereas 7 firms sold over ₹75 million in the same year (Table 10.1).

Table 10.1 Characteristics of enterprises

Sr. No.	Characteristics	Number	Percentage
1.	**Caste background of entrepreneurs**		
i.	Patel	130	73.9
ii.	Vaishya	13	7.4
iii.	Carpenter	9	5.1
iv.	Blacksmith	6	3.4
v.	Rajput	3	1.7
vi.	Brahmin	4	2.3
vii.	Tailor	6	3.4
viii.	Others (cobbler, mason and Ahir)	5	2.8
	Total firms	176	100.0
2.	**Engineering sub-sectors covered**		
i.	Machine tools	39	22.16
ii.	Foundry	29	16.48
iii.	Submersible pumps	33	18.75
iv.	Bearing	18	10.23
v.	Diesel engine	27	15.34
vi.	Auto parts and components	28	15.91
	Total	176	100.00
3.	**Nature of ownership**		
i.	Proprietary	74	42.00
ii.	Partnership	76	43.20
iii.	Private limited	25	14.20
iv.	Public limited	1	0.60
	Total	176	100.00
4.	**Year of establishment**		
i.	Before 1970	12	6.80
ii.	1970–1980	25	14.20
iii.	1981–1990	28	15.90
iv.	1990–2000	60	34.10
v.	2000–2010	42	23.90
vi.	After 2010	9	5.10
	Total	176	100.00
5.	**Nature of unit**		
i.	Registered under Factories Act, 1948	152	86.37
ii.	Unregistered	24	13.63
	Total	176	100.00

Contd.

Table 10.1 *contd.*

Sr. No.	Characteristics	Number	Percentage
6.	Investment size plant and machinery (₹ lakh)		
i.	Up to 25	42	23.90
ii.	25–50	10	5.70
iii.	50–100	33	18.80
iv.	100–200	37	21.00
v.	200–500	35	19.90
vi.	500–750	10	5.70
vii.	More than 750	9	5.1
	Total number of units	176	100.00
	Average investment (₹ lakh)	45.6	
7.	Size of sales turnover (₹ lakh)		
i.	< 25	13	7.4
ii.	25–50	20	11.4
iii.	50–100	35	19.9
iv.	100–200	49	27.8
v.	200–300	21	11.93
vi.	300–500	19	10.79
vii.	500–750	12	6.8
viii.	> 750	7	4.0
	Total units	176	100.00
	Average turnover (₹ lakh)	28.38	
8.	Employment size (nos.)		
i.	1–5	4	2.3
ii.	6–9	20	11.4
iii.	10–25	54	30.7
iv.	25–50	60	34.1
v.	50–100	33	18.8
vi.	100+	5	2.8
	Total units	176	100.0
	Average employment	36.03	
9.	Size by export (₹ lakh)		
i.	<10	4	9.80
ii.	10–25	6	14.60
iii.	25–50	7	17.10
iv.	50–100	8	19.50
v.	100–200	7	17.10
vi.	> 200	9	22.00
	Total firms	41	100.00
	Average exports (₹ lakh)	301	

Source: Author's field survey.
Note: 1 lakh = 100,000.

Emergence of the Rajkot Engineering Cluster and the Role of Technology

Clusters tend to go through a life cycle. They emerge, grow and decay. The primary reason for this decay has often been ascribed to technological obsolescence (Sood and Pal 2004). However, a few clusters reinvent, adopt a new technological trajectory and pursue a new growth path. The Rajkot engineering cluster can be considered as a reasonably successful example of this kind. The emergence of engineering industries in Rajkot dates back to the late 1930s. Many artisan-based micro enterprises were operating in Rajkot, manufacturing agricultural tools and equipment, during this period. They were also engaged in the maintenance and repair of Lister Petter diesel engines that were being imported from England. However, during the Second World War, it became difficult to import diesel engines and spares.

This triggered the development of the Rajkot engineering industries. The initial entrants were diesel engine parts manufacturers and foundries. They also started sourcing their parts and components from within Rajkot. Thus, the base for the diesel engine industry was laid. It emerged as a major cluster of diesel engines in the country during the 1960s and the 1970s. Of the 500,000 engines being produced in the country, close to 300,000 were being manufactured in Rajkot, but using almost 100-year-old designs of the Lister (slow speed) and the Petter (high speed) engines. Therefore, though a flourishing cluster, Rajkot was considered as technologically weak (Basant 1997). However, due to competition from China, the focus of the government on energy efficiency, withdrawal of subsidies in the late 1980s and technological obsolescence, the industry witnessed a significant downturn during the late 1980s and 1990s.

This decay led to significant diversification of the industrial base of Rajkot to auto parts and components, computerised numerical control (CNC) machines, bearings, electric pumps, and so on. This became possible because the basic skills and raw material required were not very different from those used to manufacture diesel engines. The Rajkot industry had gained substantial experience in handling pig iron, backed up by close to 600 foundries which had taken root while supporting diesel engine manufacturing. Since there was a major thrust on new-age industries such as CNC machines, auto parts, defence, and aerospace and on exports, the quality became the prime concern. These products required more technology content to meet the complexity of products and quality standards.

Moreover, since the production in Rajkot is primarily being organised through subcontracting, it became necessary for the subcontractors also to upgrade their technology. As a result, in Rajkot, technology has been upgraded across the value chain. Rajkot is no more an exporter to only the Gulf and African countries. Its export destinations now include North America, Europe, Japan and even China.

Recent Growth Performance of the Rajkot Engineering Cluster

The growth performance in terms of investment in plant and machinery and total investment (net of land and building), output (gross sales turnover), employment and factor productivity has been analysed for the last five-year period, from 2012–13 to 2017–18. Without any exception, all the six engineering segments have grown faster than the national average (Table 10.2). Overall, the sector has registered a robust growth of a little over 17 per cent compared to 4.3 per cent at the all-India level. Auto parts topped the growth chart with the compound annual growth rate (CAGR) of 23.47 per cent between 2012–13 and 2017–18 compared to 18.3 per cent at the all-India level. There seems to be one-to-one relationship between productivity and growth in sales (Table 10.2). Overall, it could be stated that engineering firms in the Rajkot cluster are performing better than the national average across the sub-sectors.

Subcontracting, Key to Success

It is worth mentioning that the engineering cluster is vertically integrated. Subcontracting is the pivot around which all the production activities are organised in Rajkot. The manufacturers are primarily assemblers who outsource most of their tasks, except final assembly, labelling and inspection. Each of the manufacturers across the segments manages a large supply chain of vendors. Subcontracting has been a significant part of the industrial organisation in Rajkot since the early 1940s. It is considered as a major source of efficiency, competitiveness, survival and growth in the cluster. It provides the base for cost reduction, spreading the risk and optimum utilisation of various levels for skills. The emergence of the diesel engine industry in Rajkot and the subsequent diversification, to a great extent, owes to subcontracting. Our field investigation indicates that close to 79 per cent firms outsource their low-end 'job work' such as casting, machining, grinding, turning, washing/rough work, assembling, and so on. Besides outsourcing firms, there are 90 subcontracting

Table 10.2 Sectoral annual compound rates of growth 2012–13 and 2017–18

Sr. No.	Sectors	Annual compound growth rates (%)					Number of firms	National average annual growth (%)
		Sales	Investment in plant and machinery	Total capital investment	Employment	Factor productivity		
1.	Machine tools	20.72	3.89	1.78	5.54	16.69	39	14.00[1]
2.	Foundry	18.86	2.24	0.86	5.33	15.32	30	12.00[2]
3.	Pumps	12.96	3.59	1.42	6.14	8.70	33	10.00[3]
4	Bearings	21.47	3.55	1.80	6.04	17.13	18	4.30[4]
5	Diesel engine	4.91	2.76	1.94	5.52	0.82	27	NA.
6	Auto parts	23.48	2.50	1.054	5.70	19.47	29	18.3[5]
	Average growth	17.05	3.11	1.52	5.69	13.02	-	4.3,[6]
	Number of firms	176	176	176	176	176	176	-

Sources: [1] Indian Brand Equity Foundation (2017: 39).

[2] India Brand Equity Foundation (2018).

[3] 'Pump Industry in India: An Overview', available at accessed on 19 June 2019.[4]

[5] India Brand Equity Foundation, 'Auto Component Industry in India', available at https://www.ibef.org/industry/autocomponents-india.aspx, accessed on 19 June 2019. [6]This is the overall growth rate of gross value added between 2012 and 2018 in the engineering industry in India. See India Brand Equity Foundation, 'Manufacturing Sector in India', available at https://www.ibef.org/industry/manufacturing-sector-india.aspx, (accessed on 19 June 2019.

firms, including job-work units. Of the total, 33 firms are both subcontractors and outsourcing firms. Of the 105 firms that outsource, close to 81 per cent are registered under the Factories Act. Similarly, 65 per cent of subcontracting firms are registered. In the case of unregistered firms also, 75 per cent do outsourcing, and a little over 58 per cent are subcontractors (Table 10.3).

Often, subcontracting refers to inter-firm relationships between small and large enterprises, wherein the large firms procure parts, components and other services from the small firms (Nagaraj 1984). It is generally construed as a one-way transaction. However, Rajkot appears to be at a variance where two-way relationships are widespread. It is not uncommon to find a micro enterprise outsourcing its work to another micro or even small enterprise. Even a relatively large (a medium-sized) firm could operate as a subcontractor, sometimes to a smaller firm. Moreover, most of the studies look at subcontracting as a 'formal–informal sector' phenomenon. For example, a study by Ramaswamy (1999) and a more recent study by Sahu (2010), besides many other studies, focus on this duality. Once again, Rajkot is an exception. It belies the general notion that informal or small firms are pushed to undertake only job work and can seldom outsource (Table 10.3).

The extent of outsourcing is quite large. On average, a 35 per cent share of sales turnover, ranging between 5 and 35 per cent, is outsourced. As many as

Table 10.3 Number of firms engaged in outsourcing and/or subcontracting

Sr. No.	Nature of unit		Outsourcing*		Subcontracting firms*	
			No.	%	No.	%
i.	Registered	Yes	75	80.64	65	65.00
ii.	Unregistered	Yes	30	75.00	25	35.00
	Total		**105**	**100.00**	**90**	**100.00**
i.	Registered	No	18	19.35	35	58.14
ii.	Unregistered	No	10	25.00	18	41.86
	Total		**28**	**100.00**	**53**	**100.00**
i.	Total	Yes	105	78.94	90	62.94
ii.	Total	No	28	21.06	53	37.06
	Total firms		**133**	**100.00**	**143**	**100.00**

Source: Author's field survey.

Note: *33 firms do both outsourcing as well as sub-contracting, and 14 firms do not enter into outsourcing or subcontracting.

65 firms outsource between 25 and 50 per cent of their sales. Only 4 relatively larger firms outsource more than 75 per cent of their sales to subcontractors (Table 10.4). These are primarily assembling firms. Unlike outsourcing, the proportion of sales from subcontracting appears to be much larger. As many as 47 per cent of firms generate more than 75 per cent of their revenues by subcontracting.

Our inquiry as to why firms outsource and what determines the 'make or buy' decision indicated that, in the view of about 77 per cent respondents, it made more economic sense to outsource. It released resources for higher-end use on the one hand and avoided labour-related issues on the other. The specialisation that subcontractors develop over time (Adam Smith's [1776/2003] pin example is very appropriate here) possibly leads to lower costs than an outsourcing firm would entail.

Usually, the outsourcing firms have the final say in the process and dictate production relations and terms of contracts, including pricing. Paying about 7–10 per cent over and above the cost to their subcontractors is the norm. Most of the subcontractors (suppliers) are satisfied with this arrangement and have long-standing relationships with their buyers. Some of the subcontractors have relationships with their principals as enduring as 30 years.

The analysis brings out four key points: (*a*) the process of subcontracting is very deep-rooted in Rajkot, (*b*) it is not unidirectional (from large to small) but all-pervading, (*c*) it is not necessarily primarily an informal sector phenomenon and (*d*) the subcontracting relationship is based on sound economic logic and not necessarily exploitative, as is usually observed in the literature.

Labour, Employment and Skills

As stated earlier, the employment grew at over 5.69 per cent per annum between 2012–13 and 2017–18, much higher than the growth in investments. Healthy and cordial industrial relations in Rajkot seem to have played a significant role. It is worth mentioning that Rajkot does not have any active trade union, despite a very large number of firms and the considerable number of workers. There is virtually no strike or lockout. There is an ecosystem of overall trust between employers and workers, including a large number of migrants. For example, most of the foundries have a majority of workers from Uttar Pradesh (UP) and Bihar. We were not surprised to find that a majority (about 60 per cent) of the 6,364 workers, in the sample firms, belong to other states, with the predominance of Bihar (23 per cent) and UP (21.35 per cent). Other states

Table 10.4 The proportion of outsourcing as a share of sales turnover

Sr. no.	Share of sales spent on outsourcing		Sales turnover 2017–18 (₹ lakh)							Total
			25	25–50	50–100	100–200	200–500	500–750	> 750	
1	<10	No.	1	1	2	1	2	1	1	9
		%	20.00	7.70	10.50	4.00	8.00	8.30	16.70	8.60
2	10–25	No.	0	3	2	7	3	0	2	17
		%	0.00	23.10	10.50	28.00	12.00	0.00	33.30	16.20
3	25–35	No.	2	2	9	8	9	6	1	37
		%	40.00	15.40	47.40	32.00	36.00	50.00	16.70	35.20
4	35–50	No.	0	7	5	5	8	3	0	28
		%	0.00	53.80	26.30	20.00	32.00	25.00	0.00	26.70
5	50–75	No.	2	0	1	3	2	0	2	10
		%	40.00	0.00	5.30	12.00	8.00	0.00	33.30	9.50
6	> 75	No.	0	0	0	1	1	2	0	4
		%	0.00	0.00	0.00	4.00	4.00	16.70	0.00	3.80
	Total	No.	5	13	19	25	25	12	6	105
		%	100.00	100.00	100.00	100.00	100.00	100.00	100.00	100.00

Source: Author's field survey.

Note: 1 lakh = 100,000.

represented are Haryana, Madhya Pradesh, Maharashtra, Jharkhand, Orissa and Rajasthan. The main reasons for preferring outside workers are their being hardworking, better skilled, regular, disciplined and docile. Recently, the Government of Gujarat has a policy that any enterprise which has received any benefit from the state government is expected to employ at least 85 per cent workers who are domicile of Gujarat. The respondents felt that such a move would cripple the industry, as local persons are neither available nor willing to take up a job that requires hard physical labour. A few industry associations have already taken up the issue with the government.

There is an acute shortage of skilled and semi-skilled workers in Rajkot. It was corroborated by 169 of the 176 respondents. A four-hour overtime is the norm. Most workers are paid on a piece-rate basis, which they prefer. It is not uncommon to find notice boards outside the factory gates announcing vacancies for positions such as fitters, machinists and turners. The dominant mode of skill development is on-the-job training. Close to 99 per cent of the respondents claimed to have been providing in-house training to workers. The so-called training institutions like the Industrial Training Institutes, polytechnics and even engineering colleges are not seen to be up to the mark, as they are not producing 'industry-ready' workforce. They were asked, if there was indeed such a deep crisis, why did the industry not come forward to set up skill development facilities to train potential worker as per its requirements? The answer was that it required a substantial investment which was difficult for the industry to meet. Moreover, 'where is the time with us for this' was stated by many. In this direction, the initiative taken by the Gujarat Industrial Development Corporation (GIDC) Lodhika Industrial Association is worth mentioning. It has recently added a Skill Development Centre to its portfolio, with a facility to train 300 technicians at a time. However, in the long run, extensive training facilities will need to be created by the government to bridge this demand and supply gap. The respondents also argued that they also needed several finishing schools, at least one tool room, a design school and testing facilities, as it was not possible for them to create this kind of infrastructure.

The above discussion indicates that (*a*) harmonious industrial relations have contributed significantly to the overall growth momentum of employment as also of the cluster and (*b*) shortage of skilled and semi-skilled workers could jeopardise this momentum, unless some concrete steps are taken sooner rather than later.

Anatomy of Markets and Competition

Firms in Rajkot experienced positive growth in sales, with increased demand from both old and new customers, besides exports. The number of exporting firms increased from 27 (15.3 per cent) in 2012–13 to 44 (25 per cent) by 2017–18. The major exporting destinations have been about 30–35 countries that include the USA, Germany, France, Latin America, Gulf countries, South East Asia, China, South Asian countries, African countries and Australia. In effect, engineering firms in Rajkot export to all continents of the world.

The field data also suggest that competition has increased during the last three to five years. Close to 81 per cent respondents felt that (*a*) the industry is facing tougher competition now than before and (*b*) it has also affected them adversely due to pressure on prices and the consequent decline in profitability. This has led to the adoption of various strategies to face the competition. The most important strategy has been to improve the quality of their products, followed by reducing the cost by improving production efficiency (Table 10.5). As mentioned earlier, clusters are characterised by intense inter-firm competition. As expected, 96 (66.66 per cent) of the 144 respondents stated that major competition emanates from within the cluster. Only 27 (18.75 per cent) felt that they have to compete with international firms.

Is China a Threat?

During our interactions with larger enterprises, we were given to understand that China is not a threat, though it remains their competitor. Of course,

Table 10.5   Strategies to face competition*

Sr. No.	Strategies to face competition	No.	%
1.	Diversified/introduce new product lines	29	20.42
2.	Improved quality	100	70.42
3.	Cost reduction	95	66.90
4.	Reduced price	92	64.80
5.	Gave higher commission/discounts	15	10.60
6.	More advertisement/publicity	18	12.76
7.	Punctuality in delivery	60	42.30
8.	Increased personal contacts with buyers	23	16.20
9.	Any other	3	2.11
	Total respondent	**142**	**100.00**

Source: Author's field survey.

Note: * Multiple responses.

most of them accepted that China has higher production and technological capabilities. However, in the last 15 years or so, Rajkot engineering firms have been able to cope with Chinese competition, especially in the global markets. It is primarily because of (*a*) the lower labour cost, as wages in China have been steadily rising (the average wages in China are about US$800–US$1,000 a month, compared to US$200–US$300 per month in India), (*b*) the cost of environmental compliances having gone up substantially in China, compared to India, (*c*) indigenous dexterity, core engineering skills and designing ingenuity that make Rajkot unique and (*d*) India being way ahead in supplying customised products that require high engineering skills and orders that are smaller in quantity though the Chinese invariably gain in terms of costs and prices of products that are mass-produced. India's advantage is in niche products. However, the cost of capital, power and land is far cheaper in China. These together give them a certain edge over India. Moreover, government support to Chinese firms is also substantial, especially in exports, technology development and skill development. Infrastructural investment by the Chinese government is also at a much larger scale than in India.

Collaboration, Networking and Social Capital

Besides intense competition, another essential characteristic of a cluster is the high interdependence among firms, leading to a significant degree of co-operation. This is greatly facilitated by social capital, emanating mostly from caste/community-based networks. It is often argued that since economic activities are mostly socially embedded, it facilitates building and nurturing contacts that promote trust and offer various kinds of economic and non-economic externalities (see Basant 1997; Awasthi 1997; Akbar 1997; Swaminathan and Jeyaranjan 1997; Colman 1988; Portes and Landolt 2000; Anderson and Miller 2002; and Nee, Liu and Della Posta 2017, among others).

Such relationships have evolved in Rajkot due to family ties, friendships, being neighbours or of the same religion, or membership in the same industry association and/or social clubs. Such linkages not only support a person at an individual level but extend far and beyond, through referrals (Granovetter 1985; Burt 1992). These informal ties have benefitted MSMEs in Rajkot enormously through information sharing, establishment of business linkages (buyer or supplier relations) and access to capital. However, our fieldwork indicated that it is becoming less important in content and practice. Enterprises have become more formal over time, and commercial interests now play a significant role. The implementation of the GST has further accelerated the process of formalisation of businesses ties.

How does this social capital formation take place? What are the routes of social networks? It was noted that among Patels (the dominant community), family ties emerged as the most crucial route to the formation of social capital, followed by the community. Of course, acquaintance, the reputation of the other party and the neighbourhood in terms of their firms' location also play an important role in developing and nurturing the networks (Table 10.6).

Industry Association as a Platform for Networking

Industry associations have been an important source of networking and collective actions. In this regard, Rajkot has a very vibrant ecosystem. As per the field survey, there are 27 active associations. Of all, the Rajkot Engineering Association (REA) is the largest association of the engineering sector which works as an umbrella association. The industry associations offer mainly (*a*) real services such as legal advice, information on technology and markets, raw material supply and capacity building programmes, (*b*) infrastructure support such as the creation of common facility centres (testing centres) or pollution control-related common facilities and general improvement in infrastructure, (*c*) governance support such as sorting out disputes among the members and (*d*) training and capacity building programmes and/or trade fairs. However, during our interactions, we observed a general refrain that associations work for office bearers and not for the members.

Strengths of the Cluster and Key Issues

Given the advantages of operating in a cluster, one would expect that if a firm operated elsewhere, it would lose out on the collective efficiency. An overwhelming majority (90 per cent) of the respondents opined that they would not have been able to perform as well had they been operating from elsewhere. They can perform and compete globally primarily because of the advantages of being in a cluster. Rajkot, they emphasised, provides strong backward and forward linkages, sizeable local market, local availability of machinery, peaceful and skilled workforce, social capital, and so on, which are the key strengths of the cluster (Table 10.7). Soft infrastructure such as several universities, a District Industries Centre, many legal and accounting firms, traders and raw material suppliers further add to the ecosystem of Rajkot.

Table 10.6 Sources of social capital

Sr. No.	Sources*	No. and %	Castes								Total
			Patel	Vaishya	Carpenter	Blacksmith	Rajput	Brah -min	Tailor	Others**	
1	Acquaintance	No.	63	5	5	4	1	3	4	1	86
		%	52.90	62.50	100.00	66.70	100.00	75.00	80.00	100.00	57.71
2	Family and friend	No.	75	4	1	1	1	0	0	0	82
		%	63.03	50.00	20.00	16.67	100.00	0.00	0.00	0.00	55.03
3	Reputation of quality	No.	59	6	2	4	0	3	4	0	78
		%	49.58	75.00	40.00	66.67	0.00	75.00	80.00	0.00	52.34
4	Own community	No.	66	2	1	1	1	2	0	0	73
		%	55.46	25.00	20.00	16.67	100.00	50.00	0.00	0.00	48.99
5	From factory in neighbourhood	No.	38	4	4	4	1	1	3	1	56
		%	31.93	50.00	80.00	66.67	100.00	25.00	60.00	100.00	37.58
6	From my village	No.	16	1	1	1	0	2	0	0	21
		%	13.45	12.50	20.00	16.67	0.00	50.00	0.00	0.00	14.09
7	Others	No.	2	0	0	0	0	0	0	0	2
		%	1.68	0.00	0.00	0.00	0.00	0.00	0.00	0.00	1.34
	Total	No.	119	8	5	6	1	4	5	1	149
		%	79.87	5.37	3.36	4.03	0.67	2.68	3.36	0.67	100.00

Source: Author's field survey.

Note: *Multiple responses; ** Others include cobblers, Ahirs, mason, and so on.

Table 10.7 Advantages of operating in Rajkot engineering cluster*

Sr. No.	Strengths	Type of enterprise								Total	
		Micro		Small		Medium					
		No.	%	No.	%	No.	%			No.	%
1	Backward and forward linkages	22	62.86	88	83.8	8	44.44			118	74.68
2	Large market	14	40.00	77	73.3	11	61.11			102	64.56
3	Availability of machines locally	18	51.43	67	63.8	12	66.67			97	61.39
4	Peaceful and skilled labour	6	17.14	74	70.5	13	72.22			93	58.86
5	Networks and social capital	2	61.00	80	76.2	8	44.44			90	56.96
6	Rajkot as a brand	6	17.14	60	57.1	14	77.78			80	50.63
7	Good infrastructure	10	28.57	55	52.4	14	77.78			79	50.00
	Total	35	22.15	105	66.46	18	11.39			158	100

Source: Author's field survey.

Note: *Multiple responses.

Despite the strength that the cluster has, several concerns were voiced too. A large proportion of respondents showed their concern about business volatility, mainly demand fluctuations. Close to this was inadequate financing, particularly after the implementation of GST. The GST has to be paid upfront at the time of sale which, more often than not, has a trade credit of 60–90 days. During this period, the GST paid upfront has severe implications for working capital, which adversely affect their liquidity, and banks do not consider this while granting working capital. As noted earlier, skill shortages are another major concern; they want the government to address this issue sooner rather than later.

Land has also become a contentious issue, especially across the medium-sized towns in India, including Rajkot. All the four industrial estates in the town are brimming to their full capacity. Land prices in the open market have gone up substantially. The cost of 1 acre of land is over ₹10 million. 'If they have to invest this much in the land, how do they make their enterprise sustainable?' they asked.

The prices of the major raw material, that is, pig iron, had gone up within a few months (November 2017 to May 2018) from ₹18,000/tonne to 26,000/tonne. Such fluctuation of prices, argued the respondents, has to be absorbed by the manufacturer even at the cost of viability, as the buyers usually pay at the rate in vogue at the time of placing the order. Similarly, they argued that the industries in Gujarat not only pay more for electricity than that paid by industries elsewhere in India but also pay 1.5 times more than that of their Chinese counterparts (₹10 in Gujarat versus ₹6 per KwH in China). It constitutes 8 per cent to 18 per cent of the input cost, which adversely affects their competitiveness.

The cost of developing technology is also a significant concern for the industry. Several respondents argued that the government research infrastructure is not doing enough to help industries develop cutting-edge technologies the way China does. We were told that China imports hi-tech machinery, does reverse engineering, develops drawing and designs and offers them to its industry to manufacture. As a result, the cost of technology comes down substantially, and industries become competitive.

Overall Business Environment and Policy Imperatives

Gujarat's business environment is often seen in a very positive light across the country. It is often said that all the governments in Gujarat in the past, irrespective of their political affiliation, have been business-friendly. As a result, one finds reasonably good industrial infrastructure, flexible rules, proactive bureaucracy and, above all, enterprising communities. A significantly large proportion (81.14 per cent) of the respondents felt that either the overall business environment had improved or had remained unchanged over time (Table 10.8). On the whole, one may conclude that the business environment in Rajkot has at least not worsened. This could be ascribed at least partly to the dynamics of clustering that offers a conducive ecosystem for growth. Overall, the engineering industry in Rajkot is upbeat. Most of the respondents felt that the future of their industry was bright (or good). Only about 12 per cent were somewhat pessimistic about their future.

Perceived Impact of Recent Policies

The three significant policies, namely demonetisation, GST and 'Make in India', announced by the Government of India recently could have significant implications for businesses. We tried to assess their impact on the overall functioning of enterprises. In all, 61 (36.7 per cent) respondents opined that GST was good for the industry. If we add the opinion that initially there were problems in managing the GST but now it is fine, the proportion goes up by 5.4 per cent to 42.17 per cent. However, 84 respondents felt that GST had made an adverse impact on their operations because of the liquidity problems, shifting to new procedures, and so on (Table 10.9). Though there were significant variations across the size of firms, the overall impression we got was that GST was a welcome step that will bring more transparency in business.

As far as 'demonetisation' is concerned, the opinion was split vertically. The survey results indicate that for 50 per cent respondents, its impact was either good or nil on business. However, the other 50 per cent, particularly micro enterprises, felt that it hurt their business (Table 10.9). The next probe was about the 'Make in India' campaign. In all, 81 (62.30 per cent) of the total 130 respondents felt that it was a good strategy that would benefit the industry as it would increase competition, and such pressure would improve the quality of the products substantially. In this case also, the positive impact was perceived more by medium-sized firms rather than small and micro ones. However, the respondents felt that the government should support industries during the initial phase, as they might find it challenging to face the likely competition from hi-tech, large domestic and foreign enterprises.

Table 10.8 The direction of changes in business environment in Rajkot*

Sr. No.	Parameters	Type of change						Total		% of the total respondents
		Improved		No change		Deteriorated				
		No.	%	No.	%	No.	%	No.	%	
1	Raw material supply	81	49.39	68	41.46	15	9.15	164	100.00	93.71
2	Market demand	46	28.05	72	43.90	38	23.17	156	100.00	89.14
3	Sales	67	40.85	59	35.98	30	18.29	156	100.00	89.14
4	Quantity of orders	60	36.59	69	42.07	25	15.24	154	100.00	88.00
5	Number of customers	76	46.34	51	31.10	20	12.20	147	100.00	84.00
6	Number of suppliers	60	36.59	80	48.78	5	3.05	145	100.00	82.86
7	Product quality	73	44.51	66	40.24	2	1.22	141	100.00	80.57
8	Profitability	35	21.34	64	39.02	40	24.39	139	100.00	79.43
9	Government support	13	7.93	71	43.29	52	31.71	136	100.00	77.71
10	Labour supply	30	18.29	68	41.46	38	23.17	136	100.00	77.71
11	Duties and tariffs	28	17.07	57	34.76	41	25.00	126	100.00	72.00
12	Product range	46	28.05	73	44.51	7	4.27	126	100.00	72.00
13	Availability of skills	24	14.63	64	39.02	35	21.34	123	100.00	70.29
14	Others	1	0.61	7	4.27	0	0	8	100.00	4.57
	Total respondents							175		100.00

Source: Author's field survey.

Note: * Multiple responses.

Table 10.9   Perceived impact of recent policies and government campaigns*

Sr. No.	Perceived impact		GST	Demonetisation	Make in India	Total
1	Positive impact	No.	70	7	81	158
		%	42.17	4.73	62.23	35.58
2	Negative impact	No.	84	74	17	175
		%	50.60	50.00	13.07	39.41
3	Negligible or no impact/can't say	No.	60	70	79	209
		%	36.14	47.97	60.76	47.07
	Total	No.	166	148	130	444
		%	100.00	100.00	100.00	100.00

Source: Author's field survey.

Note: * Multiple responses.

Policy Implications and Expectations from the State

Several concerns were raised by the entrepreneurs in Rajkot, as highlighted earlier. Among these, credit-related issues, the land issue, the issue of skill deficit, concerns related to the high and fluctuating cost of inputs and the cost of developing technology were the key issues facing the industry in Rajkot.

The government should mandate banks to take into consideration the increased working capital requirement of the industries and accordingly enhance the working capital limits.

While the 'land concern' is genuine, land acquisition by any government is fraught with severe consequences anywhere in the country. Moreover, land also has competing claims and will always remain scarce. However, the Government of Gujarat has announced the creation of another industrial estate at Devgam Khirasara in Lodhika *taluka* of Rajkot. Recently, the district administration has acquired a piece of 97 hectares of land against the 341 hectares demanded by the industry. The shortage of skilled workforce also emerged as a serious concern.

The respondents also wanted the Government of Gujarat to rationalise power tariffs, which constitute between 8 and 18 per cent of their input costs. It may be recalled that the electricity rates are the highest in Gujarat compared to the other states. The state government may also give impetus to solar energy and encourage industries to adopt 'green energy' methods (Table 10.10).

Skill deficit remains the cluster's Achille's heel. There is a need to accurately map the skill gaps and involve industry on the lines of the German vocational

Table 10.10 Policy wish list of firms in the Rajkot engineering cluster*

Sr. No.	The wish list	Type of enterprise						Total	
		Micro		Small		Medium			
		No.	%	No.	%	No.	%	No.	%
1.	Provide loans on low-interest rates	34	91.89	76	71.03	1	5.26	111	68.10
2.	Make land available at reasonable rates	10	27.03	88	82.24	11	64.70	109	67.70
3.	Reduce GST and its slabs/Revamp GST	13	35.14	78	72.90	12	63.16	103	63.19
4.	Ease of doing business, bring more transparency	16	43.24	71	66.36	12	63.16	99	60.74
5.	Improve Skills development facilities. Set up finishing schools, Tool Room and design school	25	67.57	60	56.70	12	63.16	97	59.51
6.	Create infrastructure for testing facilities, locally	25	67.57	67	62.62	2	10.53	94	57.67
7.	Improve BDS	11	29.73	47	43.93	10	52.63	68	41.72
8.	Ease imports and exports and support them	2	5.41	63	58.88	1	5.26	66	40.49
9.	Have more stable tax policy	3	8.11	7	6.54	15	78.95	25	15.34
10.	Others (control steel prices, reduce power rates, make government tenders more transparent)	14	37.84	17	15.89	14	73.68	45	27.61
	Total	37	22.70	107	65.64	17	11.66	161	100.00

Source: Author's field survey.

Note: * Multiple responses.

training system. The government should also promote tool rooms (on the lines of the German tool rooms), finishing schools, testing laboratories and design schools to support industry (Table 10.10). The government should also desist from bringing rules such as the domicile component in employment. The Government of Gujarat should roll back its recent rule that mandates industries to hire 85 per cent of their workforce from the population that is domicile of Gujarat.

Concerning technology development, costs in China are relatively low due to the government's direct participation. The Government of India should, likewise, participate aggressively in technology development through its Council of Scientific and Industrial Research (ICSIR) network and make it more industry-friendly. The government may also encourage industry–academia interactions and make research more applied in nature so that industry could benefit from academic research. However, we hasten to add that several schemes have been evolved by the Government of India to make the research industry-oriented, and industry is also being encouraged by the government to participate in a public–private framework. However, all these schemes, by and large, do not touch micro and small industries and a large section of medium-scale industries. The government must play a more proactive role in reaching out to the MSME segment to help it upgrade technologically.

Given the criticality of cluster dynamics, the Government of India should craft a sound 'cluster development policy' to augment the competitiveness of MSMEs.

Concluding Observations

Rajkot is one of the largest engineering clusters in the country. The cluster is quite upbeat about its future. Besides attaining higher growth in production vis-à-vis all India, the engineering cluster in Rajkot has also generated substantial employment. The axiom that engineering industries are highly capital intensive and therefore less employment-generating does not hold in the case of Rajkot. The entrepreneurs are optimistic about their future, are resilient and have focused on quality, productivity and efficiency to sustain themselves in a challenging environment. Consequently, competition from China is not seen as a threat, though it remains a major competitor. Having said this, one should admit that the industry in Rajkot has a long way to go as far as technology and research and development are concerned. The skill gap is going to prove detrimental to the growth in the long run. It is high time for the industry to pitch in for large-scale skill development by utilising the government's public–private partnership scheme for the purpose. Taking a cue from the high performance of clusters such as the Rajkot engineering cluster, it is strongly recommended that the government come up with a sound cluster development policy and commit significant resources to promote them.

Notes

1. The database pertains to the third census of small-scale industries conducted by the Development Commissioner Small Scale Industries (DCSSI) in 2001. No information on clusters is available for the subsequent period.
2. At the outset, we would like to clarify that the information on the size of the sectors is based on the information provided by various industry associations and knowledgeable persons. We tried to get information from the Industries Commissioner, Government of Gujarat. However, their information pertains to the registration of firms. Whether the firm is still working or not is not recorded. Therefore, we were constrained to not use that data, as it did not tell anything about the current status of MSMEs in Rajkot.
3. It may be mentioned that the gross output (sales turnover) and capital investments in plant and machinery have been brought to 2011–12 prices by using sector-wise deflators.

References

Akbar, M. 1997. 'Industrial Clusters in Uttar Pradesh: Meerut and Moradabad'. Unpublished research report, Indian Institute of Management, Lucknow.

Anderson, R. A. and C. Miller. 2002. '"Class Matters": Human and Social Capital in Entrepreneurial Process'. *Journal of Socio-Economics* 32 (1): 17–36.

Awasthi, Dinesh. 1997. 'The Brass Part and Component Industry Cluster, Jamnagar'. Unpublished report, Entrepreneurship Development Institute of India, Ahmedabad.

———. 2004. 'Labour Process and Productivity in Micro and Small Enterprises'. *Indian Journal of Labour Economics* 47 (4): 871–90.

———. 2005. 'Dynamics of Cluster Development in India: Emerging lessons and Future Strategies'. Unpublished report, Institute of Economy and Development, New Delhi, Observer Research Foundation (ORF), 19 July.

Bagchi, A. K. 1999. 'Indian Economic Organisations a Comparative Perspective'. In *Economy and Organisations: Indian Institutions under the Neo-Liberal Regime*, edited by A. K. Bagchi, 19–62. New Delhi: Sage Publications Private Pvt. Ltd.

Basant, Rakesh. 1997. 'The Diesel Industry Cluster: Rajkot'. Unpublished research report, Indian Institute of Management, Ahmedabad.

Branco, Amelia and Joao Carlos Lopes. 2013. 'The Economic Performance of Cluster and Non-Cluster Firms along the Different Phase of the Cluster Life Cycle: The Portuguese Cork Industry Case'. Working Paper, WP/26/2013/DE/UECE/GHES, Department of Economics, University of Lisbon.

Burt, R. S. 1992. 'The Network Structure of the Social Capital'. *Research in Organisational Behaviour* 22: 345–423.

Colman, J. S. 1988. 'Social Capital in the Creation of Human Capital'. *American Journal of Sociology* 94: S95–S120.

Gade, Sunder. 2018. 'MSMEs' Role in Economic Growth: A Study on India's Perspective'. *International Journal of Pure and Applied Mathematics* 118 (18): 1727–41.

Granovetter, M. 1985. 'Economic Action and Social Structure: The Problem of Embeddedness'. *American Journal of Sociology* 91 (3): 481–510.

Humphrey, J. and H. Schmitz. 1995. 'Principles for Promoting Clusters and Networks of SMEs'. Paper commissioned by the Small and Medium Enterprises Branch, No. 1, October, Institute of Development Studies, Sussex.

ICRA Research Services. 2018. 'Indian Bearing Industry'. Available at https://blog. pawealthadvisors.com/2018/11/29/understanding-the-indian-bearing-industry-its-key-players/#:~:text=Indian%20bearing%20market%20is%20estimated,remaining%20 is%20met%20through%20imports, accessed on 19 June 2019.

Indian Brand Equity Foundation. 2017. 'The Best of India in Engineering: Machine Tools'. Available at https://www.ibef.org/the-best-of-india-in-engineering-2017.pdf, accessed on 19 June 2019.

———. 2018. 'Indian Engineering and Capital Goods Industry Report'. September, New Delhi. Available at https://www.ibef.org/download/Engineering-and-Capital-Goods-Report-Sep-2018.pdf, accessed on 19 June 2019.

Katua, Ngui Thomas. 2014. 'The Role of SMEs in Employment Creation and Economic Growth in Selected Countries'. *International Journal of Education and Research* 2 (12): 461–72.

Krishna, K. V. S. M and Dinesh Awasthi. 1994. 'Responsiveness of Small Scale and Tiny Enterprises to Policy Reforms in India'. *Journal of Entrepreneurship* 3 (2): 163–89.

Marshal, Alfred. 1974 [1890]. 'Industrial Organization: The Concentration of Specialized Industries in Particular Localities'. In *Principle of Economics*, Book IV, Chapter 10, 154–60. Available athttps://eet.pixel-online.org/files/etranslation/original/Marshall,%20 Principles%20of%20Economics.pdf, accessed on 19 June 2019.

Nadvi, K. and H. Schmitz. 1994. 'Industrial Clusters in Less Developed Countries: A Review of Experiences and Research Agenda'. Discussion Paper 339, Institute of Development Studies, University of Sussex, January.

Nagaraj, R. 1984. 'Sub-contracting In Indian Manufacturing Industries: Analysis, Evidence and Issues'. *Economic and Political Weekly* 19 (31–33): 1435–53.

Nee, V., L. Liu and D. Della Posta. 2017. 'The Entrepreneur's Network and Firm Performance'. *Sociological Science* 4: 552–79.

Papola, T. S. 2014. 'Employment Growth in Indian Manufacturing: Post Reform Trends and Implications for the Labour Flexibility Debate'. *The Indian Journal of Labour Economics* 57 (4): 351–72.

Piore, M. and C. Sabel. 1984. *The Second Industrial Divide: Possibilities for Prosperity*. New York: Basic Books.

Porter, M. 1990. *The Competitive Advantage of Nations*. London: Macmillan.

Porter, M. E. 1998. 'Cluster and the New Economics of Competition'. *Harvard Business Review* 76 (6): 77–91.

Portes, A. and P. Landolt. 2000. 'Social Capital: Promises and Pitfalls of Its Role in Development'. *Journal of Latin American Studies* 32 (2): 529–47.

Ramaswamy, K. V. 1999. 'The Search for Flexibility in Indian Manufacturing: New Evidence on Subcontracting Activities'. *Economic and Political Weekly* 34 (6): 363–68.

Sahu, P. P. 2010. 'Subcontracting in India's Unorganised Manufacturing Sector: A Mode of Adoption or Exploitation?' *Journal of South Asian Development* 5 (1): 53–83.

Schmitz, H. 1989. 'Flexible Specialisation: A New Paradigm of Small-Scale Industrialisation'. IDS Discussion Paper No. 261, Institute of Development Studies, University of Sussex.

Schmitz, Hubert. 1999. 'Collective Efficiency and Increasing Return'. *Cambridge Journal of Economics* 23 (4): 465–83

Shah, Amita. 1994. 'Inter-Firm Scalar Linkages in India: A Class within the Small-Scale Industry'. *Small Business Economics: An International Journal* 6 (3): 237–47.

Smith, Adam. 1776/2003. *An Inquiry into the Nature and Causes of the Wealth of Natures*, Chapter 1, Book 1. Available at https://ocw.mit.edu/courses/literature/211-448j-darwin-and-design-fall-2003/readings/lecture8.pdf, accessed on 9 February 2021.

Sood, Kunal, and Sanjay Pal. 2004. 'Report on Dynamics of Growth and Stagnation of Industrial Clusters in India: Emerging Issues and Policy Imperatives'. Unpublished report, Entrepreneurship Development Institute of India, Ahmedabad.

Swaminathan, P. and J. Jeyaranjan. 1997. 'The Knitwear Cluster of Tiruppur: Potential Industrial District?' Unpublished research report, Madras Institute of Development Studies, Chennai.

Tendler, J. 1987. 'The Remarkable Convergence of Fashion on Small Enterprises and the Informal Sector: What Are the Implications for Policy Mimeo, Department of Urban Studies and Planning, Massachusetts Institute of Technology, Cambridge, MA.

Trigilia, C. 1989. 'Small-firm Development and Political Subcultures in Italy'. In *Small Firms and Industrial Districts in Italy*, edited by E. Goodman, J. Bamford and P. Saynor, 174–87. London: Routledge.

United Capital. 2018. 'Impact of Small Businesses to the Overall US Economy'. 1 January. Available at https://www.ucfunding.com/impact-of-small-business-to-the-overall-us-economy/, accessed on 19 June 2019.

CHAPTER 11

Manufacturing and Automation

SUNIL MANI

Introduction

The initiation of the Make in India programme is yet another statement of the desire of the government to increase employment in the country through the manufacturing route. Under this programme, the manufacturing sector is expected to contribute at least a quarter of India's gross domestic product (GDP) by 2020. However, recent events and discussions have brought to the fore the pessimism that not much employment possibilities emanate from the manufacturing sector due to its capital-intensive nature, which the sector had become for quite some time now. The worst fears on this issue have been accentuated with the increasing automation of manufacturing processes elsewhere in the world. Industrial automation is thought to have a deleterious effect on the creation of employment in different sectors of the economy, manufacturing included. This has given rise to an important debate, primarily in the context of developed countries where industrial automation has diffused manifold and that too over a much longer period of time. This debate, although originally in the popular press, has now been brought to the formal academic table by the publication of an influential and highly cited piece of research by Frey and Osborne (2013). Subsequently, one of the leading academic journals, namely the *Journal of Economic Perspectives*, organised a symposium on the theme of 'automation and labour markets' in its 2015 summer issue.[1] Thereafter, there has been a series of studies by academic economists and multilateral institutions such as the Organisation for Economic Co-operation and Development (OECD 2016) as well.[2]

In the context, the purpose of the chapter is to understand the extent of the diffusion of automation technologies in Indian manufacturing and then analyse its effects on manufacturing employment.

Concept of Automation

A range of technologies are involved in industrial automation which manifests itself as both hardware and software. Employment implications of these various automation technologies vary considerably. The specific automation technology that has the most direct impact on employment is the use of multipurpose industrial robots. The International Federation of Robotics – IFR for short – defines an industrial robot as 'an automatically controlled, reprogrammable, and multipurpose [machine]' (IFR 2014). That is, industrial robots are fully autonomous machines that do not need a human operator and that can be programmed to perform several manual tasks such as welding, painting, assembling, handling materials or packaging. Most other types of automation technologies require a human operator, for instance, a machine tool, programmable controllers or a computer-aided design (CAD) equipment. Robots can also perform reliably and consistently in harsh and constrained environments in which a human worker cannot function satisfactorily. Robots therefore represent the most advanced and flexible form of industrial automation that can be envisioned. So, in the present study, we focus on industrial robots. In addition to industrial robots, there are service robots as well. There are two concepts of industrial robots: delivered (flow) and operational stock (stock). Since we are interested in employment implications, our focus is on the operational stock of industrial robots in Indian manufacturing. So, the concept of industrial automation used is the use of multipurpose industrial robots in manufacturing.

Motivation

In recent years, there has been a revival of concerns that automation and digitalisation might, after all, result in a jobless future. The debate has been fuelled by studies for the USA and Europe arguing that a substantial share of jobs is at 'risk of computerisation'. These studies follow an occupation-based approach proposed by Frey and Osborne (2013), that is, they assume that whole occupations rather than single job tasks are automated by technology. It is argued that this might lead to an overestimation of job automatability, as occupations labelled as high-risk occupations often still contain a substantial share of tasks that are hard to automate.

There are essentially a number of reasons as to why an understanding of the relationship between automation and employment is important in the India context. These are:

- World wide there has been an increasing concern or fear about the effect of automation on employment. An extension of the earlier Frey and Osborne (2013, 2017) study on India showed that a whopping 69 per cent of the jobs in India are considered to be automatable.
- Four industries, namely computers and electronic products, electrical equipment, appliances and components, and transportation equipment and machinery are the ones most prone to automation. In many countries, including India, these four industries, and especially the transportation equipment industry, have been given much emphasis in the industrialisation strategy.
- Automation potential is concentrated in countries with large populations or high wages – India, therefore, is a good candidate, even though currently it is considered to be a low-wage country.
- India's recent policy is aimed at raising employment through the promotion of growth of the manufacturing industry, but hitherto the scenario has been one of steady decline in the labour intensity of manufacturing employment (Sen and Das 2014).
- The most recent data from India's periodic labour force survey for 2017–18 showed that the unemployment rate among the rural male youth (persons of age 15–29 years) was 17.4 per cent, while the unemployment rate among the rural female youth was 13.6 per cent in 2017–18. The unemployment rate among the urban male youth was 18.7 per cent in the same period, while the unemployment rate for urban female youth was 27.2 per cent (Ministry of Statistics and Programme Implementation 2019).

All these issues motivate us to understand the process of automation that is taking place in Indian manufacturing and its potential and actual effects on manufacturing employment.

Significance

The rate of diffusion of automation technologies is likely to increase in the manufacturing sector in the near future. The following factors highlight the significance of the study:

- First, a late manufacturing country such as India can skip stages and start with the latest manufacturing technologies.
- Second, with increasing globalisation and with increasing pressure on manufacturing companies to be more productive and thereby competitive internationally, the pressure on adopting productivity-enhancing technologies is much more now than ever before. According to estimates by the Boston Consulting Group (2015), the use of robots can decrease labour costs by as much as 16 per cent.
- Third, with developments in artificial intelligence and machine learning, the nature of tasks that machines can do has seen a quantum jump. For instance, industrial robots are now much more intelligent and can perform a wide variety of operations which they could not do earlier.
- Fourth, the declining cost of automation and its increasing supply are still another factor that can hasten the rate of diffusion. Again, according to the Boston Consulting Group (2015), the average price of industrial robotic systems has declined from US $182,000 in 2005 to US$133,000 in 2014 (Sirkin, Zinser and Rose 2015).

Research Questions, Analytical Framework and Data Sources

In the context, the study attempts to answer the following two research questions:

- What has been the rate of diffusion of automation technologies in Indian manufacturing during the post-globalisation period?
- What has been its effect on manufacturing employment? What is the relationship between the rate of diffusion of automation and the intensity of manufacturing employment and also what are the likely trends in this relationship in the years to come when the size and composition of manufacturing are bound to increase and become more sophisticated?

In order to understand the diffusion of industrial robots in manufacturing, we adopt a task-based approach. This is because an occupation may contain several tasks that are not prone to easy automation. So, a task-based approach may provide us with a more accurate picture of diffusion. Also, in the framework, we measure diffusion by the number of operational stocks of industrial robots per unit of employment. This framework is influenced by Arntz, Gregory and Zierahn (2017).

The main data source consulted is the annual survey of robotics titled *World Robotics*. The data source presents annual and time series data on the number of delivered robots and its operational stock industry-wise and country-wise. Further, it presents the task-wise distribution of robots within occupations. Data are available for over 32 countries, including India. The data on manufacturing employment are taken from the Annual Survey of Industries. This is available industry-wise, up to and including 2014–15. Further details on the data are presented in Appendix 11A to the chapter.

Engagement with the Literature on Automation and Employment

The literature on the effect of automation on manufacturing employment is a subset of the general discussion on the effect of technological development on employment creation. There are two different phases in the development of this literature. The first phase is the late 1980s, when the first of the cross-country studies on effect of industrial automation on employment was completed (Flamm 1988). The second phase is from 2013 onwards, beginning with the publication of the Frey and Osborne (2013) study. The publication of this study has unleashed a wave of extreme concern about the deleterious effect of faster diffusion of automation technologies on manufacturing employment. This has spawned a number of studies analysing the effect of automation on employment. These studies in turn can be divided into three groups: the first is a study which analyses the diffusion of industrial robots in a range of countries, the second group of studies shows an inverse relationship between the extent of the diffusion of automation and manufacturing employment in the sense that increased automation leads to decline in employment, and the third group shows that increased automation has not really resulted in hefty job losses. In the following, we review these studies in detail.

Diffusion of Industrial Robots in Developing Countries

One of the earliest studies on the changing pattern of industrial robot use is the one by Flamm (1988). He analysed the rate of diffusion of robot use in Belgium, France, Germany, Italy, Japan, Sweden, the UK and the USA during the period from 1970 to 1984. His survey focused on two related issues: how and where industrial robots were used in manufacturing and how robot use in the USA compares with manufacturing practices abroad. Robot use is uneven across industries with their use being confined or concentrated in certain specific tasks and industries. Historically, they were first used in hazardous and unpleasant operations associated with metal processing, in relatively small numbers. The Japanese auto manufacturers, after 1975, began to use them in large numbers for spot welding operations on their assembly lines and late in that decade expanded their field of application to arc welding. Their foreign competitors followed suit. In fact, it was welding activities that have hastened the diffusion of industrial robots across the developed world. Since 1980, once again led by Japanese manufacturers, more sophisticated industrial robots began to be used in electrical and electronics industries. The majority of the industrial robots, according to Flamm, are found in electronic assembly and automotive welding. The reasons as to why the use of robots has not diffused are because there are only a handful of major uses in which they are currently a cost-effective solution to manufacturers. In fact, industrial robot use has not shown a secular increase but only in fits and starts.

In the context, Flamm is of the opinion that 'one would be well advised to be sceptical of technological optimists who, on the basis of broad statistical job classifications for industrial workers, project veritable tidal waves of robots inundating manufacturing in the medium term'.

Another interesting finding is that robots' diffusion has lagged in the US manufacturing industry when compared to Japan, Sweden and Germany. Cross-country variation in the relative prices of capital, labour and other factors of production does not seem to explain the differential rate of diffusion. The shift to greater product variety that requires a more flexible manufacturing plant may be a more plausible explanation.

Studies Finding an Inverse Relationship

One of the studies in this genre is World Economic Forum (WEF) (2016). The study covered 15 major developed and developing countries based on a large-scale survey of major global employers, including 100 largest global employers in each of the WEF main industry sectors, to estimate the expected level of changes in job families between 2015 and 2020 and extrapolate the number of jobs gained or lost. Automation and technological advancements could lead to net employment impact of more than 5.1 million jobs lost due to disruptive labour market changes between 2015 and 2020 with a total loss of 7.1 million jobs, two-thirds of which are concentrated in the office and administrative job family, and a total gain of 2 million jobs in several smaller jobs.

Another study in this category is by the McKinsey Global Institute (2017) which covers 46 countries accounting for about 80 per cent of the global labour force. The study showed that almost half of work activities globally have the potential to be automated using current technology. Technically speaking, automatable activities touch 1.2 billion workers and US$1,404 trillion in wages. China, India, and the USA will account for over half of the automatable jobs. The study also notes that automation's boost to global productivity could be 0.8 to 1.4 per cent annually over two decades.

A more systematic study of the diffusion of robots in US manufacturing is done by Acemoglu and Restrepo (2017). In specific terms, the study analysed the impact of robot use on the US labour market during the period from 1990 to 2007. Using a model in which robots compete against human labour in the production of different tasks, they show that robots may reduce employment and wages, and that the local labour market effects of robots can be estimated by regressing the change in employment and wages on the exposure to robots in each local labour market – defined from the national penetration of robots into each industry and the local distribution of employment across industries. Using this approach, they estimate large and robust negative effects of robots on employment and wages across commuting zones. They supplement this evidence by showing that the commuting zones most exposed to robots in the post-1990 era do not exhibit any differential trends before 1990. The impact of robots is distinct from the impact of imports from China and Mexico, the decline of routine jobs, offshoring, other types of information technology (IT) capital, and the total capital stock (in fact, exposure to robots is only weakly correlated with these other variables). According to their estimates, one more robot per thousand workers reduces the employment-to-population ratio by about 0.18–0.34 percentage points and wages by 0.25–0.5 per cent.

Occupation versus Task-based Approach

The main problem with these studies is that they consider only very broad occupations and not tasks within occupations. In short, they follow the occupation-based approach of Frey and Osborne (2013). Very often, the assumption that whole occupations are automated by technology is invalid; rather, it is only that single job tasks are prone to automation. This may lead to an over-estimation of job automatability as occupations labelled as high-risk occupations often still contain a substantial share of tasks that are hard to automate. An important cross-country study that has considered a more task-based approach is by Arntz, Gregory and Zierahn (2017).

The main conclusion from the Arntz, Gregory and Zierahn (2017) study is that automation and digitalisation are unlikely to destroy large numbers of jobs. However, low-qualified workers are likely to bear the brunt of the adjustment costs, as the automatability of their jobs is higher compared to highly qualified workers. Therefore, the likely challenge for the future lies in coping with rising inequality and ensuring sufficient (re-)training, especially for low-qualified workers.

A still another study (Graetz and Michaels 2017) using cross-country data on robot adoption by the IFR (the same data source used in our study) analyses robot adoption within industries in 17 countries during the period from 1993 to 2007. Employing panel data on robot adoption within industries in these countries, and new instrumental variables that rely on robots' comparative advantage in specific tasks, it is found that increased diffusion of robotic technology contributed approximately 0.37 percentage points to the annual labour productivity growth. Simultaneously, it has raised total factor productivity and wages, and lowered output prices. Further, the estimates suggest that robots did not significantly reduce employment, although they did reduce low-skilled workers' employment share.

In sum, the following inferences can be drawn from the studies that we have reviewed here:

- Industrial robots are basically used in certain specific industries such as automobile, electrical and electronics, and metal tending. Even within these industries, they are used for certain tasks such as spot and arc welding, which are both harsh and repetitive for human beings to perform. In fact, their usage does not seem to have diversified into other manufacturing industries over the last four decades.
- Studies which have analysed the relationship between the diffusion of automation and employment have yielded results that are diametrically opposite to each other. Some studies suggest an inverse relationship between the two variables, while others have not detected any such relationship. A careful analysis of the former studies shows that they have used an occupation-based approach while dealing with employment as opposed to a task-based approach. An occupation-based approach tends to exaggerate the impact of automation on employment, as there are many tasks within an occupation that are not automatable,

- According to Varian, 'Automation doesn't generally eliminate jobs. Automation generally eliminates dull, tedious, and repetitive tasks. If you remove all the tasks, you remove the job.' He illustrates this statement by referring to the US Census Bureau which listed 250 separate jobs in 1950. Since then, the only one to be completely eliminated is that of elevator operators. But some of the tasks carried out by elevator operators, such as greeting visitors and guiding them to the right office, have been distributed to receptionists and security guards (Snyder 2019).
- The proxy that is used for identifying automation has varied across studies. Some studies define automation in terms of computerisation, while others identify it in terms of use of industrial robots.
- All the studies, without exception, refer to the situation in developed market economies. None of the studies refer to any of the developing countries.

Thus our engagement with the literature shows that there is a real case for a study analysing the relationship between automation and manufacturing employment in the context of a late industrialising country, such as that of India. Further, in our study, we define automation in terms of its highest form, namely the use of industrial robots, and use a task-based approach to measure its effect on employment. This, we feel, will provide us with better and meaningful results on the effect of automation on manufacturing employment.

Main Findings with Respect to India

The operational stock of industrial robots in manufacturing has been increasing both in the world and in India. In India, it has increased from just 70 in 2000 to 16,026 in 2016 (see Figure 11.1). The operational stock has been increasing by 44 per cent per annum during the same period. According to the IFR (2017), there are five major markets representing 74 per cent of the total sales volume in 2016. These are China, South Korea, Japan, USA and Germany. China has now become the largest with a share of almost a third of the total market in 2016. At a total sale of 87,000 robots, the total number of industrial robots sold in the country is almost equal to the total number of industrial robots sold in Europe and America together. Apart from China, the other important markets for industrial robots are Taiwan, Thailand and India. In India, sales of industrial robots increased by 27 per cent in 2016 to reach 2,627 units. The estimated worldwide operational stock of industrial robots in the 15 largest markets is presented in Figure 11.2.

Figure 11.1   Trends in operational stock of industrial robots in the world and in India (in thousands)

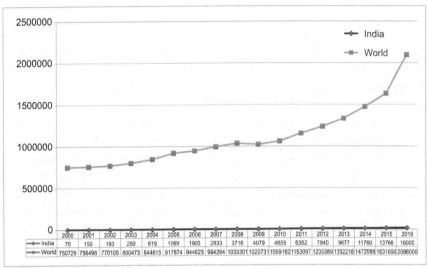

	2000	2001	2002	2003	2004	2005	2006	2007	2008	2009	2010	2011	2012	2013	2014	2015	2016
India	70	150	193	250	619	1069	1905	2833	3716	4079	4855	6352	7840	9677	11760	13768	16000
World	750729	756498	770105	800473	844615	917874	944823	994264	1035301	1020731	1059162	1153097	1235389	1332218	1472088	1631650	2098000

Source: IFR (2017).

Figure 11.2   Estimated worldwide operational stock of industrial robots in the 15 largest markets, 2016

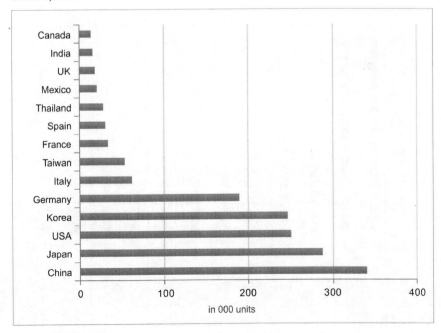

Source: IFR (2017).

Despite having the largest operational stock of robots, in terms of its density, China is still below the world average. India appears to have the lowest density, although there is some underestimation. This is because the IFR has overestimated the employment in the organised sector; so the density of robots appear to be lower than what it really is. This will be made clear in our own estimates of the density of industrial robots. The Republic of Korea, or South Korea, has had by far the highest robot density in the manufacturing industry since 2010 (see Figure 11.3). It had 631 industrial robots in operation in 2016 per 10,000 employees. The rate has been increasing from 311 units in 2010 due to continued installation of a large number of robots since 2010, particularly in the electrical/electronics industry and in the automotive industry. Singapore follows with a rate of 488 robots per 10,000 employees in 2016. Due to a very low number of employees in the manufacturing industry – some 240,000 employees are estimated by the International Labour Organisation (ILO) – and a large number of installed robots, the robot density is very high. About 90 per cent of the robots are installed in the electronics industry in Singapore, which has increased its number of robot installations significantly in recent years.

Figure 11.3   Density of industrial robots across both developed and developing countries, 2016

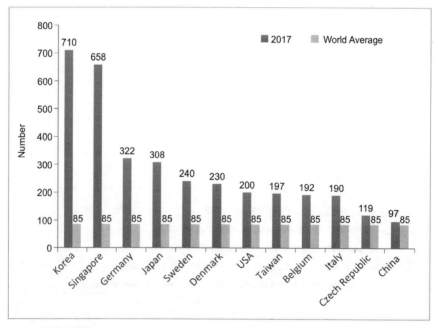

Source: IFR (2017).

Now we analyse the industries and the tasks within these industries where the robots are being used. It will be instructive to explore whether this has undergone any changes compared to what was observed by Flamm (1988) during the late 1980s. Three industries account for about 80 per cent of the operational stock of industrial robots: metal, electrical and electronics, and automotive (see Table 11.1). Within the three, the automotive industry itself accounts for about 43 per cent – in fact, it is the only industry which has increased its share. What is most interesting is the fact that the same industry accounted for the largest share in the 1980s as well (Flamm 1988). We now analyse the tasks or application areas within these industries where industrial robots are used (see Table 11.2).

Table 11.1 Industry-wide distribution of the operational stock of industrial robots worldwide (percentage shares)

Year	Metal	Electrical and electronics	Automotive	Total for the three
1993	17.07	31.97	27.83	76.86
1994	17.16	31.63	27.76	76.55
1995	16.77	30.77	27.97	75.52
1996	16.25	30.20	28.74	75.20
1997	15.62	29.74	28.89	74.25
1998	14.75	28.95	29.84	73.53
1999	13.91	27.76	30.53	72.20
2000	12.90	26.83	31.47	71.20
2001	13.20	24.06	33.98	71.24
2002	12.96	22.24	35.96	71.17
2003	12.66	20.91	38.11	71.68
2004	11.87	20.04	40.95	72.86
2005	11.06	20.46	42.43	73.95
2006	11.36	19.02	44.59	74.98
2007	11.54	18.63	44.95	75.13
2008	12.16	18.23	44.90	75.30
2009	12.19	17.92	45.26	75.38
2010	11.97	18.78	45.92	76.67
2011	11.55	20.42	45.57	77.54
2012	11.28	21.51	45.44	78.23
2013	11.16	22.18	45.58	78.92
2014	11.21	22.48	45.76	79.45
2015	11.55	23.58	44.71	79.84
2016	11.46	25.77	43.21	80.43

Source: Computed from IFR (2017).

Table 11.2 Task-wise distribution of industrial robots in world manufacturing 2011–16 (percentage shares)

IFR class	Application area	2011	2012	2013	2014	2015	2016
110	Handling operations/machine tending	41.3	44.3	43.6	47.1	48.4	47.4
111	Handling operations for metal casting	1.0	1.1	0.9	0.9	1.1	1.5
112	Handling operations for plastic moulding	6.9	7.5	6.9	8.1	8.4	6.9
113	Handling operations for stamping/ forging/bending	0.8	0.9	0.7	1.0	0.9	0.9
114	Handling operations at machine tools	3.9	4.4	5.6	4.2	5.6	5.1
115	Machine tending for other processes	1.9	1.5	1.4	1.0	1.6	0.9
116	Handling operations for measurement, inspection and testing	1.6	0.6	1.0	0.7	0.7	0.5
117	Handling operations for palletising	2.8	3.3	3.2	3.3	3.9	3.5
118	Handling operations for packaging, picking and placing	7.5	9.7	7.2	12.2	10.7	10.0
119	Material handling not elsewhere classified	15.0	15.2	16.7	15.6	15.3	18.0
120	Handling operations/machine tending unspecified						
160	Welding and soldering (all materials)	28.9	28.4	28.0	26.2	23.9	22.1
161	Arc welding	12.7	13.2	12.8	11.2	9.8	8.6
162	Spot welding	14.9	14.7	13.5	13.0	12.5	11.6
163	Laser welding	0.4	0.2	0.3	0.2	0.2	0.2
164	Other welding	0.5	0.2	1.2	0.9	0.6	0.7
165	Soldering	0.5	0.0	0.0	0.8	0.9	0.9
166	Welding and soldering unspecified						
170	Dispensing	4.2	4.0	4.9	3.6	3.6	3.3
171	Painting and enamelling	2.8	2.7	2.8	2.4	2.1	2.3
172	Application of adhesive, sealing material or similar material	0.9	1.0	1.2	0.4	0.6	0.3
179	Dispensing others/spraying others	0.5	0.2	1.0	0.8	0.9	0.6
180	Dispensing unspecified						
190	Processing	1.4	2.0	1.8	2.5	2.1	1.3
191	Laser cutting	0.1	0.5	0.2	0.2	0.3	0.1
192	Water jet cutting	0.1	0.1	0.2	0.2	0.1	0.1
193	Mechanical cutting grinding/deburring/ milling/polishing	0.6	0.9	1.1	1.8	1.4	0.7
198	Other processing	0.6	0.5	0.3	0.3	0.3	0.3

Source: IFR (2017).

The use of industrial robots is concentrated in two main tasks: handling/machines tending, and welding and soldering. The single largest application or task where robots are used is welding, and within it, arc and spot welding. In fact, there is a remarkable stability in the tasks where robots were used in the late 1980s and now. The only difference is that more of them are used for the same kind of tasks. The only task that has improved its share is in material handling and machine tending, which shows that industrial robots are primarily used for those tasks which are difficult for human beings to perform.

Firms employ robots to automate specific tasks – many of them harmful to human health. The range of automatable tasks is continuously increasing and will continue to increase through advances in vision and end-effector technologies.[3] But this does not imply that jobs will be wiped out.

We now turn our attention to the Indian case. As seen earlier in Figure 11.1, the operational stock of industrial robots has shown some tremendous increase from just 70 in 2000 to 16,026 in 2016. However, its growth rate has been fluctuating. Although there has been a fall in the growth rate, it has been in double digits. The share of the manufacturing sector has been rising steadily and now accounts for about two-thirds of the operational stock (Table 11.3). It is also interesting to note that the number of robots being used in both construction and education/research and development (R&D) has also shown some impressive increase. However, the industry-wise usage to a certain extent is coloured by a large number of robots whose usage cannot be ascribed to any specific sector.

However, within the manufacturing industry, much of the robot installations are in five industries, namely automotive; electrical and electronics; metal; chemical; and rubber and plastics. There has been a 27 per cent increase in the number of delivered robots in 2017 compared to 2016 and, on average, it has increased by 64 per cent per annum during the period under consideration.

An analysis of the industry-wise operational stock of industrial robots shows that it is very much concentrated in the automotive industry, followed by plastics, rubber and chemical products and the metal industry (Figure 11.4). The pattern that one observes in India is very similar to the international pattern that we observed earlier. In short, within India, it is the growth of the automotive industry which explains largely the growth of robotic installations.

Task-based Installations

Once again, the pattern that we observe in India is exactly the same as we have observed internationally (Table 11.5). Basically, robot usage is confined to

Table 11.3 Trends in operational stock of industrial robots in India (number)

	All industries	Manufacturing	Electricity, gas and water supply	Construction	Education R&D	Other manufacturing	Unspecified
1999	50	0	0	0	0	0	50
2000	70	0	0	0	0	0	70
2001	150	0	0	0	0	0	150
2002	193	0	0	0	0	0	193
2003	250	0	0	0	0	0	250
2004	619	0	0	0	0	0	619
2005	1069	0	0	0	0	0	1069
2006	1905	497	0	6	5	0	1397
2007	2833	799	0	14	8	0	2012
2008	3716	1201	0	15	8	0	2492
2009	4079	1302	0	16	10	0	2751
2010	4855	1517	0	16	11	0	3311
2011	6352	2189	0	17	17	1	4127
2012	7840	3526	1	18	23	1	4270
2013	9677	5189	1	27	40	1	4417
2014	11760	7138	1	29	53	1	4536
2015	13768	8953	1	30	62	1	4718
2016	16026	11237	1	30	82	1	4671

Source: IFR (2017).

Note: The manufacturing sector accounts for the lion's share of delivered robots, as also indicated by Table 11.4.

Table 11.4 Trends in the number of delivered robots

	All industries	Manufacturing	Electricity, gas and water supply	Construction	Education, R&D	Others manufacturing	Unspecified
1999	50	0	0	0	0	0	50
2000	20	0	0	0	0	0	20
2001	80	0	0	0	0	0	80
2002	43	0	0	0	0	0	43
2003	57	0	0	0	0	0	57
2004	369	0	0	0	0	0	369
2005	450	0	0	0	0	0	450
2006	836	497	0	6	5	0	328
2007	928	302	0	8	3	0	615
2008	883	402	0	1	0	0	480
2009	363	101	0	1	2	0	259
2010	776	215	0	0	1	0	560
2011	1547	672	0	1	6	1	866
2012	1508	1337	1	1	6	0	163
2013	1917	1663	0	9	17	0	227
2014	2126	1949	0	2	13	0	162
2015	2065	1815	0	0	0	0	250
2016	2627	2284	0	0	0	0	343

Source: IFR (2017).

Figure 11.4   Industry-wise operational stock of industrial robots in India, 2006–16

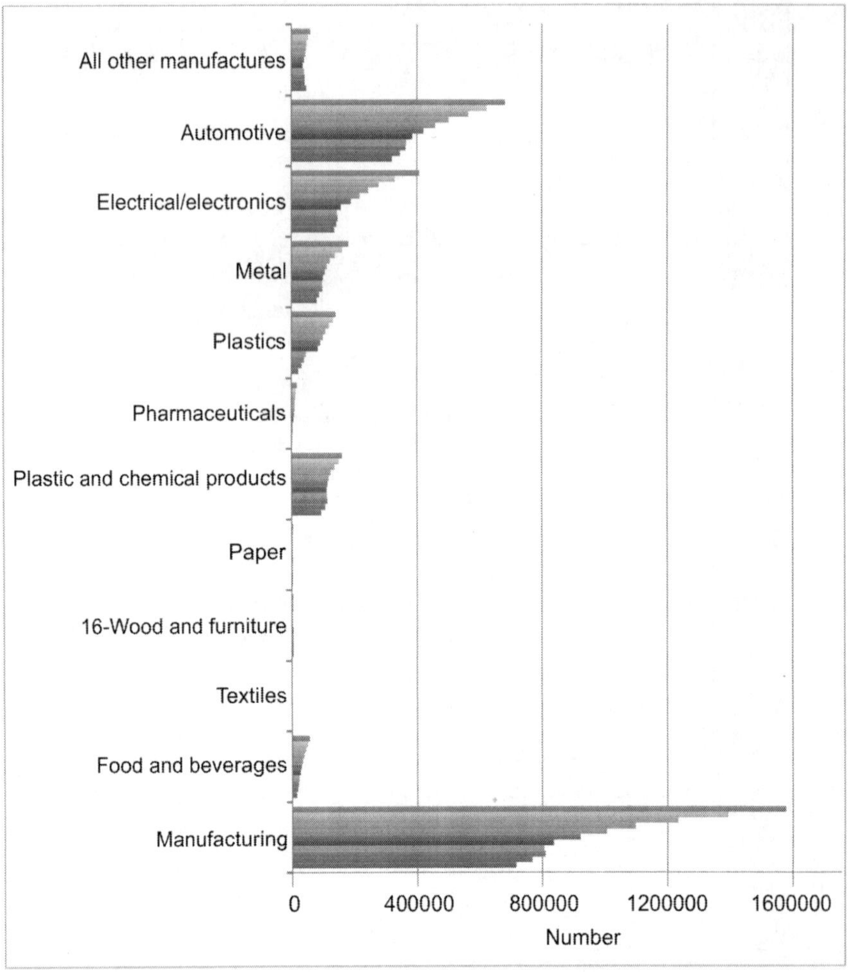

Source: IFR.

two tasks, namely welding and soldering, and handling and machine tending. Within the former, it is almost entirely concentrated in arc and spot welding. This is followed by material handling, wherein material handling for plastic moulding and machine tools accounts for the second largest share. This was more or less the pattern observed historically even in developed countries.

This finding has very deep implications for employment. Industrial robots are currently being used for tasks that are inhospitable for human labour and where much precision is required.

Table 11.5 Task-based operational stock of industrial robots in India, 2011–16

Task	2011	2012	2013	2014	2015	2016	CAGR 2011–2016
Handling operations/Machine tending	2,101	2,531	2,903	3,404	3,948	4,760	18%
Handling operations for metal casting	44	58	62	68	93	111	20%
Handling operations for plastic moulding	538	676	790	905	1,097	1,387	21%
Handling operations for stamping/forging/bending	78	91	100	109	117	158	15%
Handling operations at machine tools	390	440	472	519	622	789	15%
Machine tending for other process	42	48	51	51	51	51	4%
Handling operations for measurement, inspection, testing	6	8	8	9	9	10	11%
Handling operations for palletising	49	63	74	87	99	114	18%
Handling operations for packaging picking and placing	29	47	63	65	78	90	25%
Material handling n.e.c.	925	1,100	1,283	1,591	1,782	2,050	17%
Handling operations/machine tending unspecified							
Welding and soldering (all materials)	2,720	3,561	4,775	6,095	7,324	8,800	26%
Arc welding	1,707	2,354	3,073	3,736	4,415	5,264	25%
Spot welding	938	1,125	1,602	2,250	2,780	3,380	29%
Laser welding	9	15	25	27	34	38	33%
Other welding	55	56	62	69	82	102	13%
Soldering	11	11	13	13	13	16	8%
Welding and soldering unspecified							
Dispensing	640	776	982	1,127	1,286	1,392	17%
Painting and enamelling	467	582	740	847	924	1,015	17%
Application of adhesive, sealing material or similar material	136	155	190	219	231	233	11%

Contd.

Table 11.5 *contd.*

Task	2011	2012	2013	2014	2015	2016	CAGR 2011–2016
Dispensing others/Spraying others	37	39	52	61	131	144	31%
Dispensing unspecified							
Processing	90	130	172	223	235	259	24%
Laser cutting	5	6	7	8	8	9	12%
Water jet cutting	5	7	7	9	11	16	26%
Mechanical cutting grinding/debarring/milling/polishing	21	37	73	109	117	133	45%
Other processing	59	80	85	97	99	101	11%
Processing unspecified							
Assembling and disassembling	71	93	139	184	261	366	39%
Fixing, press-fitting	61	83	129	170	229	328	40%
Assembling mounting/inserting	5	5	5	9	10	16	26%
Disassembling							
Other assembling	5	5	5	5	22	22	34%
Assembling and disassembling unspecified							
Others	113	129	147	206	240	271	19%
Cleanroom FPD	5	5	5	5	5	6	4%
Cleanroom for semiconductors							
Cleanrooms for other							
Others	108	124	142	201	235	265	20%
Unspecified	617	620	559	521	178	178	–22%
Total	6352	7,840	9,677	11,760	13,768	16,026	20%

Source: IFR.

However, in order to understand the employment implications of robot use, one has to analyse in detail the density of robots per unit of employment.

Density of Industrial Robots

We had earlier noted that the density of robots in India is one of the lowest among robot-using countries. The density is an important indicator of the labour-displacing effect of industrial robot use. We provide here two different estimates of density: first is the density of robots in the manufacturing industry and second is its density in the automotive industry. Both are showing an increase, although, as expected, it is much higher in the automotive industry than in the general manufacturing industry (Figure 11.5).

How does the density of robots in India compare with other countries? This is attempted in Table 11.6.

This once again confirms the proposition that India has one of the lowest densities of robot usage in the world even when compared to her Asian

Figure 11.5   Trends in density of industrial robots in India, manufacturing versus automotive industry

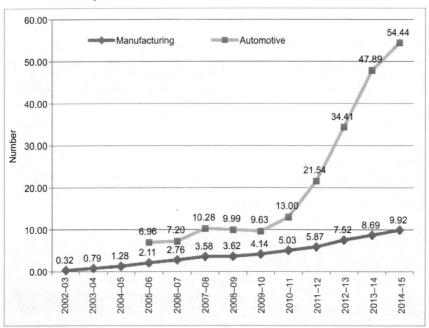

Source: IFR (2017) and Central Statistical Organization (2015).

Table 11.6 Extent of the diffusion of automation technologies in India compared with other countries, 2015 (density of industrial robots per 10,000 manufacturing employment)

	India	China	Brazil	Thailand	Malaysia	Korea	Japan
Manufacturing	10	49	11	52	33	531	305
Automotive	54	392	125	859	281	1218	1216
All other industries	1	24	5	22	22	411	213

Source: IFR (2017).

counterparts, although robot usage in India's automotive industry is much higher than other Indian industries. Since the automotive industry in India is dominated by affiliates of multinational corporations (MNCs), and given the fact that the parent MNCs have a much longer history and experience with respect to the usage of industrial robots in various manufacturing operations, it is only natural that their affiliates in India with newer vintage plants will be using industrial robots (Table 11.7).

It is seen that the robot density of these state-of-the-art plants are significantly higher than the average for the Indian automotive industry discussed earlier. Even the domestic automotive manufacturers such as Tata Motors (See Box 11.1) are deploying industrial robots although at a much lower density.

Table 11.7 Industrial robot usage in MNC affiliates in India's automotive industry

Company	Location of plant	Number of industrial robots	Number of employees	Density of robots
Ford Motor India	Sanand, Gujarat	453	2,500	1,812
Hyundai Motor India	Irugattukottai, Tamil Nadu	400	4,848	825
Volkswagen India	Chaken, Pune	123	2,000	615

Source: Compiled by author from company sources.

Box 11.1

Tata motors uses industrial robotics and automation for production. Reports reveal that the production force in Tata Motors came down by 20 per cent. At the same time, its turnover increased by 250 per cent. In a single plant in Pune, Tata is said to have installed 100 robots.

Source: Tata Motors.

Highly labour-intensive industries such as paper and wood products, textiles, non-metallic products, food products, metal products and machinery are the least automated. The most automated industries, such as the automotive industry, rubber and petroleum, basic metals and chemicals, are less labour intensive. So, the effect of automation (read as the use of industrial robots) has only an insignificant effect on the quantum of employment in the manufacturing industry.

Manufacturing of Industrial Robots in India

Some of the world's leading firms in factory automation such as Fanuc, Kuka, Gudel and ABB have manufacturing and sales operations in India, which can hasten the diffusion of industrial robots even in non-traditional industries. One of them has even established a training academy or college in the Indian city of Pune for training young engineering graduates in robotics. Further, TAL Manufacturing Solutions, a subsidiary of Tata Motors Ltd., has launched its much-awaited TAL Brabo robot in two variants, with payloads of 2 kilograms and 10 kilograms, priced between ₹500,000 and ₹700,000. Indigenously developed, the TAL Brabo is apparently a solution developed to cater to micro, small and medium enterprises, as well as for large-scale manufacturers who require cost-competitive automated solutions in manufacturing. Designed and styled in-house at TAL Manufacturing and Tata Elxsi, respectively, Tata AutoComp manufactured some of the critical components of the robot. Conceptualised to complement human workforce and perform repetitive, high volume, dangerous and time-consuming tasks, the TAL Brabo robot can be deployed across industries. Having successfully tested the TAL Brabo in over 50 customer work streams so far, TAL Manufacturing is ready to supply these robots to several sectors, including automotive, light engineering, precision machining, electronics, software testing, plastics, logistics, education, aerospace and engineering.

Implications of Impending Automation on Traditionally Labour-intensive Industries

One of the most labour-intensive industries in India is the cotton textile industry, especially the making of ready-made garments. The 'Sewbot' technology, being developed by Softwear Automation (a US company), aims to automate the entire clothes-making process. However, the technology is so highly priced that its diffusion in the textile industry will take years to fructify. There are four processes that go into making an item of clothing: (*a*) picking up the item, (*b*) aligning it, (*c*) sewing it and (*d*) disposing of it. Of these, only the sewing has so far been automated, and the sewing machine came in a long time ago. The other parts of the process are still done more quickly and more cheaply by humans. In fact, as can be seen from Figures 11.6a and 11.6b, the most automated industry in India – the automotive industry – accounts for only about 10 per cent of the manufacturing employment in the country. Within this industry, we have already seen that only certain specific tasks are automated.

However, automation technologies are fast improving with significant developments in the following three areas: (*a*) artificial intelligence (AI) and machine learning, especially a technique known as deep reinforcement learning, (*b*) a number of technologies relevant to the development of robotics are improving at exponential rates and (*c*) China's AI boom. The country's tech industry is shifting away from copying Western companies, and it has identified AI and machine learning as the next big areas of innovation. Chinese investors are now investing heavily in AI-focused start-ups, and the Chinese government has signalled a desire to see the country's AI industry blossom, pledging to invest about US$15 billion by 2018. A combined effect of these three can make industrial robots more intelligent and capable of performing

Figure 11.6a   Trends in employment in India's automotive manufacturing industry

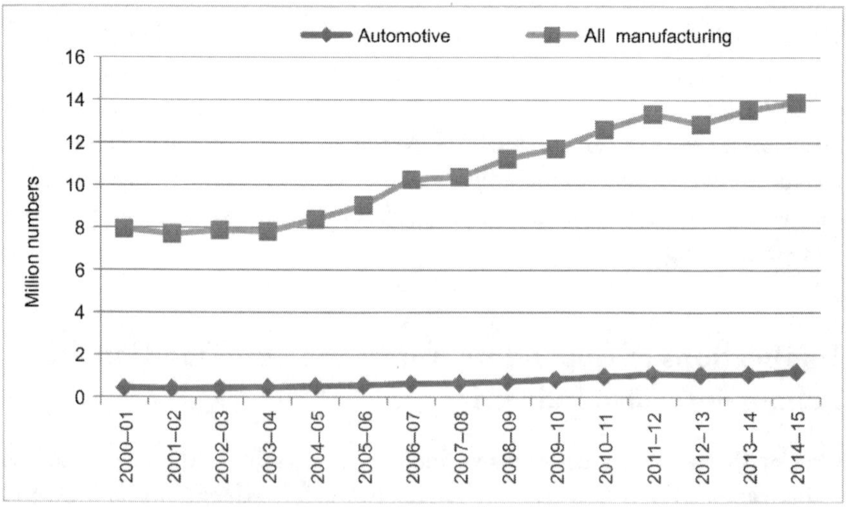

Source: Computed from Annual Survey of Industries.

Figure 11.6b   Share of automotive sector employment in total organised manufacturing sector employment

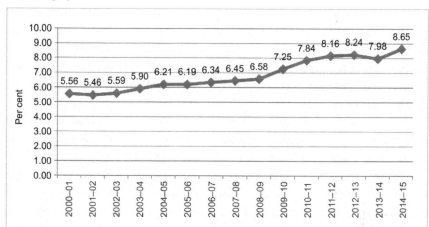

Source: Computed from Annual Survey of Industries.

tasks that are still impossible for robots to perform. Further, the entry of China can make robots much cheaper as well, increasing the probability of it being affordable to even new industries as against traditional adopters of robotic technology such as the automotive industry. Faster adoption of these new automation technologies can have deleterious effect on employment intensities in Indian manufacturing, for instance, in the labour-intensive industries such as textiles and clothing.

Further, there are eight technologies in which improvements will have a strong positive effect on faster diffusion of automation technologies:-

- Exponential growth in computing performance
- Improvements in electromechanical design tools and numerically controlled manufacturing tools
- Improvements in electrical energy storage
- Improvements in electronics power efficiency
- Exponential expansion of the availability and performance of local wireless digital communications
- Exponential growth in the scale and performance of the Internet
- Exponential growth of worldwide data storage
- Exponential growth in global computation power

Conclusion

In this chapter, we have analysed the possible links between the diffusion of automation technologies and employment. Automation technology is narrowly defined in terms of the highest form of automation – namely the use of industrial robots – primarily because of the unavailability of good quality data on the use of automation technologies at the level of tasks within occupations. Analysis of the data shows that, although the density of robots has increased, its usage is restricted to one or two manufacturing industries, the automotive industry being the most important user. Within the automotive industry, the use of industrial robots is concentrated in tasks that are historically speaking less labour intensive. So, for the present, automation does not pose a threat to manufacturing employment. However, with the fast developments in technology, the situation can change. Therefore, there has to be a policy on automation for a labour-abundant economy such as that of India's.

Appendix 11A   The World Robotics Database

The most comprehensive database on the use of robots, country-wise and, within a country, industry-wise and, within an industry, task-wise, is by the International Federation of Robotics (IFR). The definition of industrial robot used is as defined by ISO 8373:2012: 'An automatically contolled, programmable, multipurpose manipulator programmable in three or more axes which can be either fixed in place or mobile for use in industrial automation applications.' Data are available in the annual publication *World Robotics, Industrial Robots*. It is available since 2006, and the latest one is for 2017 covering data up to 2016. The statistical data are based on consolidated data provided by nearly all industrial robot suppliers worldwide. The statistics collected by national robot associations and robot suppliers are processed by the IFR's statistical department and made internationally comparable so as to allow the analysis of the distribution of robots worldwide and in individual regions and countries. The database has year-wise data on annual shipments of industrial robots, their operational stocks, and the industry-wise distribution of both sales and operational stocks and tasks within industries where the stocks are installed. Further, it has also worked out the density of robots per unit of employment in the industrial sector as a whole, and tasks within industries where these installations are available. Data are available for a range of countries, including India. For India, data on stocks and shipments are available since 1999. Industry-wise distribution dof both sales and operational stocks is available since 2006, but task-wise distribution is only available since 2011. The database can thus be used for doing not just specific country-level studies but also inter-country comparisons of the diffusion of robots. There are, of course, some points that is worth remembering. When calculating the operational stock, it is assumed that the average service life is 12 years and that there is an immediate withdrawal of the robots after 12 years. Where countries actually do surveys of the robot stock or have routines for their own calculation of operational stock, for instance, in Japan, then those data are naturally used as the operational stock of robots. The source of the data on employment that is used for computing the density of robots is not always mentioned. For India, we have used the total employment as reported by the Annual Survey of Industries. The very high price tag attached to this dataset limits its large-scale usage by academic researchers.

Notes

1. See symposium on 'Automation and Labor Markets', *Journal of Economic Perspectives* 29, no. 3 (Summer, 2015), https://www.aeaweb.org/issues/381 (accessed on 17 April 2020). The three papers in the symposium are Autor (2015), Mokyr, Vickers and Ziebarth (2015) and Pratt (2015).
2. See Acemoglu and Restrepo (2017), Autor (2015), Brynjolfsson and McAfee (2014), Chang, Rynhart and Huynh (2016) and Hallward-Driemeier and Nayyar (2018).
3. In robotics, an end effector is the device at the end of a robotic arm designed to interact with the environment.

References

Acemoglu, Daron and Pascual Restrepo. 2017. 'Robots and Jobs: Evidence from U S Labour Markets'. Working Paper 23285, National Bureau of Economic Research, March. DOI: 10.3386/w23285. Available at https://www.nber.org/papers/w23285, accessed on 5 January 2021.

Arntz, Melanie, Terry Gregory and Ulrich Zierahn. 2017. 'Revisiting the Risk of Automation'. *Economic Letters* 159 (C): 157–60.

Autor, David. 2015. 'Why Are There Still So Many Jobs? The History and Future of Workplace Automation'. *Journal of Economic Perspectives* 29 (3, Summer): 3–30.

Boston Consulting Group. 2015. 'The Robotics Revolution: The Next Great Leap in Manufacturing'. Available at https://circabc.europa.eu/sd/a/b3067f4e-ea5e-4864-9693-0645e5cbc053/BCG_The_Robotics_Revolution_Sep_2015_tcm80-197133.pdf (accessed on 13 September 2017).

Brynjolfsson, E. and A. McAfee. 2014. *The Second Machine Age: Work, Progress, and Prosperity in a Time of Brilliant Technologies*. New York: W.W Norton and Company.

Central Statistical Organization. 2015. 'ASI Summary Results 2014–15'. Ministry of Statistics and Programme Implementation, Government of India, Delhi. Available at http://mospi.nic.in/asi-summary-results/808, accessed on 9 February 2021.

Chang, Jay-Hee, Gary Rynjhart and Phu Huynh. 2016. *ASEAN in Transformation: Textiles, Clothing and Footwear, Refashioning the Future*. Geneva: International Labour Organization.

Frey, Carl B. and Michael A. Osborne. 2013. 'The Future of Employment: How Susceptible are Jobs to Computerisation?' Mimeo. Oxford Martin School.

———. 2017. 'The Future of Employment: How Susceptible are Jobs to Computerisation?' *Technological Forecasting and Social Change* 114: 254–80.

Flamm, Kenneth. 1988. 'The Changing Pattern of Industrial Robot Use'. In *The Impact of Technological Change on Employment and Economic Growth*, edited by Richard M. Cyert and David C. Mowery, 267–328. Cambridge, MA: Ballinger Publishing House.

Graetz, Georg and Guy Michaels. 2017. 'Robots at Work'. Centre for Economic Performance Discussion Paper 1335, London School of Economics. Available at http://cep.lse.ac.uk/pubs/download/dp1335.pdf (accessed on 16 November 2017).

Hallward-Driemeier, Mary and Gauvrav Nayyar. 2018. *Trouble in the Making? The Future of Manufacturing-led Development*. Washington, DC: The World Bank.

International Federation of Robotics (IFR). 2017. *World Robotics, Industrial Robots 2017*. Version 1.1.14, Online database.

Ministry of Statistics and Programme Implementation. 2019. *Periodic Labour Force Survey 2017–18*. New Delhi: National Statistical Office, Government of India

Mokyr, Joel, Chris Vickers and Nicolas L. Ziebarth. 2015. 'The History of Technological Anxiety and the Future of Economic Growth: Is This Time Different?' *Journal of Economic Perspectives* 29 (3, Summer): 31–50.

Pratt, Gill A. 2015. 'Is a Cambrian Explosion Coming for Robotics?' *Journal of Economic Perspectives* 29 (3, Summer): 51–60.

OECD (Organisation for Economic Co-operation and Development). 2016. 'Automation and Independent Work in a Digital Economy'. Policy Brief on the Future of Work, OECD Publishing, Paris.

Sen, Kunal and Deb Kusum Das. 2014. 'Where Have the Workers Gone? The Puzzle of Declining Labour Intensity in Organised Indian Manufacturing'. DEPP Working Paper No. 36, IDPM, University of Manchester.

Sirkin, Harold, Michael Zinser Justin Rose. 2017. 'How Robots Will Redefine Competitiveness?' Boston Consulting Group. Available at https://www.bcgperspectives.com/content/articles/lean-manufacturing-innovation-robots-redefine-competitiveness/ (accessed on 16 November 2017).

Snyder, Bill. 2019. 'Our Misplaced Fear of Job-Stealing Robots'. Available at https://www.gsb.stanford.edu/insights/misplaced-fear-job-stealing-robots (accessed on 25 June 2019).

About the Contributors

Dinesh Awasthi, an economist by training, is former Professor and Director, Entrepreneurship Development Institute of India, Ahmedabad. He was a Professor of Strategic Management at the Indian Institute of Management, Lucknow, before joining EDI as Director in 2003. Currently, he is Vice-Chancellor, Lok Jagrut Kendra University, Ahmedabad. He has over 70 research papers and 8 books, besides several research studies on small and medium enterprises (SMEs), technology, and entrepreneurship, to his credit. Areas of his professional interest are dynamics of micro, small and medium enterprises (MSMEs), social and rural entrepreneurship, cluster development, and issues related start-ups.

Judhajit Chakraborty is currently a Ph.D. student at Michigan State University, East Lansing, USA. He completed his M.Phil from Indira Gandhi Institute of Development Research (IGIDR), Mumbai. Judhajit's primary areas of interests are development economics, labour, and political economy.

Keshab Das is a Professor at the Gujarat Institute of Development Research, Ahmedabad. He holds M.Phil. (applied economics) and Ph.D. (economics) degrees from the Jawaharlal Nehru University, New Delhi (through the Centre for Development Studies, Thiruvananthapuram). He also holds a bachelor's degree in journalism and mass communications. He is a recipient of the VKRV Rao Prize in Social Sciences (Economics). His research focuses on issues in local and regional development; industrialisation strategies; the informal sector; micro, small and medium enterprises (MSMEs), clusters and globalisation; innovation; labour; basic infrastructure; and politics of development.

Kshiti Gala is an independent researcher based in Mumbai. She read the MSc Development Economics at SOAS, University of London, as a Chevening Scholar with a research focus on smallholder farming in Indian agriculture. She was a Young India Fellow at Ashoka University, Sonepat, a Management Associate with the UNDP's Energy and Environment Unit, and a Research Officer at Samaj Pragati Sahayog, a non-governmental organisation in Madhya Pradesh.

Tareef Husain is an Assistant Professor in the department of economics, Galgotias University, Greater Noida. His research area includes small and medium enterprises, their internationalisation and export, industrial clusters, and regional and sectoral analysis. He has published several research articles in reputed journals and participated in national and international conferences. He is a member of academic associations like the Indian Society of Labour Economics, the Indian Economic Association and the Indian Political Economy Association. He enjoys writing on contemporary and theoretical economic issues.

Varinder Jain is an Assistant Professor at the Institute of Development Studies, Jaipur. He holds M.Phil and Ph.D. degrees in economics, through the Centre for Development Studies, Thiruvananthapuram, from Jawaharlal Nehru University, New Delhi. Small-scale industrial growth is his prime area of interest. He has also done research on various issues related to energy economics and labour economics. He has published widely in both national and international refereed journals and edited volumes. His research is grounded in both field work and rigorous secondary data analysis.

Sunil Mani is Director and RBI Professor, Centre for Development Studies, Thiruvananthapuram. His field of specialisation is the economics and policy aspects of technology and innovation.

R. Nagaraj is currently Visiting Professor at the Centre for Development Studies, Trivandrum, Kerala. His areas of academic work include India's industrialisation, applied macroeconomic issues, public sector performance, industrial labour market in India, and official economic statistics. His most recent book is *Political Economy of Contemporary India,* co-edited with Sripad Motiram (Cambridge University Press, 2017).

Satyaki Roy is an Associate Professor at the Institute for Studies in Industrial Development, New Delhi. His initial research focuses on industrial clusters in India and the nature of spatial concentration of production in the context of late industrialisation. His current areas of interest include global production network, its implications on the process of industrialisation in developing countries and the emerging nature of global hegemony in the context of globalisation. He is the author of *Contours of Value Capture: India's Neoliberal Path of Industrial Development* (Cambridge University Press, 2020) and *Small and Medium Enterprises in India: Infirmities and Asymmetries in Industrial Clusters* (2013).

Madhuri Saripalle is an Associate Professor of Economics at the IFMR Graduate School of Business, Krea University, Sricity, Andhra Pradesh. She received her doctorate in economics from the University of Connecticut, Storrs, USA. Her research analyses contemporary issues related to the impact of technology and trade on industry and agri-business. She has conducted research related to environment-friendly policies, employment generation, labour practices and supply chain in the manufacturing sector, specifically in the automobile and electronics industries. She teaches postgraduate courses on microeconomics, empirical industrial organisation and game theory.

Amita Shah, an economist, is former Professor and Director, Gujarat Institute of Development Research, Ahmedabad. She has published over 75 papers in national and international journals, on dry land agriculture and forestry, environment, employment, chronic poverty, industry–agriculture interface and migration-related issues. She also has five books to her credit. She was President of the Indian Society for Ecological Economics (INSEE) for 2012–14. She has worked extensively with government and non-government organisations and bilateral and multilateral international agencies.

M. Vijayabaskar is a Professor at the Madras Institute of Development Studies, Chennai. His research centres on the political economy of regional development with a focus on labour and land markets, industrial dynamics and rural–urban transformations. In addition to publishing in numerous scholarly journals and media outlets, he has also co-edited monographs including *Rethinking Social Justice* (2020), *Participolis: Consent and Contention in Neoliberal Urban India* (2012) and *ICTs and Indian Social Development: Diffusion, Governance, Poverty* (2008). He is on the editorial advisory board of *Oxford Development Studies* and has also served as a consultant to the ILO and UNRISD.

Index

Ad-dharmis, 143
*adi dravida*s (Dalits), 201
Agra leather cluster, 203
Aligarh lock cluster, 9, 18, 154, 158
    automobile locks, 155–56
    business associations, effective
        functioning of, 165–67
    distributional aspects, 164–65
    educational level of owners and
        employees, 161–62
    firms' performance, 169
    foreign locks and, 154
    historical development and overview,
        159–61
    horizontal bilateral relationship, 167–68
    import of Chinese locks and, 158
    imports and exports, 156
    incidental external economies, 167
    inter-firm cooperation, 167–68
    marketing options for, 164–65
    policy implications, 168–70
    technological development and
        innovation, 162–64
    technological support programme, 169
    trade deficits, 155–56
Aligarh Lock Manufacturers and Traders
    Association (ALMTA), 166
Aligarh Small Scale Lock Manufacturers
    Association (ASSLMA), 166
Aligarh Udhyog Vyapar Pratinidhi Mandal
    (AUVPM), 166
All India Lock Manufacturers Association
    (AILMA), 165
Ambattur automotive cluster, 82–83
annual survey of industries (ASI), 73
antidumping duty, 60

Apparel Export Promotion Council
    (AEPC), 44, 50–51
artificial intelligence, 6
artisanal cluster, 26, 29, 32, 40, 45
auto-ancillary industry, 11–13, 19
automation technologies, 251
    diffusion of, 271, 273
    effect of artificial intelligence (AI) and
        machine learning, 272
    industrial robots (*see* industrial robots)
    literature on effects of, 254–56
    motivation for, 251–52
    occupation-based approach *vs* task-
        based approach, 256–58, 263
    significance of, 252–53
automotive industry, 5, 270, 272–75

Banerjee Haat market, 34
Bangalore, 11, 13, 52
Bangladesh, 3
Bangla Readymade Garments
    Manufacturers and Traders Welfare
    Association, 32, 42
Bengali community, 187
Bharatiya Janata Party (BJP), 126
Burberry (brand), 21n12

Cambodia, 3
capital-intensive industries, 5, 75
Capital Subsidy Scheme, 148
Center for Monitoring Indian Economy
    (CMIE), 74, 86
ceramic tile industry, 6, 8
*chamar*s (Dalits), 143, 201
Chennai automotive cluster, 82–83

China, 1–2, 49, 54
  industrial wages, 3
  share in India's exports and imports of
      ceramic products, 103–04
  sports goods manufacturing industry,
      149
Chinese ceramic tiles, 16
Chinese imports, impact of, 9–10, 116, 158
cluster, definition, 29
Coimbatore foundry cluster, 181
collective actions, 116, 119, 121, 154,
      166–67, 178, 224, 238
collective efficiency, 28
Common Effluent Treatment Plant
      (CETP), 59
Commonwealth Games, 129
comparative advantage, 3
competition, 10, 16, 26, 28–29, 46–47, 74,
      79, 101, 119–21, 131, 137, 145–47,
      153–54, 158–59, 165–70, 178, 203,
      211, 215–16, 225, 229, 236–37, 242,
      246
competitive advantage, 157
competitive market, 24
competitiveness, 53, 68, 119–21, 154,
      224–25
cooperative competition, 26
cooperative efficiency, 28
Council of Scientific and Industrial
      Research (CSIR), 246
Covid-19 crisis, 202, 220n1

demonetisation and its impact, 18, 64
  on ceramic business, 117–18
design studios, 56
Dharavi, 11, 19–20, 21n12, 197
  neighbourhood, 199
  population, 198
  water and sanitation services, 199
Dharavi leather goods cluster, 11, 13,
      197–98, 219–20
  adaptive strategies, 204
  awareness on institutions and their
      membership benefits, 213–15

brand development, 212–13
  competitive advantage, 201
  demand for leather-based products, 215
  education level of entrepreneurs and
      workers, 211
  evolution of, 204–05
  future, 209
  historical and anthropological accounts,
      200
  impact of GST, 217
  impact of international competition
      and national policy changes, 216
  indirect and direct exporters in, 208
  investment needs and profit margin,
      206–07
  level of mechanisation, 210–11
  locational advantage, 202–03, 220n2
  marketing outreach, 212
  nature of employment, 199
  organic process, 205–06
  policy implications, 216–19
  primary surveys and in-depth case
      studies, 203–04
  relationship between small enterprise
      owners and large exporters, 206
  role of community, religion, caste and
      kinship networks, 202
  sentiment among Dharavi's
      entrepreneurs, 215
  skilled workers, 201
  sources of credit, 209–10
  spatial constraints, 207–08
  subcontracting, 213
Dharavi Redevelopment Plan, 215, 218
Director General of Trade Remedies
      (DGTR), 117
directory manufacturing establishment
      (DME), 194n2
District Industries Centres (DICs), 7
Dollar (brand), 11
domestic manufacturing, 3
domestic-market-oriented clusters, 11
domestic production, 2–3
Duty Drawback Scheme, 148

Duty Entitlement Passbook Scheme, 148
Duty Free Import Scheme, 148

e-bikes, 81
electrical and electronics industries, 3, 74,
    76–77, 84, 86–90, 92, 215, 255, 257,
    260–61, 263, 271
electronics industry, 89
employee state insurance (ESI), 66–67
employment, 1
    generation, 8–9
    Howrah foundry cluster, 181
    Indian automobile industry, 73
    in India's automotive manufacturing
        industry, 272–73
    Kolkata garment cluster, 36–38
    manufacturing, 191–93
    in manufacturing sector, 223–24
    Morbi cement tile industry, 102,
        109–12
    Rajkot engineering cluster, 233–35
    small and medium enterprise (SME)
        clusters, 154
    sports goods industry, 142–46
    subcontracting, 52
endogenous growth theory, 27
engineering goods, 8
equilibrium–disequilibrium dynamics, 29
European Enhanced Vehicle-safety
    Committee (EEVC), 96n6
export-oriented growth strategies, 25
Export Promotion Capital Goods
    (EPCG), 117
exports
    of ceramic products, 103–04
    garment, 42–43
    Indian automobile industry, 76–77, 92
    leather goods, 206, 208
    of locks, 156
    sports goods, 134–40

Factories Act, 1948, 8, 52
Federation Internationale de Football
    Association (FIFA) World Cup, 129

fieldwork-based research, 7–8
    industrial fieldwork, 8
finishing schools, 12
firm-level technological activities, 158
Focus Market Scheme, 148
Focus Product Scheme, 148
foreign direct investment (FDI), 53
foundry cluster, 6
fragmentation, 26, 40, 44–45, 65
free trade zones, 11

generalised method of moments (GMM)
    technique, 89
global financial crisis, 2008, 2
goods and services tax (GST), 9, 46, 64, 68,
    217, 241
    on ceramic business, 118–19
    in Jalandhar, 135, 151n5
gross domestic output (GDP), 24
    share of manufacturing and industry
        in, 1
Gujarat Industrial Development
    Corporation (GIDC) Lodhika
    Industrial Association, 235
Gujarat's ceramic industry, 102. *See also*
    Morbi cement tile industry
Gulf Cooperation Council (GCC), 117
Guru T-Shirts, 56
Gwalior Rayons, 60

Hosur, 11
Howrah foundry cluster, 15, 17–18, 35,
    174–75
    contractual labour, 181
    forms of production organisation,
        184–85
    institutional and technological
        challenges, 185–90
    inter-sectoral collaborations, 187
    literature review, 176–79
    manufacturing output and employment,
        180–81
    perceptions on, 188–89
    pig iron suppliers, 182–83

pollution-related problems, 189
shortcomings of, 186
sources of demand, 183–84
working conditions, 181
Howrah *haat* (market), 30, 32, 40
Huawei, 2

imitative innovation, 163
immiserising growth, 66
imports, 3. *See also* Chinese imports,
    impact of
Aligarh lock cluster, 156
of ceramic products, 103–04
Indian automobile industry, 76–77, 92
technology, 85, 89, 91
index of industrial production (IIP), 2
India, competitive advantage of, 201
Indian automobile industry, 72–73
auto component firms, 81, 93
automated programmable logic
    controller (PLC) machine, use
    of, 78
compound annual growth rate
    (CAGR), 76
contribution to employment, 73, 75,
    83, 92
data sources and descriptive statistics,
    86–88
direct employment, 73
export and import, 76–77, 92
free trade agreements (FTA), 78–79, 92
growth in production and turnover,
    74–75, 94
major import sources, 76
quality requirements and inventory
    challenges, 76
R&D capabilities and skill gaps, 79–81,
    87–88, 91–92, 97n7–8
restructuring, 78
robot installations, 77
technology acquisition strategies, 83–91
technology imports, 85, 89, 91
tier 1 and 2 supplier of automobile
    system, 73

unorganised sector, 81–83
Indian Leather Products Association, 189
Indian Premier League (IPL), 129
individual effluent treatment plants
    (IETPs), 59
industrial automation, 250
industrial clusters, 196–97
competitiveness, 224–25
definition, 224
in developing countries, 157
operational dynamics of, 224
study and methodology, 27–30
industrial district, 28–29, 224
industrial park, 33
industrial policy, 16, 20, 74, 168–70, 216–
    19, 241–46
industrial robots, 253–54
density of, 260, 269–71
diffusion of, 250, 252–56
distribution of, 274–75
markets for, 258
operational stock of, 258–61, 263–69
task-wise distribution of, 254, 262, 267,
    275
use of, 263
Industrial Training Institutes, 235
industry associations, 15, 30
information technology (IT) services, 1
infrastructure facilities, 14–15
institutional governance, 50
internet of things, 6
IT outsourcing services, 3

Jalandhar, 9, 14, 17, 129, 132–34
average monthly wage of unskilled
    workers in, 146
contribution to India's sports good
    exports, 134–40
production of unbranded products, 14
state-sponsored skill development
    and sport-goods promotional
    facilities, 13
surgical instrument cluster, 154
wage rates for factory workers, 145–46

Jalandhar's sports goods industry, 16
jobless or *job loss* growth, 100
job losses, 2

knit global supply chains, 19
knitwear industry, 6
knowledge spillover theory, 27–28
Kolkata garment cluster, 11–12, 18, 29
    activities, 33
    average monthly occupational wages, 39
    brands, 42–43
    categories of workers, 29–30
    cluster study and methodology, 29–30
    cost structure of a jeans garment, 36
    economic agents and their roles, 29, 38
    exports, 42–43
    forms of labour contracting, 36–37
    gents' shirts, 32
    history, 30–32
    home-based units, 34, 36, 38
    jeans trousers, 32
    labour force and processes, 36–40, 46
    layers of units, 33
    machines used, 34
    major centres, 30
    market and trade, 40–44
    Muslim tailors, 37
    production processes, 33–36
    production quality, 35
    raw material sources, 34
    readymade garment producers, 32
    second-hand clothes, 32
    self-employment, 38
    skilled labour pool, 35
    women's labour, 37–38
Krugman, Paul, 27

labour-abundant countries, 3
labour demand, determinants of, 84–85
labour-intensive industries, 3–6, 17–19,
    25, 36, 49, 65, 72, 109, 132, 140,
    142, 153–54, 159, 164, 168, 174,
    197, 201, 205–06. *See also* Aligarh

lock cluster; Dharavi leather goods
    cluster; sports goods industry
    implications of automation, 271–73
leather goods, 9
    exports, 11, 206, 208 (*see also* Dharavi
        leather goods cluster)
locks, international trade composition of,
    155–57. *See also* Aligarh lock cluster
Lodhika Industrial Association, 15
Louis Vuitton (brand), 21n12
low-end domestic demand, 53, 103, 116,
    215. *See also* Kolkata garment cluster
low road syndrome, 100
Lucknow, 30
Ludhiana, 69, 196
    subcontracting levels, 52

machinery manufacturing, 11
'Make in India' initiative, 2, 20, 217, 250
man-made fibres (MMF) garments, 51, 55,
    60, 67
    competitiveness of, 53
manufacturing employment
    share in GDP, 191
    state-wise distribution, 192–93
    in total employment, 191–93
manufacturing sector (industry), 1, 250
    growth of, 223, 225
manufacturing stagnation, 1, 24, 49–50, 68,
    173–75, 178–81, 190
Market Access Innovation Scheme, 148
Market Development Assistance Scheme,
    148
Marshallian notion of externalities, 27
Maruti Suzuki India Limited (MSIL),
    96n4
Marwari community, 187
Meerut, 129, 132–34
    average monthly wage of unskilled
        workers in, 146
    wage rates for factory workers, 145–46
Meghs, 143
Merchandise Exports from India Scheme
    (MEIS), 117

Metiabruz, 30, 32, 35, 40–42, 44–45
    popular brands from, 42
Mexico shoe cluster, 157
micro, small and medium enterprises
        (MSMEs), 4, 16, 100–01, 223–24,
        246
    definition, 5
    definitions of, 21n4
    gross value added (GVA), 4
monoethylene glycol (MEG), 60
Moradabad brass cluster, 154
Morbi cement tile industry, 10, 14–16, 18,
        22n14, 101–08, 154
    access to Middle Eastern markets, 16
    annual turnover, 112
    benefits of anti-dumping duties,
        116–17
    challenges with clusters, 122–23
    Chinese imports and, 116
    competitiveness, 119–21
    contribution to employment, 102,
        109–12
    cooperation and mutuality in, 121–22
    demonetisation and its impact, 117–18
    export performance, 10
    exports and imports of ceramic
        products, 103–08
    facilities offered to workers, 112
    firm strategies for business expansion,
        123–24
    goods and services tax (GST) on,
        118–119
    industry and business infrastructure,
        growth and upgradation of, 125
    in-house changes/innovations
        undertaken, 115
    policy support, 124–26
    production process and subcontracting,
        111–13
    profile of enterprises, 108–09
    quality control procedures, 116
    range of ceramic tiles and sanitaryware
        products, 101–02
    skilled and unskilled workers, 110–11
    skill requirement, 111
    source of finance, 109
    technological upgradation, 113–16
    trade balance in ceramic products, 105
Morbi Ceramic Association (MCA), 110
MSME Development Act, 2006, 4–5
multi-fibre arrangement (MFA), 49
multinational corporations (MNCs), 74,
        270

National Capital Region (NCR), 52, 154
National Fibre Policy of 2010, 53
National Industrial Classification (NIC)
        codes, 73
National Institute of Fashion Design, New
        Delhi, 15
National Institute of Fashion Technology-
        TEA (NIFT-TEA), 51, 60
    anti-microbial properties fabric project,
        59
National Manufacturing Policy, 2011, 2
National Skill Development Corporation
        (NSDC), 61
National Skills Qualifications Framework
        (NSQF), 61
National Small Industries Corporation
        (NSIC), 13, 163
National Textile Policy of 2000, 53
neoclassical production functions, 25
NIVIA Sports, 141–42
North American Free Trade Agreement
        (NAFTA), 78

Olympic Games, 129
organised manufacturing, 100
original equipment manufacturers
        (OEMs), 73–74, 86
Oudh, 30

Panipat, 196
parallel economy, 198
Paridhan, 32, 39, 44
'partial-proletarianisation' of labour force,
        25

private engineering colleges, 13
'Project Uptech' scheme, 186, 194n3
purified terephthalic acid (PTA), 60

quality of employment, 100

Rajkot, 18, 22n13
    computer numerical control (CNC)
        machine tool manufacturers, 13
    precision engineering firms, 12
    support of industry association, 15
Rajkot engineering cluster, 225
    advantages, 238, 240
    annual compound rates of growth
        2012–13 and 2017–18, 231
    business environment and policy
        imperatives, 241–46
    China imports and, 241
    collaboration and networking, 237–38
    contribution to employment, 233–35
    development of, 229
    diversification of, 229
    growth performance, 230
    impact of GST, 241–42
    industry associations, 238
    market and competition, 236–37
    outsourcing and subcontracting, 230–34
    production in, 229–30
    profile of MSMEs, 226–28
    social capital, 237–39
ready-made garment (RMG)
    exports of India, share of fabrics in,
        52–54
    retail chains and supermarkets, 54
    transaction costs, 54
    value chain, 54–55
Regent Garment Park, 33, 39, 42–43
re-industrialisation, 2
Reliance, 60
rescaling space, 101, 126
research and development (R&D), 13, 74,
        77, 85–89, 91–93, 97n8, 150, 169,
        187–88, 263
    Indian auto industry, 79–81

institutional failures in knitwear, 62–63
revolt of 1857, 30
robotics, 6
Rupa (brand), 11

service centres, 28
'Sewbot' technology, 271
Shah, Nawab Wajid Ali, 30, 32
Shops and Establishments Act, 1948, 200
Sialkot, 16
    soccer ball industry, 148
    surgical instrument cluster of, 157
skill requirements/development, 12–13
    institutions for, 12
    as opportunity for upward mobility, 12
    for self-employment, 12
small and medium enterprises (SMEs), 28,
        148, 153–54, 224
    competitiveness of, 154
    employment-generating capacity, 154
    inter-firm linkages, benefits of, 224
    operational dynamics of, 224–25
small industrial clusters (SICs), 196
Small Scale and Cottage Industries
        Development Corporation, 148
South Indian Textile Research Association
        (SITRA), 62–63
space, 25–27
sports goods industry, 6, 9, 129
    contribution to employment, 142–46
    effect of Chinese imports, 9–10
    export markets, 141–42
    foreign brands and Indian brands, 140,
        149
    hand-stitched footballs/rugby balls
        export, 10
    home-based piecerate workers, 144–45
    interventions aimed at promotion of,
        150
    Jalandhar and Meerut clusters, 129
    post-1990, 130–32
    state policy framework, 147–50
    wageworkers' exposure to job insecurity
        and economic insecurity, 146–47

Sports Industries Development Centre (SIDC), 148
state-level promotional agencies, 14
subcontracting, 52, 112–13, 199, 230–33
    Kolkata garment cluster, 37
'sweatshop' regime, 40

TAL Brabo robot, 271
TAL Manufacturing Solutions, 271
Tamil Nadu automotive cluster, 82–83, 95
Tata Metallics, 186
technical efficiency, 85–86
technical progress, 13–14
technological capabilities, 158
technological maturity, 126
technology upgradation, 126
Technology Upgradation Fund (TUF) scheme, 53
textiles and clothing (T&C) sector, 51
tier 1 and 2 supplier of automobile system, 73
Tiruppur Exporters' Association (TEA), 50–51
Tirupur, 10, 13, 32
    environmental issues in, 17–18
    training school and design centre, 14–15
Tirupur knitwear clusters, 18, 50, 154, 168
    barriers to bypassing intermediaries, 61–62
    branding, 56
    competitive edge, 52
    constraints in upgrading, 60–61
    constraints of geography and capital, 56–57
    coping strategies by exporters, 64–65
    ecological upgrading, 59–60
    economic/social/ecological upgrading, 65–67

'green products,' 17
growth and expansion of exports, 57
infrastructure constraints, 63
policy implementation, 64
R&D support and innovations, 62–63
skill upgrading, 61
spinning mills, upgradation of, 58
subcontracting levels, 52
turnover, 51
upgrading initiatives, 57–59
user–producer networks, 62
vertical integration, 58
yearly international trade fairs, benefits of, 59
zero liquid discharge (ZLD) technology, use of, 59
trader–producer relation, 158, 164–65
training centres, 28
Trans-Pacific Partnership Agreement, 55
transportation costs, 27

ustagar, 33, 37

value chain, 10–11, 33, 45–46, 54–55, 60, 62, 64, 91–92, 178, 180, 184–85, 189, 205, 217, 219–20
    buyer-driven, 200
    upgrading, 50, 54–55, 67, 72, 230
Vardoon's law, 3
Vietnam, 3
virtual reality, 6

West Bengal, 17–18, 174
    real per capita total manufacturing NSDP, 173–74
West Bengal Industrial Development Corporation, 43
West Bengal Pollution Control Board (WBPCB), 188